D1272823

IMAGINING EACH OTHER

SUNY series in

Modern Jewish Literature and Culture

Sarah Blacher Cohen, EDITOR

IMAGINING
Each Other

*Blacks and Jews in
Contemporary American Literature*

ETHAN GOFFMAN

State University
of New York Press

PS173
.N4
G64
2000

Published by   i 0791446778
State University of New York Press

© 2000 State University of New York

All rights reserved

Printed in the United States of America

No part of this book may be used or reproduced in any manner
whatsoever without written permission. No part of this book may be
stored in a retrieval system or transmitted in any form or by any
means including electronic, electrostatic, magnetic tape, mechanical,
photocopying, recording, or otherwise without the prior permission
in writing of the publisher.

For information, address the State University of New York Press,
State University Plaza, Albany, NY 12246

Marketing by Michael Campochiaro • Production by Bernadine Dawes

Library of Congress Cataloging-in-Publication Data

Goffman, Ethan, 1961–
     Imagining each other : Blacks and Jews in contemporary American literature / Ethan Goffman.
         p.   cm.—(SUNY series in modern Jewish literature and culture)
     Includes bibliographical references and index.
     ISBN 0-7914-4677-8 (alk. paper)—ISBN 0-7914-4678-6 (pbk. : alk. paper)
     1. American literature—Jewish authors—History and criticism. 2. Afro-Americans in
literature. 3. American literature—Afro-American authors—History and criticism. 4.
Literature and society—United States—History—20th century. 5. American
literature—20th century—History and criticism. 6. Afro-Americans—Relations with Jews.
7. Ethnic relations in literature. 8. Blacks—Relations with Jews. 9. Race relations in
literature. 10. Blacks in literature. 11. Jews in literature. I. Title. II. Series.

PS173.N4 G64 2000
810.9'355—dc21
                                                                                      99-054982

1   2   3   4   5   6   7   8   9   19

To My Parents

Contents

Acknowledgments

I am indebted to many individuals for advice and support over the course of this project, the writing of which often resembled the longest distance between two points. Thanks to Michael Rosenblum for his patience and vision; to Carolyn Mitchell for her font of ideas, her crucial early guidance, and her continuing useful suggestions; to Patrick Brantlinger for his immeasurable knowledge of cultural studies and theory; and to Christoph Lohmann for his editorial recommendations. For their helpful comments on various portions of this manuscript, and for much needed moral support, I am grateful to Shakir Mustafa and Darrin Pratt. For intriguing discussions and useful suggestions regarding source material, I thank Yusef Komunyakka. For help regarding various annoying practical matters I thank William J. Palmer. I am indebted to the three anonymous readers, whose comments greatly improved both the historical context and the cohesiveness of this manuscript. I also wish to thank James Peltz for his support, and for his helpful responses to a variety of vexing questions. For enlivening conversations and friendship I am grateful to Shelly Barnard, Amy Baum, Robert Hausladen, M. A. Y. Jamal, Eric Jeschke, Crystal Keels, Sara Prigan, Ed Schelb, Elizabeth Starr, and Marianne Szlyk. For helpful comments and for encouragement, I am indebted to many family members: Lisa Goffman and Bill Saxton, Carolyn and Dan Goffman, and of course my parents for their tireless (and rather quixotic) support.

Introduction

Fractured by competing racial and ethnic voices, contemporary American literature is one element in a clamorous social dialogue, a conversation inherent in multiethnic democracy. Transcending the model of assimilation into a preformed society, America increasingly views itself as an evolving project marked by continuing transformation under the influence of numerous peoples and traditions. This evolution, marked initially by the term "melting pot," which implies movement toward a homogenous standard, is now referred to as a "mosaic," "stew," or "salad" in recognition of its multivariegated nature. The Black-Jewish dialogue is a dialectical enactment, in miniature, of this process, one that dramatizes how, if social and political events influence literature, literature in turn engages society. This book is a relatively straightforward analysis of this clamorous dialogue in which Blacks and Jews are portrayed in each other's literature, in solidarity and in conflict. Although the works discussed extend from World War II to the 1990s, the book focuses on the 1960s and early '70s, a period pivotal not just in transforming Black and Jewish relations but in moving America's self-conception toward a multicultural vision.

Replete with tensions of acculturation, the Jewish-Black relationship is a touchstone of interethnic relations. Key transformations in both Black-Jewish relations and in the larger movement toward an acknowledgment of America's multicultural nature have occurred partly in the medium of literature. A chronological analysis of key literary works is therefore simultaneously a reading of historical and social events. Although this book concentrates on social and historical readings, this should not be taken to imply that aesthetic considerations are of lesser importance. After all, if there were no beauty and artistry in literature, we would all be reading sociology textbooks.

Nevertheless, if a strictly social reading of literature is necessarily limited, so too is a strictly aesthetic reading. While social and, at least indirectly, political factors are present in virtually all literature, aesthetics has often been seen as the only legitimate approach to literature. Drama-tizing the belief that literature is an inviolate realm, Stendhal comments ironically that "Politics in a work of literature is like a pistol-shot in the middle of a concert, something loud and vulgar, and yet a thing to which it is not possible to refuse one's attention" (quoted in Howe 1957, 15).[1] The argument that political consciousness drains a work of its artistry and complexity is still employed by opponents of ethnic and cultural studies. Roger Kimball, for instance, complains that the "self-righteous emphasis on 'diversity,' 'relevance,' and 'sensitivity' provides a graphic example of the way in which the teaching of the humanities in our colleges and universities has been appropriated by special interests and corrupted by politics" (1990, 3). Kimball may be right that a single-minded political agenda often flattens a work (though such a work may subvert itself and add interest through gaps in ideological consistency, and may besides be worth studying as part of a cultural record). However, a sophisticated political and social awareness only adds complexity and enhances textual interpretation, and may be impossible to avoid, since, as humans, we are all embedded within networks of political assumptions.

Indeed, a text may have an overall didactic thrust and still succeed as a work of art, as does Toni Morrison's *Beloved* or, to cite a European classic, Vergil's *Aeneid*, a work written to justify the hegemony of the Roman Empire. From Plato's *Republic* to Shakespeare's history plays, texts are enriched by a knowledge of the historical circumstances that surround their genesis, the social and philosophical debates that permeate their language. So Shakespeare's Caliban may be considered a misshapen subhuman, a figure morally cramped, incapable of higher aesthetic vision, or may just as easily—and even simultaneously—be perceived as Prospero's victim, colonized and brutalized, the creation of Eurocentric arrogance. Caliban is both intensely constrained and capable of voicing in an intensely poetic, perceptive way the nature of this constraint. Kimball himself admits a didactic purpose for art, but only if it upholds the exist-ing order: "[T]he humanities *do* have a political dimension, insofar as they rest on a belief in the value and importance of Western culture and the civilization that gave birth to it" (61). Kimball is silent as to why the humanities must be limited to maintaining Western culture, the primacy of which he assumes.

However important Western culture is to our society, to claim it as the sole grounding is to ignore a huge part of the American experience. If art is an expression of a given culture, and our current culture is composed of a theoretically Western center under continuous alteration by numerous other cultures, then we must have a literature that rests upon the "value and importance" of the polyglot moment. If Black and Jewish literature are constrained by a specific time and place, by historical boundaries to consciousness, this does not hinder their artistry; what a text does within its given constraints determines its success (though success is itself provisional, depending largely upon the perceptions and needs of its community of readers). In fact, it is questionable whether innovative artistry exists outside of social conventions. To imagine a work of art without a social context is rather like playing tennis not just without a net but without a court or a set of agreed-upon rules; boundaries define both sports and literature. Literature, of course, differs from sports in the capacity to alter these boundaries (if only in a historically channeled way).

Aesthetic and social considerations, then, cannot be separated; it is the evolving relationship between the two that makes the works discussed herein so fascinating. One might view social and historical conditions as the raw clay that individual artists shape into aesthetic objects. Although this particular study concentrates mainly on the social and political, hopefully it will lead its readers to a deeper appreciation of all aspects of the literature discussed herein.

One last word about method. Chapters are generally structured as a brief discussion of historical events followed by close analysis of key literary texts. The development of broad historical themes largely occurs through the literary texts themselves. Texts are defined as "key" if they illustrate a continuity among Jewish-Black dialogue and illuminate that dialogue within a larger context regarding issues of ethnic identity and assimilation. Authors with an important role in defining the place of Black or Jewish literature within the American canon are given priority, as are those who develop themes relevant to Black-Jewish relations over a span of time. For instance, Saul Bellow's *Henderson the Rain King*, *Mr. Sammler's Planet,* and *The Dean's December*, published over a twenty-two-year period, depict Blacks from shifting perspectives that can be linked to the dates of their publication. To further ensure continuity, works with detailed portraits of Blacks, for Jewish authors, and Jews, for Black authors, are given priority, while those with incidental or fragmented references are only briefly mentioned. This methodology, whatever its constraints, does allow for a relatively contained discussion that combines the scope of a social history with some of the immediacy of literature.

Monologues and Dialogues

*Without the reference to the Jew who is corroding the social
fabric, the social fabric itself would be dissolved.*
        —Slavoj Žižek, *The Sublime Object of Ideology*

*Merely a concrete test of the underlying principles of the great
republic is the Negro problem.*
        —W. E. B. DuBois, *The Souls of Black Folk*

*The question of color, especially in this country, operates to
hide the graver questions of the self.*
        —James Baldwin, *Nobody Knows My Name*

The narrative of Black and Jewish relations in America encompasses dramatic political alliances and conflicts, dilemmas of identity and assimilation, and persistent questions of ethnic division and economic inequality. Despite radically differing experiences in this country, the two groups share powerful memories, religious identifications, and historical traumas. The catastrophes inflicted upon Jews in Europe, centuries of pogroms followed by the Holocaust, provide a rough analogy to the Black experience of Middle Passage, slavery, and lynching. However, the shape and meaning of these events is evolving and contested. As with all historical analogies, comparisons between Jewish and African American experiences acquire meaning through the perspective of the beholder. Both Black and Jewish thinkers have described a mutual sympathy, at times a common global status or mission, through memories of oppression. Nevertheless, economic and social divergence in the United States threatens such connections.

Religion provides an originary narrative common to Blacks and Jews. The tale of a people escaping from slavery, finding their way to the Promised Land, is remembered by diaspora Jews for whom redemption is always just over the horizon: "Next year in Jerusalem." A similar hope is held by African Americans, evident as long ago as slavery's appropriation of "Go Down, Moses" as a parable of the Black struggle for freedom. As happened to European Jews for centuries, for African Americans this tantalizing promise has been endlessly deferred; full social acceptance and economic equality have repeatedly seemed imminent and repeatedly been withheld, most prominently after Emancipation and, a hundred years later, following the Civil Rights era. American Jews, in contrast, have finally seen millennia-old religious and historical promises fulfilled in the creation of Israel and, for many, in the attainment of affluence. In America, then, Blacks have suffered the mythic-historic Jewish role of hope incessantly deferred. The experience of trauma may be memorialized as an important part of historical identity; as easily it can be reified as an event beyond meaning. Trauma and the recovery from trauma, the attempt to repair and reconstitute an identity, link the Jewish and African diasporas. Conversely the memorialization of trauma may become a site of contestation, of rivalry, as is occurring in debates about which people's experience constitutes the "true" Holocaust.[1]

Relations between African and Jewish Americans have been shaped by each group's struggle to define its status, to balance group identity with Americanization. African American reactions to the Jewish presence mix identification, admiration, and resentment. Religious identification is fundamental, with Jews conceived as a people whose suffering has a special meaning, a redemptive quality often transposed to the Black experience in America. This framework often yields a sympathetic view of American Jewry, yet it may also produce hostility. While some Blacks see America's Jews as hypocritical usurpers, often they are regarded as positive role models, a minority group that has succeeded despite oppression. These perceptions are inextricably mixed, though to greatly varying degrees depending upon time, place, and individual experience.

Jewish perceptions of Blacks are torn between identification with majority culture and an awareness of past Jewish marginalization. To further define themselves as Americans, Jews may adopt conventional racial stereotypes. Yet the Black presence may fissure the mythic American (w)hole into which assimilationist Jews seek to disappear. Given their stake in the ideal of a society that accepts all ethnic groups, Jews have long had a special interest in an America free from historical injustices and divisions. So a Jewish playwright, Israel Zangwill, coined the term "melting pot," and a Jewish woman, Emma Lazarus, wrote the poem engraved on the Statue of Liberty, "Give me your tired, your poor, / Your huddled masses yearning to breathe free." Such a harmonious vision is difficult to sustain, given the presence of an exploited minority who remind Jewish Americans of their own past and of the shortcomings of their adopted country. Struggling to eradicate their stigma as the Other, a status inflicted in Europe and lingering in America, Jews have been a strong presence in movements toward a universal society, notably socialism and civil rights (often to the point of effacing their own traditions).

Black and Jewish representations enact a multilayered history of identification and estrangement. A minority group tends to view another based on (at least) three elements: actual cultural traits, dominant stereotypes, and reflections of the perceiving group's own status and needs. This last is crucial; Jews and Blacks define their status within American society, their social and cultural identity, partly through their relationship with each other. African Americans may thus measure themselves against another marginalized group, one that nevertheless seems closer to the American center, while Jewish Americans often compare their status to groups positioned farther from the center. Negative stereotypes, for instance of Blacks by Jews, reflect an acceptance of dominant cultural values. Sympathetic portrayals, on the other hand, are an indirect means of narrating one's own struggle, of identifying with one's people. How Black and Jewish writers represent each other tells at least as much about the perceiving subject position as about the group being represented. As Emily Miller Budick puts it, "For a significant number of African and Jewish American writers, the other group becomes a vehicle by which to think through their own ethnic identities" (1998, 1). This dialogue, then, often resembles two simultaneous monologues in which each group holds up a mirror to the other and perceives: Itself. The process is one of "missteps and trespasses, as, losing the distinctions between self and other, one constructs the other as oneself and causes the other similarly to misconstrue and misconstruct oneself" (8). If misunderstandings are pervasive here, though, so too is constructing something new, a multivocal identity, one marked by constant change, but an identity nevertheless. Such racial and ethnic tensions and paradoxical identifications are part of an American dialogue, a continual self-invention narrated at least partly through the medium of literature.

I

A Jew is a nigger turned inside out

—Joke

In America it is we who are the Jews. . . . [The] star of David is all over us.

—Julius Lester, *Lovesong: Becoming a Jew*

Eurocentric hegemony lingers in the postcolonial mind. African and Jewish Americans, educated (both formally and informally) into dominant culture, are among those whose minds have historically been "colonized," who must fight off a psychological "invasion" (though one ultimately capable of symbiotic behavior). European racial hierarchies, albeit in varied forms, extend around the earth, structuring relations between various ethnic groups. Edward Said describes a world totally transfigured by colonialism: "The great imperial experience of the past two hundred years is global and universal; it has implicated every corner of the globe, the colonizer and the colonized together" (1993, 259). Beyond actual geographic alterations, humanity's mental terrain has been reconfigured in the image(s) of the colonizer. European ideology has been exported to faraway colonies as part of a "civilizing" mission, an attempt to replace barbarism and anarchy with, in the words of Matthew Arnold, "sweetness and light" (1950, 54). Since this civilization's definitive character is a fiction, it has failed to eradicate the (purportedly nonexistent) native culture except in those cases in which it physically eliminates the natives. Instead—as Homi Bhabha describes—it generates a hybrid through which native cultures adapt European culture and technology to local conditions. Center and periphery engage in a dialectic, but an unequal one; periphery must engage in indirect, subversive cultural building.

Western Europe has codified a set of beliefs about the peoples outside its borders. Incessant scrutiny and classification are principles of the rationalism that justified colonialism, especially in its later phases. Mary Louise Pratt discusses "the totalizing classificatory schemas that coalesced in the mid-eighteenth century into the discipline of 'natural history'" (1992, 28), through which "one by one the planet's life forms were to be drawn out of the tangled threads of their life surroundings and rewoven into European-based patterns of global unity and order" (31). So Linnaeus, a founder of natural science, progressed from classifying plants and animals to humans. He grouped humans into five basic types: Wild Man, described as "mute"; American, "Regulated by customs"; European, "Governed by laws"; Asiatic, "Governed by opinions"; and African, "Governed by caprice" (Pratt 1992, 32). Although such schemes began with physical characteristics, these were quickly linked to social and moral values. As part of the rationalist project, the external was to be scrutinized, characterized, mapped out, explored, and explained by scientific means. Rationalism, as Pratt describes it, documents racial traits in unprecedented and excruciating detail, providing a pseudoscientific justification for colonial domination.

These schemes classify non-Europeans (including Jews and Gypsies) as either subhuman or extrahuman, the first incapable of rational development, the second only pseudointelligent, clever perhaps but lacking the power and originality of the European intellect. Morally, too, these outsiders are considered inferior to the blend of Hellenic and Christian principles that typifies Europe and defines the White race. The two peoples who most clearly represent these (seemingly) bipolar groupings of inferior humans are Blacks and Jews, the first representing emotional and mental primitivism, the second hyperrational detachment. Frantz Fanon describes this bipolar differentiation, which categorizes Blacks as physical and sexual and Jews as abstract, greedy presences: "[T]he Negro symbolizes the biological danger, the Jew, the intellectual danger" (1967, 165). In the New World, Leslie Fiedler outlines a similar division:

> The Negro . . . has always represented for the American imagination the primitive and the instinctive, the life of impulse whether directed toward good or ill. The Jew, on the other hand, stands symbolically for the uses and abuses of intelligence, for icy legalism or equally cold vengefulness. (1960, 237)

Two monumental racial myths represent all that "enlightened" humanity wishes not to be, all the deepest psychic terrors.

The bipolar construction of Blacks and Jews forms convenient poles for a hierarchical table of racial traits. Other groups, often classified under the broad rubric of "oriental," are considered to fall between these main poles, combining qualities of Black primitivism with Jewish slyness. So Edward Said describes the stereotype of the Oriental as "gullible, 'devoid of energy and initiative,' much given to 'fulsome flattery,' intrigue, [and] cunning . . . Orientals are inveterate liars, they are 'lethargic and suspicious,' and in everything oppose the clarity, directness, and nobility of the Anglo-Saxon race" (1979, 39). Traits ascribed to Blacks and Jews are mixed as needed: laziness, confused thought, shrewdness, amorality. Besides the obvious economic advantage of such stereotypes in justifying colonialism, they also serve a psychological need, an image against which the European—and American—self is defined.

European rationalism, often under the rubric of natural science, codified a system of racial ideology largely drawn from older belief systems embedded deep within the European collective consciousness. Blacks and Jews formed the poles in this system, which can be diagrammed as follows:

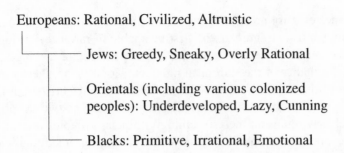

Europeans: Rational, Civilized, Altruistic

        Jews: Greedy, Sneaky, Overly Rational

        Orientals (including various colonized
        peoples): Underdeveloped, Lazy, Cunning

        Blacks: Primitive, Irrational, Emotional

This hierarchy, while varied depending upon time, place, and circumstance, is remarkably consistent as a general scheme dating before
Shakespeare's Shylock and the biblical exegesis of Ham as the progenitor
of the excluded Black races.[2] Such beliefs were incorporated in allegedly
scientific classification schemes, which actually served as maps of the
European psyche as it defined itself against Otherness. If Blacks represent suppressed emotions, particularly sexuality, Jews represent an excess, a kind of hyperrationalism lacking emotional and communitarian
impulses, rationalism's archetype of its own excesses. Both stereotypes
fulfill larger social needs: Blacks are constructed to justify exploitation of
those outside Europe's borders, while Jews provide a scapegoat within
Europe, particularly for capitalist exploitation. The key point is the classification of people according to type rather than as individuals; more specifically, within a European iconography Black and Jewish stereotypes
are at opposite ends of the diagram, poles of categorization representing
distinguishable Othernesses.

Or are they? Both are submerged beneath the European, the term representing a positive definition of humanity that defines itself against the
various "lower" races. Michael Rogin explains stereotypes of Jews and
Blacks as only apparently opposite, as connected organs of a single system: "If the patriarchal Jew of racist fantasy was the superego mirror of
the hypermasculine, sexually rampaging, black id, the hysterical or trick-
ster Jewish man blended into the feminized blackface black" (1996, 70).
The determining dichotomy is not Jewish/Black, but European/Other. As
the young Frantz Fanon was warned, "Whenever you hear anyone abuse
the Jews, pay attention, because he is talking about you" (1967, 122).
Jews are a term associated with blackness to the point of literalness: "The
Jews are black, according to nineteenth-century racial science, because
they are not a pure race, because they are a race which has come from
Africa" (Gilman 1991, 99). Furthermore, the stereotypes attributed to
various "races" change depending on local needs. As the European self-

definition evolved from religious to rational, the stereotype of Jews shifted from Christ-killers to capitalists. Concordantly the justification for colonization shifted from converting the heathen to civilizing the uncivilized or, finally, to excising those deemed metaphysically beyond the reach of civilization. Throughout, representations of Jews and Blacks had in common the image of the dark Other, rational at best in a debased, nonlinear manner, incapable of higher forms of thought and nobility.

II

I remember that I am invisible and walk softly so as not to awaken the sleeping ones.
—Ralph Ellison, *Invisible Man*

What have I in common with the Jews? I scarcely have anything in common with myself.
—Franz Kafka

The Enlightenment, which posited a rational, universal subject, both codified racial hierarchies and eventually, through assimilationism, offered a method of escaping them. Assimilation is a recurring process of the modern state, an entity that has been characterized by ruthless incorporation to a single vision of conformity. As Zygmunt Bauman explains, the word "assimilation" dates back to a scientific term meaning "the conversion by an animal or plant of extraneous material into fluids and tissues identical with its own" (1991, 103). Traditional assimilation thus demands the renunciation of old forms to conform to a standardized culture: "The meaning of the liberal offer in general, and the 'cultural assimilation' programme in particular, is the affirmation of that site in the society from which the offer has been made" (71). Acceptance of this offer usually means denial of one's own history.

The shift from national and racial exclusion toward the promise of assimilation is gradual and ambiguous, following a general evolution from biological toward environmental notions of human capabilities. At the point(s) where Enlightenment reaches beyond the confines of the European subject, declaring its secrets and benefits available to Jews, Asians, Blacks, and other excluded groups, it would seem to dissolve racial barriers. Yet the continued dominance of a European standard of civilization maintains a de facto cultural exclusion; the ideal of universal culture is, in practice, far from universal. The promise of assimilation mandates shedding traditional cultures in favor of a European standard. For Jews and Blacks, and for other marginalized groups, the attempt to assimilate leads to a divided consciousness, a self-image reflected through racial hierarchy, often a self-hatred. The relationship of colonized to colonizer plays itself out on the battlefield of the individual psyche.

Albert Memmi provides one description of the fragmentation and self-hatred generated by European hegemony, showing how the colonized emulates, imitates, envies, and finally rebels against the colonizer. Internalizing colonial stereotypes means that the colonized must reject their own traditions. In the subservient aspect of their being, the colonized gasp in awe at colonial achievements, struggling to join the colonizer, "to become equal to that splendid model and to resemble him to the point of disappearing in him" (Memmi 1967, 120). Such an approach is doomed to failure for, met with scorn by representatives of the civilization he so admires, the colonial subject is torn from his own tradition: "In the name of what he hopes to become, he sets his mind on impoverishing himself, tearing himself away from his true self" (121). The dominant culture through which the colonized has attempted to understand herself gives back an ugly, distorted image. To counteract this stereotype the colonial subject, both individually and collectively, undergoes a period of national pride giving birth to a countermyth, a reconfigured past often transforming the hated stereotype into a utopian image, for instance of "Yiddishkeit" or of "Black pride," of warmth, humanity, and creativity. This utopian reaction, an image of an idyllic, unchanging precolonial society, becomes mythologized as eternal and unitary, an essential Irishness or Africanness or Jewishness or Indianness.[3] Memmi's *The Colonizer and the Colonized* moves from myth to countermyth, yet suggests no synthesis or transcendence.

If Memmi provides a general model of psychological colonization, W. E. B. DuBois delineates how this condition affects a specific people, showing how African Americans scrutinize themselves through the assumptions of European ideology. DuBois defines the resulting internal struggle as "double consciousness,"

> this sense of always looking at one's self through the eyes of others, of measuring one's soul by the standards of a world that looks on in amused contempt and pity. One ever feels his twoness,—an American, a Negro; two souls, two thoughts, two unreconciled strivings; two warring ideals in one dark body, whose dogged strength alone keeps it from being torn asunder. (1989, 3)

In the long term this doubleness generates a rich, complex cultural mix, yet the immediate psychological effect is often confusion, dissonance, and self-hatred. African Americans are born into a society that ensures they will live the postcolonial dilemma of existing as a doubly interpellated subject. The conflict that the European colonizers won physically is refought eternally in the psyche of a defeated people, with European ideology having a terrifying advantage. Black Americans speak a language originally European, live in a political system set up by Whites, attend schools with White teachers, work largely for White bosses, and, at least until recently, have had European culture everywhere upheld as the singular ideal.

The pattern of European dominance and psychic fissuring frames Frantz Fanon's work, which argues that in Martinique the inhabitants view themselves through European social and psychological systems. His *Black Skin, White Masks* shows in great social and psychological detail the self-hatred generated by European hegemony. Fanon's training as a psychiatrist leads him to examine the relationship between social and individual psychosis, particularly in the psyches of young Africans whose identity formation is based on a negative appraisal of blackness. He reinterprets Jungian archetypes as being not biologically ingrained but deeply embedded cultural constructs. In this analysis both Freudian and Jungian psychology are based not upon a universal human condition but upon a specific time and place, nineteenth-century Europe, for "the collective unconscious, without our having to fall back on genes, is purely and simply the sum of prejudices, myths, collective attitudes of a given group" (1967, 188). Psychological problems do not originate in the individual consciousness but have a social basis, one so powerfully engraved that, regardless of conscious belief systems, the adult psyche is incapable of changing basic emotional reactions, including a hatred of one's own blackness.

Racism, then, is pervasive in the psychological terrain of every individual inhabiting a society shaped by colonialism. European cultural hegemony is impressed upon both African and Jewish Americans. Historically Blacks have suffered a deliberate obliteration of African heritage, while European Jews have faced ghettoization and cultural isolation. As assimilation became a real possibility for Europe's Jews, so too did the pressure to shed religious and cultural traditions. The phenomenon of double consciousness, with its attendant self-hatred, occurred in Jews as they played out the colonial dilemma within the boundaries of Europe. Describing one such figure, Sigmund Freud, Daniel Boyarin points out a Jewish "sense of inferiority vis-à-vis the gentile . . . closely allied to the 'inferiority complex' that Frantz Fanon identifies in the colonial subject" (1997, 239). If the European ideal is naturalized as the universal norm, the Jew, by contrast, is perceived as an oddity with a specific history and odd physiology, with a large nose and an excess of speech and gesture. This image creates a psychological crisis for Jews attempting to assimilate. As with psychologically colonized Africans, Jews have struggled to participate in a culture that disavows them. To achieve emancipation, Jews have been asked to obliterate their pasts, to make themselves anew. Sartre describes the Jew who

> considers himself the same as others. He speaks the same language, he has the same class interests, the same national interests; he reads the newspapers that the others read, he votes as they do, he understands and shares their opinions. Yet they give him to understand that he does not belong, that he has a "Jewish way" of speaking, of reading, of voting. (1976, 78)

An elusive otherness clings to the assimilating individual, in physical features, odor, gestures, speech patterns; he or she can never be entirely secure. Europeanized Jews are torn between ideals of universal self and internalized images of their own Jewishness as physically and emotionally repulsive. A Jew's self-image is divided; he or she is subject "to endless self-examination and finally [to] assuming a phantom personality, at once strange and familiar, that haunts him and which is nothing but himself—himself as others see him" (78). Double consciousness, incessant self-perception through the assumptions of a hostile society, is a recurring postcolonial and assimilationist trope. Struggling to assimilate, both Jews and African Americans project dominant cultural ideals upon themselves. Sander Gilman points out that assimilating Jews cannot avoid a self-conception as "inherently different," as "the essence of Otherness," and that "the fragmentation of identity that results is the essence of self-hatred" (1986, 3).

The Enlightenment era, together with the rise of capitalism, meant a change in anti-Semitism. If earlier stereotypes derived from Christian perspectives, capitalism intensified portrayals of conspiratorial Jews, figures useful to deflect blame for the suffering caused by early capitalism. The most important analyst of capitalist dislocation, Karl Marx, internalized such stereotypes; alienation from his Jewish heritage was one factor driving his conceptual breakthroughs. Struggling to be considered a universal human among humans he developed a vision devoid of Jewish tradition, one that rid society of that Otherness which disrupted his social/ psychological stability. Marx's "On the Jewish Question" defines Jewishness as identical with the capitalist state. When this withered away, Jewishness would vanish with it. Marx went so far as to identify the Jewish spirit as integral to capitalism:

> The Jew has emancipated himself in a Jewish manner, not only by acquiring the power of money, but also because *money* has become, through him and also apart from him, a world power, while the practical Jewish spirit has become the practical spirit of the Christian nations. (1978, 49)

Rather than understanding anti-Semitism as an escape valve for capitalism, Marx identified Jewishness with capitalism, a definition making inevitable the disappearance of Judaism when capitalism disappeared. If Jewishness was a key factor in Marx's social alienation, he now proposed it as the essence of alienation, making an effect into a cause and neatly circumventing psychological problems of assimilation.

Marx's self-hating anti-Semitism is a paradigmatic version of an incessant European phenomenon, a manifestation of double consciousness geographically distant from the circumstances that motivated DuBois's theory. In America, too, Jews moving from ghettos into mainstream society suffered alienation similar to that encountered by the Black bourgeoisie. So the young Adrienne Rich was encouraged to deny her Jewishness, to associate "scorn and contempt with the word 'Jew'" in a culture in which "'Ideals' and 'manners' included not hurting someone's feelings by calling her or him a Negro or Jew—naming the hated identity" (1986, 104). The urge to disavow their heritage, to create a generic universalism, affected also Jewish activists, heirs of Marx, who, "yearned to bleach away their past and become men without, or above, a country" (Howe 1976, 291). Jewish heritage was effaced, unspeakable thoughts unspoken (in Toni Morrison's phrasing). Qualities of Otherness, embedded in the social psyche, were simultaneously invisible and omnipresent.

The Jewish double consciousness, manifested as self-hatred, unfolds in an American context in Philip Roth's fiction. In *Portnoy's Complaint* Alexander Portnoy enacts Jewish neurosis through his simultaneous contempt for both Jewish and gentile worlds. Jewish alienation in the diaspora, an unremitting sense of dis-ease, is displayed in his family's paranoia. Portnoy asks what in this Jewish world "was not charged with danger, dripping with germs, fraught with peril?" (1967, 35). Although Portnoy's fear may be of the Jewish world, his family's is of the alien, gentile society.

Yet Portnoy feels only disgust at his family's Jewish qualities—his mother's excessive nurturing, his parents' incessant protectiveness, their physical attributes, particularly the large nose which, as he grows older, he finds sprouting on himself: "J-E-W written right across the middle of that face" (15). Dominant society's hatred is literally engraved upon his face and psychically engraved in his consciousness. Conversely he suffers from a disgust with the gentile world, the goyim, whom he views with a mixture of awe and contempt; the awe for the (perceived) physical perfection and order of the White world, the contempt due to their history of brutality and to his perceived intellectual superiority. Alienated from both Jewish and mainstream American societies, he nevertheless aches to conquer the gentile world through career success and sexual conquests. Indeed, *Portnoy's Complaint* presents such an exaggerated view of Jewish neurosis, such transparent self-awareness, as to make explicit what for most people is unconscious:

> The coincidences of dreams, the symbols, the terrifyingly laughable situations, the oddly ominous banalities, the accidents and humiliation, the bizarrely appropriate strokes of luck or misfortune that other people experience with their eyes shut, I get with mine open! (257)

This is parody with a terribly real basis, alienation made blatantly visible. A Jewish version of Fanon's collective unconscious shapes Portnoy's psyche, which inhabits a tragicomic position torn between two cultures that demonize each other.

The assimilationist Jew and the bourgeois Black, then, are replaying largely the same drama. Assimilationist zeal means rewriting values and history to conform to the ideals of a scornful society. Amiri Baraka's "Black Bourgeois," who "does not hate ofays / hates instead, him self / him black self" (1979a, 103), bluntly displays this dilemma. Through transferring such self-hatred onto the body of another, Blacks and Jews may perceive each other with heightened suspicion.

III

Just as a society must have a scapegoat, so hatred must have a symbol. Georgia has the Negro and Harlem has the Jew.
—James Baldwin

Why, why should it have been so different as between the Negroes and us? . . . Why did we hate one another so?
—Norman Podhoretz

As my father's son, as my uncle's nephew, as a Black person in this world, I say to you, that there was one band of honor and decency in America and it was Jews and blacks.
—Roger Wilkins

As historical victims of racial hatred, Blacks and Jews have long occupied an uncertain position. An intricate archaeology of hatred and identification is apparent in the ways the two groups represent each other; layers of emotion, a great psychic undercurrent, are given form in image. In times of despair and upheaval they may behold in each other hated stereotypes that they long to shed, or may feel solidarity in a mutual struggle for self-worth. In each other, beyond the veil of stereotypes, Blacks and Jews reconstruct their own struggle.

Paul Gilroy explains that the Black diaspora has long relied upon Jewish narratives to define itself: "[I]t was Exodus which provided the primary semantic resource in the elaboration of slave identity, slave historicity, and a distinctive sense of time" (1993, 207). Stuart Hall, too, comments upon this, describing the Bible as "the story of a people in exile dominated by a foreign power, far from 'home' and the symbolic power of the redemptive myth. So the whole narrative of coloniality, slavery and colonization is re-inscribed in the Jewish one" (1996, 491). Blacks in exile conceive of themselves in and through the Old Testament narrative of slavery and redemption, an originary text of identification with the Jewish people. While often silenced, this identification may erupt in intense perceptions of betrayal when American Jews take the side of "the enemy," metaphorically of the Egyptian masters rather than the oppressed slaves.

Extending biblical identification to the modern world, at least one Black declaration of sympathy with international Jewry predated Jewish involvement in African American affairs. In 1887 Edward Wilson Blyden, a Liberian intellectual born in the Caribbean, described a common Black and Jewish "mission to act as 'the spiritual saviors or regenerators of humanity'" (Gilroy 1993, 211). Suffering and exile, if integrated into a national narrative, may acquire a transhistorical sense of purpose. Beyond biblical redemption, secular redemption includes notions of a cultural gift and of a special role as conscience of a nation, or even as global conscience. Gilroy points out three basic similarities in the Jewish and Black situation:

"the notion of a return to the point of origin," "the condition of exile," and "the idea that the suffering of both blacks and Jews has a special redemptive power" (208). This last is actually a result of the first two; the notion of a fall, of suffering and redemption as marking a special purpose, is an archetypal religious and nationalist trope.

In twentieth-century America such identifications have proceeded from Jews to Blacks. Until the Black nationalist movement of the late 1960s, the tone and direction of political relations between the two peoples was largely set by Jewish Americans. With physical features and cultural background similar to other Whites, Jews have long spoken for assimilation, assuming a linking position between White and Black America. This accords with a broader historical Jewish role, described by Michael Rogin as that of "cultural and economic middlemen, disproportionately important not only in trade but also in the liberal professions and image-making businesses" (1996, 64). Economically this middleman role has occurred through Jewish ownership of businesses and housing in the Black ghettos; culturally Jews have been managers and consumers of African American music and literature; while politically Jewish activists have expounded civil rights positions. Hasia Diner explains Black-Jewish political alliances as characterized by Jewish action and Black reaction, a pattern that reinstates the colonizer/colonized relationship on a smaller, more benevolent, scale. It was Jews who first emphasized common features between the two groups, Jews who initiated the alliance.[4] Two factors directly influenced this undertaking. First, the surge of East European Jewish immigrants to America, beginning in the 1880s, provided a group sympathetic to spurned outsiders. Second, the rise of anti-Semitism in American society following World War I, including such measures as quotas and restricted social access, revealed assimilation as precarious and provoked a common legal agenda with African Americans.

Spurred by the lynching of a Southern Jew, the Yiddish press began an intense period of identification with Blacks in 1915. Coinciding with Nazism in Europe and rising anti-Semitism in the United States, the period from 1915 to 1935 was one of extreme vulnerability and anxiety for Jews, who shared with Blacks a fear of the ascendant Ku Klux Klan. Hasia Diner describes how the Yiddish press fervently emphasized parallels between the two groups, portraying Blacks as what Jews had been in Europe: "the most oppressed, the most despised, and the most victimized segment of the population. Blacks seemed, in the eyes of the Yiddish writers, America's Jews" (Diner 1977, 74). Alongside sympathy and identification, Jewish self-interest also spurred an interest in the African American situation. On the one hand, hatred directed against Blacks was hatred not directed at Jews: "The more prejudice exists in this country against the blacks, the safer we Jews will be. *They* are a lightning rod for our protection" (quoted in Katz 1967, 43). On the other hand, if Blacks as the most marginalized group could integrate into America, then surely the less precarious Jewish position would be safe. In either case, Blacks acted as a buffer protecting Jews. Uncertain of their status, Jews viewed their efforts to recruit Blacks into the cultural center as part of their effort to create an America safe for themselves. A multiethnic definition of America validates the Jewish stance of simultaneously participating in their own tradition and contributing to a larger culture. A secure African American role within a society free of racial and ethnic discrimination ensures a secure Jewish role.

That racial boundaries, quotas, and other discriminatory mechanisms affected not just Blacks but, to a lesser extent, Jews mandated a common political agenda. A strong Jewish involvement in the National Association for the Advancement of Colored People (NAACP), and later in the Civil Rights movement, has been critical in transforming the American political landscape to one relatively inclusive and encompassing. The overtures, the initial connections, the expressions of commonality, came largely from one side, from Jews who offered expertise that, in their relative powerlessness, African American leaders could not refuse. Daniel Levering Lewis goes so far as argue that the early "NAACP had something of the aspect of an adjunct of B'Nai B'rith and the American Jewish Committee." He describes how "Marcus Garvey stormed out of NAACP headquarters in 1917, muttering that it was a white organization" (1984, 85), probably the first instance of Black nationalist protest at Jewish usurpation of Black organizations.

Despite parallel historical oppression, Blacks and Jews in America have not had similar destinies. Lewis believes that "theirs was a politically determined kinship, a defensive alliance cemented more from the outside than from within" (84). This is probably true regarding the immediate alliance, but it neglects biblical and historical affinities that linger on (even when inverted into divisive rhetorical tools). Although Jews have overtly articulated common suffering, Black biblical identifications may be more powerful, even if unspoken. Yet for African Americans immediate comparisons are tenuous, due to the generally higher economic and social status of Jewish Americans. Economic and cultural neglect suffered by African Americans has created a long-term power imbalance, an instability. Diner describes how "the Jewish-black alliance had emerged

from the almost total weakness of one party" (1977, 240). However, by
the 1960s African Americans became more forceful in articulating their
own circumstances and in developing the tactics of the Civil Rights movement: "Starting with Rosa Parks' historic refusal to move to the back of
the bus in Montgomery, Alabama, in December 1955, local blacks took
matters into their own hands" (Friedman 1995, 157). Propelled by a dynamic religious and rhetorical tradition, the initiative was shifting toward
African American empowerment. Nevertheless, an imbalance remained
in economic circumstances and social influence, creating resentment that
would one day surface to surprise Jewish liberals. What Jewish Americans assumed was a dialogue initiating African Americans into mainstream
society could appear to Blacks as an extension of their powerlessness.[5]

Eventual Black nationalist critiques of the Jewish role in the Civil
Rights movement, then, were merely the visible rupture in an affiliation
that, due largely to economic and social gaps, was never as close as some
Jewish Americans maintained. Murray Friedman argues that "quite early
in their relationship, it would appear, blacks held a view of Jews that
mixed admiration and respect with suspicion and hostility" (1995, 34).
Due to the urgency of immediate struggle, however, Black uneasiness
remained inert until political circumstances changed. Ironically, the Black-
Jewish alliance's success is perhaps the single most important factor in
leading to its demise. The victories of the 1960s greatly reduced common
political interests. Hence political strategies have increasingly diverged,
Blacks tending to favor a group-based approach bolstered by government
intervention, Jews teetering uneasily between assimilationism and group
rights, and between government intervention and free-market economics.

IV

*I am, as far as I can judge, the most Western Jew of them
all—which means (if I may overstate the case) that I have not
been granted a single second of tranquility, nothing has been
granted to me, everything has to be acquired, not only the
present and future, but also the past.*
                                                              —Franz Kafka

*We have admitted the dregs of Europe until America has been
orientalized, Europeanized, Africanized and mongrelized to that
insidious degree that our genius, stability, greatness, and promise of advancement and achievement are actually menaced.*
                                                              —American congressman, 1924

V

How does the tangled web of Jewish and African American interactions
play itself out in literature? Minority interaction within a majority culture, fragmented consciousness, and formation of a hyphenated group identity are tricky and ambiguous enough. The addition of another marginalized
group complicates matters. Political realities interact with social and psychological needs, shaping the ways in which each group perceives the
other. Historical subject position creates a group's view—and hence its
cultural and literary representations—of another group, refracted, however, through mainstream stereotypes of that second group, as the accompanying diagram illustrates.

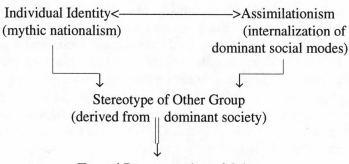

Group's Own Needs:

Individual Identity<————————————>Assimilationism
(mythic nationalism)   (internalization of
                                                 dominant social modes)

Stereotype of Other Group
(derived from dominant society)

Textual Representation of Other

Social needs are channeled through existing stereotypes, participating in
the creation of literary representations. One way of conceiving a literary
text is as a trace of an encompassing social/historical context; in the case
of Black and Jewish Americans, this requires a complex balancing of the
demands for identity both *within* and *against* a larger society. The chaotic
perceptions discussed throughout this book, the misunderstandings and
contradictions, are at least partly explicable by this perceptual split.

Although divided consciousness is unremittingly present for both
Blacks and Jews, its specific effects change according to the evolution of
social status. For Jewish Americans increasing comfort with, and acceptance by, dominant society leads to tensions regarding the significance of
historical memory. Despite awareness of past oppression, the temptation
to internalize dominant stereotypes is great. Seemingly bipolar forces interact in unexpected ways. Countermyths of Blacks often unwittingly reinstate

the original stereotype, for instance in notions of primal creativity. Accepting these countermyths, Jews may feel they are doing justice to their own history by acknowledging Black ability, yet the original stereotype persists. Furthermore, countermyths—though intimately connected to originary myth—may contribute to a conception of American culture as combining the special gifts of many peoples, a stance that justifies the Jewish role within America and intimates current theories of multiculturalism. Conversely, drawing upon a more universalist conception of humanity, Blacks may be represented as complex modern subjects, psychologically fragmented, constrained by stereotypes, struggling, as Jews have so long struggled, to be treated with respect. Overall Jewish attitudes have vacillated between maintaining dominant representations of Blacks, reworking these impressions into a more positive model, and portraying Blacks as complex people beyond stereotype.

While most African American literary portrayals of Jews combine historical sympathies with portraits of complex human beings, stereotypes, of course, have persisted, at times serving as an outlet for frustration and an explanation for continued economic and social disenfranchisement. Prior to 1968, partly reflecting the position of Black authors in an intellectual and political atmosphere replete with Jewish influence, a positive image dominated. Indeed, the predominant Black literary portrait is of a sympathetic and helpful, but ambivalent, Jewish figure; a strain of doubt remains about Jewish intentions. While the Black nationalist period employed anti-Semitic images in an expression of long-suppressed frustration, this eruption was quite brief. Overall, Black representation of Jews has moved from a historical fascination and identification, to a version of postcolonial awe at Jewish patronage, to rupture, to a partial return to an unstable liberalism marked by dissonant voices.

For both Jews and Blacks, then, the split between marginalized and dominant perception leads to a multitude of effects, often contradictory and difficult to pinpoint. Group identification may lead to either solidarity or conflict with other ethnic groups. Furthermore, group loyalties may be based on essentialist notions of difference or may operate in combination with an open-ended cultural relativism. Majority cultural identification often encourages a fetishization of European culture, which may manifest itself in traditional racial doctrine or in endorsement of Enlightenment universalism. These broad effects play themselves out in actual histories of actual peoples, evolving through time and circumstance and finally exhibited in individual beliefs and in daily contacts. All history is simultaneously individual and social; all politics is local. While people live always in specific communities, identification with larger groups demands a certain mythologization.

Literature, in its detailed social and psychological portraits, creates a unique record of the effects of larger ideological structures on individual psyches. Even works that appear to present a monologic viewpoint, ethnocentric and stereotypical of outside groups, create a version of dialectic through appropriating multiple voices. This process extends and intensifies heteroglossia. If even narrow appropriations of "minor" languages jar singular ideologies, implying plurality, a reader of many such texts experiences a larger dislodgement.

To study Black and Jewish history and literature, then, is to study a road map to the contemporary American psyche. If the alienation of double consciousness has been pervasive, a common external threat has been the final ingredient driving Blacks and Jews to a political alliance that culminated in the Civil Rights era. While telling the story of this relationship, reciprocal Black and Jewish literary portraits have taken on each other's language, engaging in a rich dialogic process. Each group has not only employed the narrative of the other in telling its own story, but has participated in a larger American drama. This multifaceted dialectic forms a historical and social narrative of intricate turns, surprising plot twists, and strange psychological manifestations. Embedded in this dialectic are powerful forces driving the human psyche, ancient suppressed traditions at war with modernity, a narrative for the postcolonial world.

When the colonizer meets the colonized both are changed forever. If a European power mandates its culture for a subject people, the occupying power, too, is invariably altered. In a process of blending and adaptation, termed "cultural hybridity" by Homi Bhabha, the past is mythologized and reconstituted under a new set of circumstances. A colonized culture implants its own characteristics into forms imposed by the colonizer: "[H]ybridity is a *problematic* of colonial representation and individuation that reverses the effects of the colonialist disavowal, so that other 'denied' knowledges enter upon the dominant discourse and estrange the basis of its authority" (Bhabha 1994, 175). Hegemony is subject to continual revision by local circumstance and resistance. The dialectic generated by colonialism, by unprecedented meetings of cultures worldwide, is characterized by incessant change, a continual process of centering, decentering, and (mutated) recentering. In response to the global experience of European hegemony, new strains and combinations have flowered everywhere. Society is reconfigured from the margins in figures at once oppositional and assimilationist, who so revise the culture that appropriates them as to query the very term "assimilation." So European Jewry, in tumultuous contact with Enlightenment Europe, bred such transgressive individuals as Marx and Freud, while African America is notable for such figures as Louis Armstrong and Martin Luther King Jr. who revise and criticize a dominant society that in turn appropriates them.

Under severe ideological and psychological pressure, then, a marginalized group is forced to drastically alter its cultural patterns; yet dominant society, too, finds itself transformed. Generating endless cultural revision, Black and Jewish artistic expressions disturb Eurocentric certainty of being the singular arbitrator of civilization. When the margins begin to speak, they by definition erode conventional categories. The diasporic figure is the catalyst for cultural hybridity, intimating a transnational, postmodern culture.

One early trope for our current period of ceaseless cross-breeding is the mythologized figure of the wandering Jew in whom East meets West, a biblical cosmology meets a Hellenic one, boundary crossings and transgressions find a focal point. The African American, too, is a transgressive figure, ostensibly made blank for the role of slave, yet in whom African and European cultures cross and breed, a cultural miscegenation threatening to the social order. If conventional stereotypes of Blacks and Jews serve to contain dominant anxieties, cultural and biological mixtures threaten the framework of dominant hierarchy. Marginalized, diasporic cultures are transgressive in their very language (codified as "nonstandard" or "broken"). Gilles Deleuze and Felix Guatari describe a "minor" language, using Yiddish as their prototypical example, as "lacking a grammar and . . . filled with vocables that are fleeting, mobilized, emigrating, and turned into nomads" (1975, 25). Yiddish, in short, is an oppositional language, one embedded within another culture and hence simultaneously addressed to an internal community and reacting to an external one. Similarly, Henry Louis Gates Jr. describes how, "free of the white person's gaze, black people created their own unique vernacular structures and relished in the double play that these forms bore to white forms. Repetition and revision are fundamental to black artistic forms" (1988, xxiv). "Minor" modes of expression are characterized by a double-voicedness, a simultaneous awareness of, and migration between, (at least) two societies, driving them to innovation and recombination, and to a sardonic awareness of language's slippery, multiple nature. The dilemma of double consciousness is thus embedded in Black and Jewish expression. Satire, experimentation, and transgression are inherent in "minor" languages.

The impulse to experiment, of course, is not unique to "minor" literature, but is a recurring feature of twentieth-century literature. The diasporic nature of Black and Jewish life is paradigmatic of the twentieth century. If Enlightenment thought is defined as the search for stable systems regarding nature and society, and of the individual self, literary modernism has been described as a period of increasing fragmentation, as "the breaking up and progressive disintegration of those meticulously constructed 'systems' and 'types' and 'absolutes'" (McFarlane 1978, 80). Mikhail Bakhtin describes modern literature as inherently transgressive, with the novel paradigmatic in absorbing, juxtaposing, and transforming older, more static forms. In contrast to closed stylistic and imagistic systems, the novel provokes a plethora of styles and voices: "Literary language is not represented in the novel as a unitary, completely finished-off and indisputable language—it is represented precisely as a living mix of varied and opposing voices . . . developing and renewing itself" (Bakhtin 1981, 49). The novel imitates, and often parodies, not only a variety of older literary forms but the voices of multiple social classes and, at times, ethnic and national groups. Authorial voice is infiltrated by external voices that disrupt unitary linguistic and ideological systems. Thus African and Jewish diaspora literature are paradigmatic of modernist fragmentation and alienation.[6]

Yet modern literature has long been claimed as part of the dominant establishment and used to enforce the status quo. Understood as an icon of the Great Tradition, literature has been fetishized to enshrine an elite group as caretakers of a mysterious knowledge. One contemporary example is Allan Bloom's claim that "men may live more fully in reading Plato and Shakespeare than at any other time, because they are participating in essential being and are forgetting their accidental life" (1987, 380). Bloom metaphorically places Plato and Shakespeare outside of time and history; yet their works are only enriched by a study of historical context. The aestheticization of a literary tradition may lead to a tame, contained approach to reading, disrupting its social and political nature (although the reverse may lead to a flat, reductive view of literature). Literature originating in a White, patriarchal Europe has long been enshrined in an educational establishment that uses notions of "liberal humanism" in a myopic, exclusionary fashion.

Claims to a monolithic literary canon are undermined by a proliferation of texts from an increasing variety of perspectives. Twentieth-century literary bricolage constitutes a clamorous assemblage of cross-connected linguistic systems (often generated from the framework of specific class and cultural needs). Burdened with excess meanings, these systems are replete with contradictions and surprising connotations. Society writes its texts on the mind of the author who, in an inextricable mixture of conscious and unconscious production, organizes, prioritizes, and symbolically encodes them. The author, of course, is not a mere mechanism for encoding social text; his or her individual situation, idiosyncratic view of life, and artistic sense all coalesce in a work of literature. The interplay between society and author, indeed, accounts for a text's richness and multiple interpretability; based as it is on a complex of implicit meanings that are themselves contested, the text threatens to overwhelm its boundaries in an overdetermined eruption. Yet if literature is overdetermined, society is even more so; the ideological structures holding it together are unstable, vulnerable to interrogation from within and without. Literature, among its many uses and pleasures, provides a vehicle for investigating this shifting amalgam, and is perhaps the vehicle best suited for illuminating the contradictions and instability that beset society and, through society, the individual psyche.

Bakhtin's theory of modernist heterogeneity describes, in an idealistic way, the multiple cultures that have inhabited both Jews and Blacks. Twentieth-century literature occurs in a terrain of unprecedented cultural and linguistic exchange: "The world becomes polyglot, once and for all and irreversibly. The period of national languages, coexisting but closed and deaf to each other, comes to an end. Languages throw light on each other" (Bakhtin 1981, 12). Language is "nomadic" and so, necessarily, is literature. Embedded within overlapping language-systems, modern literature acts as an intermediary force, undermining the hegemony of any single system. By revealing worlds of otherness, twentieth-century literature undermines claims of the academy as the sole arbiter of culture.

Beyond its dialogic function, modern literature has developed intense interior explorations of a variety of consciousnesses. Geoffrey Hartman describes romanticism—an early stage of modernism—as facilitating a widening "ability to feel for others," which allows representation of "a mad mother, an infanticide, an idiot boy, a homeless woman, a destitute shepherd, an old and disabled servant" (1997, 141). Besides broadening its subject matter, modern literature has increasingly dwelt upon subtleties of the human psyche. Milan Kundera explains how "the novel, in its quest for the self, was forced to turn away from the visible world of action and examine instead the invisible interior life" (1988, 24). Between action and interiorization, between Homer's *Odyssey* and Joyce's *Ulysses*, however, come dialogue, varieties of dialects, heterogenous linguistic layers, and an increasing focus on private worlds. To Richard Rorty the novel is the best means for the "process of coming to see other human beings as 'one of us' rather than as 'them'" (1989, xvi). Humanistic literary tradition traces a broad arc toward an understanding of others, of those outside the reader's isolated community. Paradoxically, it does so through an increasing interiorization in which individual self is somewhat illusory, entangled as it is with social and political selves. Written into consciousness is an intricate blend of social forces; dialogism invades the social interior.

Literary evolution, then, is inherently social and contradictory. In being so, it subverts attempts to use literature as an unchanging fixture of a preordained social structure by encouraging an experimentalism that incorporates "another's voice in another's language" (Bakhtin 1981, 324). This revolutionary quality is enhanced in literature by an expanding variety of authors, including women and a widening class, national, ethnic, and racial spectrum. The individual consciousness emphasized in Western literature becomes a tool of liberation. Intense explorations of the self, of various selves, counteract ethnocentricism, breaking down suppositions and stereotypes, generating a widening sympathy. Literature is one forum for society's multiplicitous clash of ideologies, a dialogue by which identity is demarcated, defined, refined, and redefined. Literature gives expression to a Babel of voices, becoming a tool of confusion, yes, but also the beginnings of understanding.

Black (E)Masculinity
and Anti-Semitism

The African-American woman, the mother, the daughter, becomes historically the powerful and shadowy evocation of a cultural synthesis long evaporated—the law of the Mother—only and precisely because legal enslavement removed the African-American male not so much from sight as from mimetic view as a partner in the prevailing social fiction of the Father's name, the Father's law.

—Hortense Spillers

Besides the Jewish role in the National Association for the Advancement of Colored People (NAACP), another key point of contact between Jews and Blacks occurred in the Communist Party. Of course the agenda of the two organizations was entirely different. Whereas the NAACP dealt specifically with racial and ethnic issues, communism considered itself a universal movement based on irrefutable laws of economic materialism. Although these, at least in theory, relegated Blacks to a subset of the proletariat, in practice the U.S. Communist Party provided a consistent antiracist platform (Wald 1994, 1). American communism was divided between following a doctrinaire party line originating in Moscow and reacting to pressing racial issues.

That ethnic issues would be an important subtext of American communism was dictated by extensive Jewish participation. While communism in no way considered itself Jewish, its strong East European roots, in combination with its internationalist character, led to a large Jewish membership. Richard Wright describes how in his initial visit to a communist organization he was introduced "to a Jewish boy who was to become one of the nation's leading painters, to a chap who was to become one of the eminent composers of his day, to a writer who was to create some of the best novels of his generation, to a young Jewish boy who was destined to film the Nazi invasion of Czechoslovakia" (1977, 62). This injection of intellectuals and artists into a setting tied to an ideology of class struggle was bound to create underlying conflict, as was the mix of Jews, gentiles, and a few Blacks. Wright peppers his discussion of Communist Party members with the adjective "Jewish"—"a Jewish chap" introduces him to the party (60), "a Jewish chap appeared at one of our meetings" (70)—yet is silent about the significance of this term. The signifier "Jewish" stands out as unexamined yet pregnant with meaning, implying both radicalism and artistic sensibility. Since Wright is rarely less than open about any issue, the unexamined juxtaposition of "Jewish" and "communist" is especially tantalizing. Wright may wish to avoid slandering the Jewish people with the oft repeated charge of communism; he may not have entirely thrown off the universalist demands of the movement he was once a part of; he may be unwilling to acknowledge the mixture of gratitude and resentment that Jewish radicalism spurs in him. Wright's self-censorship reflects a general public silence regarding the Jewish relationship with African Americans. In the Communist Party, as elsewhere, open expression of ethnicity was suppressed.

A barely spoken ethnic awareness is critical for Wright's attraction to the Communist Party:

> It was not the economics of Communism, nor the great power of trade unions, nor the excitement of underground politics that claimed me; my attention was caught by the similarity of the experiences of workers in other lands, by the possibility of uniting scattered but kindred peoples into a whole. (1977, 63)

Both the excitement and contradiction of Black participation in communism are expressed here; the racial/ethnic bridging that captured Wright assumes an acknowledgment of difference denied by the Party. African American culture was ignored; Blacks were officially considered one wing of the proletariat, to be mobilized for strategic purposes. However powerful communism's materialist conception, national and racial identity, that other great force driving twentieth-century history, was considered secondary. So the Communist Party rendered itself oblivious to dangerous fissures, ancient psychic architectures.

I

Prior to Jewish involvement in African American affairs, Jewish Americans, to Blacks, were not particularly differentiated from other Whites. For the young James Baldwin,

> Jews, as such, until I got to high school, were all incarcerated in the Old Testament, and their names were Abraham, Moses, Daniel, Ezekiel, and Job, and Shadrach, Meshach, and Abednego. It was bewildering to find them so many miles and centuries out of Egypt. (1993, 36–37)

Jews loomed large in their Old Testament roles, particularly as a slave people escaping to the promised land, a narrative elaborated upon by Zora Neale Hurston in her epic retelling of the Exodus tale in Black dialect, *Moses, Man of the Mountain*. Hebrew and African American slavery and redemption become difficult to distinguish, an archetypal formation-point of Black identity.

The New Testament, as interpreted via traditional anti-Semitism, provided Black consciousness a very different Jewish figure: the betrayer of Christ who continued century after century obstinately to reject Christianity. This lonely figure, doomed to eternal wandering and damnation, was easily adapted as a means of contextualizing Jews. So Richard Wright as a child taunted Jewish children: "Bloody Christ killers / Never trust a Jew / Bloody Christ killers / What won't a Jew do?" (1989, 70). The sadistic impulse of the European pogroms is here transposed to African American mouths (admittedly a relatively powerless agent). Yet, Baldwin argues, while the Jew is a figure of hatred, tales of Jewish suffering allow for redemption. In the Black consciousness the wandering Jew may be transformed: "The images of the suffering Christ and the suffering Jew are wedded with the image of the suffering slave, and they are one: the people that walked in darkness have seen a great light" (1955, 67). An extraordinary bipolarity of vision inhabits African American Christians: Jews are simultaneously sympathetic fellow sufferers and the enemy of God and humanity. These contradictory images are one root of the tortured ambivalence that continues to pervade African American images of Jewry.

Yet the Jewish role in America has been too variegated for biblical images to serve as more than a start to interpretation. Blending into Whites, slave owners, and oppressors, American Jews were a bizarre anachronism awaiting evaluation by African Americans. Alongside biblical images, Black conceptions of Jewish Americans were formed by their role in dominant society. After all, the situations of the two peoples have been strikingly different in America. Jewish behavior has often reflected this; Jews have not always been any kinder or more sympathetic to Blacks than have other Whites. Wright describes how when he worked as a hospital janitor, "daily I saw young Jewish boys and girls receiving instruction in chemistry and medicine that the average black boy or girl could never receive" (1977, 47). This occurred prior to the Second World War, during the height of American anti-Semitism, when Jews were kept out of universities through quotas, when select neighborhoods and clubs were barred to Jews. Yet from the Black vantage point Jews participated fully in American society. If Whites often treated Blacks as invisible, Wright makes clear, so did Jews: "when I asked a timid question I found that even Jewish doctors had learned to imitate the sadistic method of humbling a Negro that the native-born whites had cultivated" (48).

In a strangely similar situation, Primo Levi describes himself as a Jewish chemist in the laboratories of Auschwitz where the young German women "never speak to us and turn up their noses when they see us shuffling across the laboratory, squalid and filthy, awkward and insecure in our shoes" (1961, 129). Degraded to the status of a nonhuman thing, an object, one becomes self-conscious of one's nonentity, comes to act the part. Levi imagines

> a man who is deprived of everyone he loves, and at the same time of his house, his habits, his clothes, in short, of everything he possesses: he will be a hollow man, reduced to suffering and needs, forgetful of dignity and restraint, for he who loses all often easily loses himself. (23)

Regarded as nothing, one becomes functionally nothing, merely a silent part of the operations of a machine. The Jew in Europe and the Black in America underwent parallel degradation, deliberate destruction of social identity. In this process American Jews have at times participated. So a young Jewish boy, an efficiency expert, times Richard Wright when he cleans a room, assuming that, like a machine, he should be able to continue work at this maximum rate all day without a break, without a change of pace. Finally the "object" protests: "'Why don't you work for a change?' I blurted" (1977, 50). Such eruptions in the face of an ideologically imposed silence are a continuing feature of Wright's work, his portrayal of the dehumanized object speaking itself into being, a violation of the mask of humility imposed upon African Americans. Individual language and agency was long denied in a torment designed to keep Blacks functioning at society's most unrewarding labor.

If Jews could act as ruthlessly as any other member of dominant society, in remembering their own dehumanization they could also display a sympathy and common humanity with Blacks. In *American Hunger* this transgression of expected roles places the narrator in a terra incognita where long-developed defense mechanisms no longer apply. Wright describes himself working for Jewish immigrants, projecting onto them his Southern heritage of mistrust, routinely lying to them when he takes a day off for a postal exam. Questioned by his employers, he tells an escalating series of lies. The survival mechanism, routinely accepted by Southern Whites who either assumed a Black incapable of shrewdness or simply accepted lying as part of Black nature, backfires in a situation novel to both parties. Wright has acted according to one set of expectations and encountered another:

> A southern white man would have said "Get to hell out of here!" or "All right, nigger. Get to work." But no white people had ever stood their ground and probed at me, questioned me at such length. It dawned upon me that they were trying to treat me as an equal, which made it even more impossible for me ever to tell them that I had lied, why I had lied. (1977, 10)

Unprepared to engage in a dialogue with Whites in which normal human emotions and motivations are expected of him, Wright is simply unable to express himself.[1] Besides its psychological fascination, its revelation of the insufficiency of Black survival tactics under unanticipated circumstances, this incident is revealing regarding the context of the Jewish-Black alliance. It shows the difficulty Jews might have in shedding their roles as members of dominant society, in engaging in equal dialogue.

This is one small incident in a continuing ordeal of broken communication. When Jews presented themselves to Blacks as mentors with a mutual history of suffering, an invisible barrier existed, one intensified by the long African American training in hiding their beliefs from White society, in maintaining a mask. Besides the racial element, class and social differences were significant, for the Jews most likely to reach out to Blacks were usually highly educated. When Wright urges the hiring of "Charles DeSheim, a talented Jew, as director" for a Black playwright project, DeSheim's sensitivity to the need for Black empowerment and self-expression is misunderstood by the Black actors, who revolt. Steeped in the minstrel tradition they demand "a play that will make the public love us" (1977, 114). Social conditioning makes incomprehensible to them the educated intelligentsia, Wright as well as DeSheim. The barrier is due to class as well as race; the desire to please rather than engage is inherited from Southern survival tactics; they insist on maintaining the mask, the only life they know. "Don't you know your friends?" (115) Wright asks the actors, but the tortured history of race relations makes them unable to separate friend from enemy, a distinction often blurry in our perplexed society.

Jews, then, appear in a multitude of guises in relation to African Americans, from bloody Christ-killers to suffering slaves, from greedy capitalists to valiant allies. An apparently natural suspicion—actually ideologically and socially created—endures among African Americans regarding Jews, a suspicion of which Jews prior to 1968 were largely unaware. The Black mask hid African American character and motivation from Jews, as it did from all White Americans. Yet Jews, too, existed for Black Americans as a bewildering spectrum of images. Each group lived behind a murky facade of stereotypic images. When they encountered each other in the Communist Party behind a theoretical equality, Jews stood in senior positions with superior numbers and education. Behind theoretical unity was a power imbalance, behind theoretical universality cultural differences. Jews and Blacks stood largely masked to each other.

II

They kill each other & hate the sun. They have no God save
who they are. Their black selves. Their lust. Their insensible
animal eyes.
—LeRoi Jones/Amiri Baraka, *The System of Dante's Hell*

The obscuring of Black identity, particularly in the Communist Party, is an implicit theme of two African American novels of the 1940s: Richard Wright's *Native Son* and Chester Himes's *Lonely Crusade*. These novels depict polarized conceptions of communism as a movement speaking for the disenfranchised and as a conspiratorial internationalism, a split paralleling African American perceptions of Jews. Through the viewpoints of divergent protagonists the two novels cross paths, unfolding the inescapability of race regardless of class and education. The novels are balanced between the stimulus provided by Jewish articulation of the African American situation and the ultimate limitations of such intervention, showing the need to develop Black intellectual networks.

From the beginning, then, Jewish mentoring of Blacks was a relationship with natural boundaries, one destined to exhaust itself. While the relationship at times may have approached paternal status, as a familial model it was dysfunctional, with a wide gap between "fathers" and "sons" producing, for Blacks, an extended dependency. At one extreme the Jew acts as a kind of father figure, a savior appearing unaccountably from the midst of a hostile society. This role is clearest in Richard Wright's *Native Son,* in which Boris Max articulates all that the silently raging Bigger Thomas has locked within him. As represented in the White press, Thomas is the archetypal Black rapist, a savage beast independent of historical and social context. He is mute, unable to articulate himself or his crime, which is rendered as instinctual. Only the Jewish Max is positioned, through education and social status, to explain to the White jury the historical context that created Bigger Thomas (though his explanation is rejected, since in the jury's mind Thomas is guilty by definition). Max's defense is a crystallized version of a liberalism that favors material explanations over biological, cultural, or individual ones, a version, however well meaning, of the rationalism that observes, analyzes, and judges Blacks. If the explicit rhetoric of *Native Son* voices a common history between Jews and Blacks, the social and educational gap between Max and Thomas makes complex communication and understanding virtually impossible. Thomas's final realization that Max ultimately cannot understand or speak for him portends the eventual necessity of a Black split from liberal and radical, largely Jewish, benefactors. African Americans must find their own voice.

To fully illustrate the conditions that produce inarticulate people capable of extreme behavior, Wright chose an extreme figure. So *Native Son* portrays a character totally victimized by White society through the limitations in his life choices and the related limitations of his moral vision. Irving Howe calls *Native Son* a crucial statement of Black anger that "made impossible a repetition of the old lies," that forced the White man "to recognize himself as an oppressor" (1990, 121) who had created a society in which "violence is central to the life of the American Negro, defining and crippling him" (9). Contrarily, *Native Son's* limited vision of African American society has been criticized. James Baldwin considers it "a continuation, a complement of that monstrous legend it was written to destroy" (1955, 22), while Ralph Ellison reproaches the "hatred, fear and vindictiveness which Wright chose to emphasize" (1966, 121) as constricting the richness and remarkable adaptability of African American culture. The debate is recurring between two visions of Black literature: as a vehicle of protest and as a rich portrayal of humanity and of culture. Ultimately, the two categories represent a false opposition, since Black literature may do either or, most often, both. However, the search for a contained set of works canonized as prototypical for African American literature, as Howe attempts, polarizes the debate. If one refuses to search for *the* Black voice, considering African American literature as polyphonic, multivoiced, and ever changing, novels can then be appraised for what they accomplish rather than for what they fail to accomplish. Given this, *Native Son* remains a powerful statement of African American frustration and rage.

Native Son's claustrophobic vision of Black helplessness and anger is reprised in a nonfiction work, Price Cobbs and William Grier's psychiatric study *Black Rage* (1968). As Fanon had done for the Martinician, Cobbs and Grier delineate the African American psyche as hopelessly distorted by dominant conceptions that cultivate a "desperate dread of blackness . . . an unreasoning self-hatred and . . . pitiful wish to be white" (1968, 79). These emotions accord with a mechanism of control that erases African history:

> The experience of slavery was unbelievably efficient in effacing the African. . . . American Negroes provide a unique picture of a people whose history was destroyed and who were offered in its stead a narrow ledge of toil on which to live and grow and nurture children. (102)

Such a loss of cultural roots breeds despair and self-negation, especially when contrasted to an idealized picture of White society. For this reason (among others) Ralph Ellison defends the richness of Black culture and the multiplicity of Black possibility. Yet such an understanding is difficult in a society where Blacks, trained to view themselves as inferior, are unable to criticize a standard they believe themselves incapable of attaining. So our society's physical ideal "is the blond, blue-eyed, white-skinned girl with regular features" (Cobbs and Grier 1968, 40); even the word "regular" here is interpellated by a White social norm. The omnipresence of such role models is fictionally compressed in Toni Morrison's *The Bluest Eye*, which graphically illustrates how a poor Black girl is coerced into praying for blue eyes. Her family's poverty is naturalized as an inescapable condition of blackness: "It was as though some mysterious all-knowing master had given each one a cloak of ugliness to wear, and they had each accepted it without question" (Morrison 1970, 34). Such ideologically ingrained self-hatred is at the root of Cobbs and Grier's analysis, and of Bigger Thomas's psyche.

From a condition of existential nothingness *Native Son* portrays perhaps the only route by which the protagonist can act himself into being. The novel is largely about the transgressing of boundaries that in America in 1940 were not meant to be crossed—a crossing into a utopian White zone forbidden Blacks not just by a physical police force but by dominant society's interpellation of the collective Black psyche. Bigger Thomas is deposited in a situation utterly alien to him regarding a White society in which his training as a "Negro," shy and outwardly respectful, allows him only a superficial perspective. Far more than Wright's Jewish employer in *American Hunger*, Mary Dalton and Jan Erlone's friendly treatment breaks Thomas's fragile defense mechanisms. The couple simply doesn't comprehend the danger that Thomas seems to know instinctively (but actually has had culturally engraved into him): that familiarity with a White woman historically has meant torture and death for Black American males. Thomas's terror leads to his smothering of Mary Dalton, paradoxically the only event that can give meaning to his meaningless life. By foregrounding the hatred and emptiness of Black life while disregarding other elements, Wright increases White understanding—and Whites, I believe, are his primary intended audience—of the suffering they have inflicted upon African Americans.

Fulfilling his role as a symbol of hopelessness, the uneducated Thomas is unable to articulate his situation. To fill in the gap left by his silence, Wright employs the Jewish lawyer Boris Max, whose closing speech to the jury expounds some of Wright's own historical perspective as filtered through the philosophy of the Communist Party. This didactic speech risks making of the novel a flat, political tract; Harold Bloom argues that those who defend *Native Son* "must choose. Either Bigger Thomas is a responsible consciousness, and so profoundly culpable, or else only the white world is responsible and culpable, which means, however, that Bigger ceases to be of fictive interest and becomes an ideogram" (1988, 4). This either/or vision ignores the novel's progression, in which Thomas begins as an ideogram, a cramped stereotype of the hopeless victim, and blossoms outward (albeit it is an ugly blossoming) through being selected by the Daltons and through murder, to become a moral agent able to ponder his social status and its implications. As Donald Gibson contends, those critics are wrong who claim that Thomas never speaks for himself. True, he remains silent publicly, in the courtroom, but in individual conversations, particularly in a murmured speech largely neglected by Max, he finally articulates his position. Gibson argues, rightly I believe, that "the focus of the novel is not on the trial nor on Max, but on Bigger and on his finally successful attempt to come to terms with his imminent death" (1972, 97).

Native Son's ideological summation comes in two speeches: Thomas's rambling one and Max's final polished address. For the Black voice is substituted the Jewish radical who fills in the spaces of the African American experience left blank to White society. To the prosecuting attorney's narrative of a "demented savage" eager "to rape and kill" (Wright 1966, 378) Max presents a counternarrative of victim of the state, dehumanized by a cruel society that needs to atone for its sins: "[H]is life and fate are linked to ours" (354). Max's overarching vision exemplifies the religious intensity of the Communist Party. Not that Max is like the myopic communists of Ralph Ellison's "Brotherhood" in *Invisible Man,* who subsume all character, both individual and racial, to the higher purposes of "the Party." A humane, flexible communist, even Max ultimately blurs his vision through excessive social analysis. So he explains of Thomas, "the complex forces of society have isolated for us here a symbol, a test symbol" (Wright 1966, 354). It is Max, not—as Bloom claims—Wright, who reduces Thomas to a polemical ideogram.

Thomas's own development, however, is inexorably away from being a test symbol, toward being a complete human being who grapples with his fate to create a newly conscious self. This identity develops against a backdrop of negation, a society that denies humanity to Blacks and to the impoverished. So Bigger Thomas qualifies his affirmation—"I wanted to do what the white boys in school did" (328)—with a denial, with the belief that "his life was not worth the effort that Max had made to save it" (371). The only definition of full humanity allowed him is the freedom and achievement of the "white boys" that he can never possess. A more comprehensive definition of freedom, the ability to define and explain one's own life and social experience, remains embryonic; in articulating his troubles to Max, Thomas finally feels a recognition, a "new sense of the value of himself" (334). Still, this value is never his; his fate is not his own to decide or even to express in public: "But Bigger wanted to save his *own* life. Yet he knew that the moment he tried to put his feelings into words, his tongue would not move" (337). Only an outsider can defend him before the White mass—the judge, the jury, the crowds, the tabloids who collectively judge him, or rather render once again old judgments, for, like K. in *The Trial,* Bigger Thomas is always already guilty. Before this prejudicial omnipotence only Boris Max—White, communist, Jewish—can "put his [Thomas's] feelings into words." Claiming his background gives him a special identification with Thomas—"I'm a Jew and they hate me, but I know why and I can fight" (332)—Max takes on the guise of the absent father figure, able to speak for Thomas.

Yet Max cannot feel Thomas's feelings, has not raised him, has not experienced his life; Jewish American alienation proves only partly analogous to Black experiences. Thomas zigzags wildly between a desperate need for Max's sympathy and a realization of the gulf between them: "Max was upon another planet, far off in space" (386). Thomas simply cannot explain his motive in the killing of Mary Dalton, for "the telling of it would have involved an explanation of his entire life" (286). Despite his understanding, he lacks the education to articulate his situation (defined by constraints that, in 1940, had barely begun to be articulated in academia). Trapped in a barren culture of poverty, lack of education, and constant wariness and envy of White society, he cannot speak about the dilemma most crucial to him. Max can understand him only partially, on an intellectual rather than an emotional level. When he asks Thomas if he liked Mary Dalton, the intensity of the reply stuns him:

> Bigger leaped to his feat; his eyes widened and his hands lifted midway to his face, trembling.
> "No! No! Bigger. . . ." Max said.
> "*Like* her? I *hated* her! So help me God, I hated her!" he shouted.
> (323)

Max is simply unable to comprehend this response to someone who treated Thomas only with kindness; he cannot understand how Mary Dalton had threatened Thomas's entire worldview. Even as relations between Thomas and Max unfold, even as Thomas explains himself as straightforwardly as possible, a gap remains.

Despite Max's protestations about his Jewish identity, the two simply do not share the same world vision or speak the same emotional language. Both the power and source of Thomas's hate remain beyond Max's understanding. As Thomas explains: "Mr. Max we're all split up. What you say is kind ain't kind at all. . . . All I know is they kill us for women like her" (324). The source of Thomas's terror, abstract and inexplicable to Max, is extremely concrete to Thomas. He finally begins to articulate that which drove him to murder. The mystery is left not unspoken, but spoken in a fragmented way lacking larger contextualization and analysis. Those critics who are confounded by Thomas's actions or who believe Max's speech to be the novel's ideological summation repeat Max's mistake, remaining bound within their own assumptions. For them, as for Max, Thomas is a symbol, part of a larger ideological battle. At the deepest emotional level the sympathy is not there. Max remains unable to comprehend the urgent drives behind the murder: "'No; no; no . . . Bigger not that.' . . . Max's eyes were full of terror. . . . Max groped for his hat like a blind man" (392). Just as the white-haired Mrs. Dalton gave generously to Negro charities yet (both literally and figuratively) could not see Bigger Thomas, so Max, despite his ideological commitment, cannot finally see, cannot comprehend, Bigger Thomas as a human being. Both communist ideology and Jewish sympathy are insufficient. The Jewish history of oppression is geographically, chronologically, and culturally removed from that of Black America. African Americans must articulate their own situation, their own passion, a battle that Richard Wright fought his entire life. The conclusion of *Native Son* implies the force that would propel the Black Power movement of the 1960s, the search for a voice capable of articulating this anger.

III

Chester Himes's largely neglected novel *Lonely Crusade* (1947) develops many of *Native Son*'s themes regarding Black emasculation, though from a different class perspective. The dehumanized Bigger Thomas, driven to murder and employing this murder as his only act of agency, has an analogue in Lee Gordon, a member of the Black intelligentsia whose education and activist background do little to protect him from the frustrations that plague Thomas; their common murderous (self-)hatred is due to racism, not social class. Himes's portrait of Jews, too, develops on a course opposite that of *Native Son*; the anti-Semitic Gordon could never place faith in a Jewish patron in the way that Thomas does. Yet perceptions of Jews cover a similar spectrum, from role model to object of alienation. Gordon's paranoia is a prototypical example of how the humiliations inflicted upon African Americans may find an outlet in the figure of the Jew. Only through conversations with, and growing support from, the Jewish Abe Rosenberg does Gordon begin to feel the affinities that Thomas early has for Boris Max. Gordon's resistance ultimately makes this process a far more substantial one than Thomas's too easy attachment to Max. Rosenberg not only wins Gordon's trust but provides an alternative voice for his concerns, one seemingly objective and free from the claustrophobic rage that envelops Gordon. Finally Rosenberg is revealed as a paragon of stability and reason in the cruel, misogynist atmosphere inflicted upon 1940s Black America.

Gordon's anti-Semitism is really directed at his own weakness, his inability to measure up to dominant constructions of the independent male agent. These are intensified in the figuration of the hypermasculine Black; yet in reality Black males are among the most powerless in American society, forced into a position of (feminine) passivity, of silence and deference. Jewish males, contrarily represented in dominant stereotypes as feminized objects—bookish, nonviolent, symbolically castrated—may personify the passivity that Black males feel inflicted upon themselves. Despite such tensions, in a society in which bookish activities increasingly mean success, the Jewish subject provides an alternative model to the extreme vision of Black masculinity constructed by dominant society, an alternative ascendant by the novel's end.

Lee Gordon's wounded masculinity vividly illustrates how education is no escape from racial degradation and psychological torment. In *Lonely Crusade* Jews provide an image of a degraded feminization, a portrayal that spurs Steven J. Rosen to assert that the novel not only

> depicts and explores black anti-Semitism, it also ventilates an anti-Semitic streak that recurs in Himes' work in tandem with anxiety to assert masculinity. Himes tended to disparage Jews in order to construct his manhood—differentiating himself from those (Jews) who imputedly lacked masculinity or disrespected its significations. (1995, 48)

The rugged masculinity constructed around Black America encourages such interpretations of aestheticized, physically passive Jews, interpretations greatly reinforced by conventional anti-Semitic representations. Indeed, the convergence of Jewishness with an Otherness threatening to masculinity is an ancient European image; Sander Gilman describes how "the association of the image of the Jew (read: male Jew) with that of the woman (including the Jewish woman) is one of the most powerful images embedded in the arguments about race" (1993, 43). Daniel Boyarin's treatment of this image system describes circumcision as the most obvious physical sign of Jewish femininity, of a lack of human (read masculine) completeness, a susceptibility to hysteria, culminating in the myth "that Jewish men menstruate" (1997, 130). Stereotypical Jewish physical features, including voice and gesture, reinforce the image of feminine passivity. Both woman and Jew, then, are defined against the European male through difference and through lack; they are alternatively incomplete or of another species. Boyarin explains this construction as based not on anatomy but upon the hierarchy of power: "If being gendered 'male' in our culture is having power and speech—phallus and logos—the silenced and powerless subject is female" (118). The African American male, then, occupies the position of the European Jew, of enforced passivity. Already self-conscious of his difference from the European and American norm, some Black men may feel particularly vulnerable, and may display sexual bravado, misogyny, and anti-Semitism to ward off a threatening society.

Lonely Crusade provides numerous images, refracted through its Black male center of consciousness, that continue the pattern of feminizing the Jew. Overwhelmed by this explicit articulation, Rosen slights the novel's larger development, which makes of Rosenberg an increasingly trusted character able not only to articulate thoughts too dangerous to have been voiced by Gordon but opening new emotional terrain, new definitions of masculinity and racial/ethnic survival. It is this which allows Gilbert Muller, in an interpretation strikingly antithetical to Rosen's, to describe Rosenberg as "a spiritual guide for Gordon and one of the sharpest, most sympathetic characters in all of Himes' fiction . . . [who] teaches his protégé the 'habits of survival' (160) that must link all oppressed people in every form of society" (1989, 36). Both Rosen's and Muller's arguments can be thoroughly supported by textual passages; their simultaneous existence exemplifies the powerful contradictory roles the Jewish figure plays in the Black psyche. Yet Muller is wrong to claim that the "habits of survival" are the same for Jews and Blacks; these differ according to historical roots and patterns. Encouraged by dominant society, Black males use achievements in sports, dance, and the military as critical to their attainment of a masculine identity. By contrast, the Jewish emphasis on intellect and education rather than on physical accomplishment as a sign of masculinity ensures eventual success in contemporary America. A long tradition of scholarship and dialogue is manifested in Rosenberg's behavior, a social ideal that simultaneously threatens Lee Gordon's assumptions and offers an alternative model of masculinity.[2]

For Black rage and emasculation whiteness is the primary symbol of blame, from which may be displaced a hatred of women, Jews, and communists (each term in this series being a displacement from the prior terms). *Lonely Crusade*'s brooding Lester McKinley, an older and even more embittered version of Gordon, exemplifies the rage described by Cobbs and Grier through "the urge to kill white men" (Himes 1986, 70–71), a pathology that his migrations across the United States cannot dislodge (69). McKinley's knowledge of psychiatry allows him to comprehend his anger in a way unavailable to Bigger Thomas, to analyze how "the Negroes were mentally ill from this oppression—ill beyond the circumstances of their present lives" (71). Yet analysis does not imply a cure; hatred continues to torment McKinley. As with Bigger Thomas the killing of a White person, here in the mind only, becomes McKinley's release from his condition, an existential statement of being in a world where whiteness is reified as the archetypal configuration, the sole arbiter, of meaning.

The archetypal symbol of whiteness—ostensibly of civilization, refinement, and aesthetic beauty, but underlying these of superiority in the struggle for power—is White womanhood. If White men control this symbol of economic and social superiority, Black men are driven by dominant ideology to long for it. Eldridge Cleaver goes so far as to condense all White women into the symbol of "The Ogre," who "possessed a tremendous and dreadful power over me, and I didn't understand this power or why I was at its mercy" (1992, 24). In a gentler reaction to this phenomenon, McKinley rhapsodizes his desire "to possess a delicate, fragile, sensitive, highly cultured blond white woman, bred to centuries of aristocracy—not rape her, possess her" (Himes 1986, 69). The oedipal drive to kill the father and marry the mother takes on a new, terrifying life when the "parents" are a distant, hostile force and their "son" is an unwanted, disowned bastard. If, by shipping Blacks to the New World, White society established African American society, the child is illegitimate, given no rightful inheritance. By *Lonely Crusade*'s conclusion, Lee Gordon has ironically played out (though largely as a passive spectator) what for McKinley is only a fantasy through his affair with Jackie Forks and his presence at the murder of a White man. Yet Gordon can occupy a central role in the mythology of whiteness only as a disempowered object. Transgression may allow an existential self-creation, yet among the disinherited it acts more powerfully to destroy.

If White women represent possessions to be protected and treasured, Black women are reduced to objects of release. Prevented from protecting a Black woman, from endowing her with the status of White woman while elevating his own masculinity, a Black male may resort to raw force, even to rape, as occurs in *Lonely Crusade*. This may be the only available means to power, albeit a largely illusory one, a poor substitute for killing a White man, itself a poor substitute for occupying the position constructed as central to American identity. Gordon's relationship to his wife, Ruth, provides a prototypical example of the situation diagnosed in Michelle Wallace's *Black Macho and the Myth of the Superwoman*. Wallace describes how many Black men are emasculated by their inability to hold a job and support a family. In a patriarchal society that defines the role of the male as provider and protector, yet often denies that ability to Black men, anxiety and violence are inevitable. This situation is intensified by the relative availability of jobs to Black women who are thrust into the role ostensibly reserved for men. Through their achievement Black women may come to be considered as participating in the failure of Black men. Wallace disparages the way the 1965 Moynihan report characterizes the Black family as abnormal:

> [T]he primary feature of this abnormality was the "matriarch," the "strong black woman," the woman who had nearly as much or more education than the black man, who worked more frequently than the white woman, who had a greater percentage of professionals among her rank. . . . In other words, Moynihan was suggesting that the existence of anything so subversive as a "strong black woman" precluded the existence of a strong black man or, indeed, any black "man" at all. (1979, 31)

Inherent in Wallace's analysis is the belief that male rage regarding female success is a social construction, that such a role is "abnormal" only in a patriarchal society. Operating admittedly from the perspective of dominant society, the Moynihan report defines this structure as deficient. Yet, whatever Wallace's ideal, Black society has often been defined through the patriarchal narrative of strong, productive males and pampered females that it cannot fulfill. In *Lonely Crusade* the situation of the emasculated Black male is intense and explicit, with Lee Gordon's fury directed at his successful wife. Marriage, rather than an arrangement allowing mutual growth, becomes a zero-sum game in which the success of the woman means the failure of the man; as Gordon reflects, "She had no way of knowing what this particular job of hers did to him, that for each development of her own personality he paid a price in loss of self-esteem" (Himes 1986, 192). When men are written out of society, written off, made invisible, women must carry, or at least supplement, the burden of employment. This situation is apparent in *Native Son* with its family headed by a single mother, with Bessie mistreated by the chronically unemployed Bigger Thomas. Boris Max here provides—if only briefly and insufficiently—the missing father, the male role model for which Thomas has implicitly thirsted, a Jewish link to a missing identity.

Countering the patriarchal narrative of the independent, active male is the figure of the Jew, in *Lonely Crusade* an objectification of the male passivity Lee Gordon hates within himself. Jewish society has developed its own means of affirming its self-worth in the face of marginalization. Jewish males may vie for attention and power not through physical strength or even economic success—though these have their place—but through scholarly performance and cleverness in argument. Lipsett and Raab describe the pattern of scholarship for the "People of the Book," wherein

individual reading and subsequent discussion maintained a high level
of literacy, even though their intellectual pursuits were often severely
limited to religious texts. During the period of the Enlightenment, this
literacy and propensity for discussion were often easily transferred to
secular subjects. (1995, 22)

A society that traditionally makes scholarship its highest value, in which
men often stay home and study Torah while women work, is less suscep-
tible to psychological domination than one that has internalized the male
role as physically powerful provider. This is certainly not to argue that
Jewish society has lacked patriarchy, but that its patriarchy has taken different forms than the powerful, solitary figure associated with masculinity in America, a figure appropriate for the wild frontier but not for a
modern environment. Boyarin describes how the Jewish scholar was "enacting a male equivalent of the 'female pursuits' of embroidery, tatting,
and such" while his wife "was ideally robust, energetic, and economically active" (1997, 131). The reversal of dominant cultural norms that
hampers African American society stimulates Jewish American success.
The key difference is the presence of an organic Jewish tradition that
stimulates this relationship, versus the externally imposed character of
Black male passivity. The scholarly nature of the male Jewish role, while
it might be read as feminine, is crucial to Jewish American success. The
shift from Talmudic scholarship to post-Enlightenment Jew leads to a successful modern identity; Gilman describes how, "in acquiring the professional mantle of the scientist the Jew became 'masculine.' The scientist
as defined in the age of positivism did not permit any role for the Jew but
that of the 'neutral' (male) observer" (1993, 10). Patriarchy has undergone a lengthy, ambiguous shift from physical to mental domination; without such a shift contemporary use of the term "phallocentrism" in describing rationalist hierarchy would be meaningless. If Black America,
isolated from Africa, had little to draw on as a cushion against Western
European dominance, Jewish modes of coping might provide an alternative version of masculinity.

   This model, however, is problematic for those like Lee Gordon who
accept an independent, aloof masculinity, for whom Jewish males become feminized objects of contempt. Gordon initially discerns Rosenberg
through this hypermasculine social perspective. Rosenberg's seeming incapacity to defend himself verbally may not be a weakness, but one version of Jewish adaptability, relying on an incremental approach, on a soft-
spoken logic, to change perceptions. Since it is alien to Gordon, however,

it draws the contempt evident in such descriptions as "the stubby, bald-headed Jew" (Himes 1986, 86), who, with "feet dangling and his froglike body wrapped in a wrinkled tan cotton slack suit, . . . looked the picture of the historic Semite" (151). The stereotype is explicitly historicized, given the weight of generations. Beyond the visage of a specific individual, this misshapen figure is a repulsive caricature emotionally distanced from the active, physical body of the masculinized Black. Yet Gordon's repulsion is probably due to a secret, terrified identification, since Blacks too are reduced in dominant imagery into creatures hardly fit for the category of human. In the figure of the Jew, the African American, beset with anxiety regarding masculinity and social acceptance, sees his own self-image threatened from both without and within.

A corollary to Gordon's anti-Semitism is a hatred of communism, an ideology that explicitly supports a systematic attempt to change the course of history on a global scale, a conspiratorial undertaking similar to that rumored regarding Jews. Gordon's sarcastic critique of Rosenberg's politics conflates Jews and communists: "[H]ow is the second front, Karl Marx, Joseph Stalin, Leon Trotsky, and other friends of yours?" (151). This hostility is a defense of Gordon's individuality and of his place in America; moreover, it prefigures criticism that an ideology ostensibly helpful to Blacks in fact objectifies them as one component of a world revolution. The conflation of communism and Jewishness is a result not only of Communist Party demographics but of the assertive role of both groups in articulating African American rights.

If communist privileging of class struggle may undermine the significance of African American history and culture, the figure of the Jew is even more insidious and threatening to the fragile defense mechanisms of Black masculinity. While the Jewish mode of favoring intellect and business acumen over physical power seems to offer a viable role model for Black America, such behavior may be interpreted as threatening. Furthermore, prior to the 1960s, in those cases in which Black men have followed the "Jewish" route to success—that is, have achieved in the intellectual arena—they have been denied the jobs and prestige expected from such achievements. Lee Gordon himself is a case in point. Jews hold out a tantalizing model for success unavailable to Blacks in 1940s America. The Black male is again symbolically emasculated, and the Jew becomes an object of envy (simultaneously possessing the phallus and lacking the penis). Highly accomplished and economically successful, playing out an almost matriarchal supportive role, to the Black American male Jews occupy a position parallel to the Black woman. Both woman and Jew undercut Gordon's masculinity.

From a Black male subject position desperately imitating—while despising—dominant cultural norms, traditional anti-Semitism may become tantalizingly relevant. A battery of socially and historically determined difficulties, reduced and transferred onto the Jew, is displayed in Lee Gordon's exclamation: "There is a certain repulsiveness in the Jew's basic approach toward life" (158). This statement echoes Sartre's definition of the anti-Semite as metaphysically investing Jews with odious qualities that permeate the surrounding atmosphere: "[T]he Jew contaminates all that he touches with an I-know-not-what execrable quality" (1976, 35). The Jew is always already guilty; all his actions are interpreted so as to fit into this guilt. This inviolable odiousness is the wellspring for a host of charges: that Jews love money, that they spoil their children, that they scorn Blacks, and, most importantly from Gordon's point of view, "that Jews fight, and underhandedly, our struggle for equality" (Himes 1986, 159). The belief in an invisible enemy, impossible to locate, impossible to defend against, becomes an all-purpose explanation for a history of frustration and failure. Larger social and ideological structures are circumvented to explain this failure, since such structures, intangible and pervasive, are an even more insurmountable enemy than the figure of the Jew.

Gordon's difficulties with Jews are shadowed by an awareness of the Holocaust. Given that the novel takes place simultaneous with the Nazi death camps, it's striking how little sympathy Gordon shows for Jewish suffering and how silent Rosenberg remains on the subject. Historically this is accurate, for the Holocaust was initially a subject of veiled silence, an embarrassment beyond acknowledgment. In *Lonely Crusade*, instead of being a touchstone of commonality the Holocaust is used as a weapon to blame the victim for not upholding a moral standard higher than that set by dominant society. From Gordon's perspective, Jews continue their pattern of exploitation, their chameleonlike ability to epitomize the worst standards of the surrounding society. Gordon argues with Rosenberg:

> "With Jews being slaughtered in Europe by the hundreds of thousands, brutalized beyond comprehension, you Jews here in America are more prejudiced against Negroes than the gentiles."
>
> "That's silly. Have you ever heard of a Jew in a lynch mob?"
>
> "Only because the white lynchers discriminate against him. He does everything to the Negro short of lynching." (152)

Even in 1948 the Holocaust is reduced to a blatant reflection of individual needs. Gordon slyly intimates that fear and the need for acceptance drive Jews to do society's dirty work, a temptation that Gordon, as a member of the Black bourgeoisie, is himself presented with and rejects. The Jew once again finds himself cast in the position of middleman, here not in drawing Blacks into dominant society but in continuing their oppression. The most effective means of enforcing social hierarchy is not force but internalized ideology. The Jewish place in this hierarchy is, to Gordon, central: "What hasn't the Jew done?—cornered us into squalid ghettos and beat us out of our money—" (153). The beating is indirect, through the medium of the police: Jew stands in for White, which enforces Jewish property rights, themselves a construction of dominant society.[3]

From Gordon's blatant antipathy toward Jews, *Lonely Crusade* moves increasingly toward portraying a sympathetic portrayal. As a larger conversation following a thesis→antithesis structure, the novel contradicts Rosen's contention that the confrontation between Blacks and Jews amounts to "a black intellectual's tirade against Jews, occasionally interrupted by a Jew who makes not one criticism of blacks" (1995, 49). This superficially accurate statement ignores the evolving friendship between the two men. Rosenberg's seeming passivity is part of a personality—and perhaps a strategy—configured to win over Gordon incrementally. Rather than reacting to force with force Rosenberg replies with patience, teaching a greater awareness of the historical context of Black and Jewish friction. He expresses a willingness to question the social circumstances behind Gordon's anti-Semitism, whereas a more direct condemnation, or a parallel assault on Black character, would foreclose dialogue. In probing such topics as the Jewish role within capitalist hierarchies and the nature of assimilation (Himes 1986, 155ff.) Rosenberg begins to untangle not only the complexities of Black-Jewish relations but the underlying structures that deform the psyches of both peoples.

Dialogue is one method of defusing anti-Semitism; yet Rosenberg proves himself even more through his actions, for Gordon's sake sacrificing a key element in his belief system, membership in the Communist Party. Transcending his grand historical rhetoric, Rosenberg makes an individual choice for personal loyalty over the Party's demands. Beyond an acute revelation of racism's psychological effects, the novel's central theme seems to be the necessity of existential choice. Actually the two themes are related; Stephen Milliken explains

that when black American writers . . . turned up in the intellectual circles
of Paris in the early fifties they met with instant acceptance as fully
established initiates. As black men they had from the beginning of their
lives no choice but to live by the existentialist attitude; agonizing, total
awareness of the absurdity of modern Western experience. (1976, 11)

In both Wright and Himes the experience of defining oneself through an
illogical series of events in an unjust world flows naturally from their
experience as Blacks in America. Occupying a precarious intermediary
zone between racial and dominant identities, the Black intellectual
(re)makes self as a countercultural, oppositional figure. If the brutal
aloneness of this choice leaves Gordon stranded, Rosenberg too sheds his
communist ideals.

Existential philosophy precludes the ability of the Communist Party
to make one's choices for one. Despite his rhetoric, Rosenberg ultimately
acts alone. The interaction of social and individual conditions drives the
novel forward, a process culminating, for Gordon, in two bipolar statements regarding race. First the grand historical: "No doubt if he tried hard
enough he could trace all his troubles to this source [racism]. . . . By
logical process he could prove that he had been persecuted and oppressed
by white people to the point of criminal compulsion" (Himes 1986, 361).
Then the individual: "Being a Negro was a cause—yes. . . . But it was
never a justification—never! . . . Because being a Negro was, first of all, a
fact. . . . a Negro is a Negro as he is an American—because he was born a
Negro. He has no cause for apology or shame" (361). One may be confined by a certain set of definitions, yet however limiting and onerous
these are, what one does within these parameters—perhaps bending or
altering them—is the final measure of one's humanity. If the first statement is of impervious victimization, of avoiding blame for one's actions,
the second is the escape clause, the return to agency within the admittedly
severe limitations imposed by society. Through Lee Gordon, Himes expresses the existential philosophy predominant among intellectuals of his
day, the ultimate privileging of individual over society.

The maestro for Gordon's conversion has been Rosenberg. The older
Jewish male as a paternal model, a (problematic) middle(wo)man between
Black and mainstream society, is a recurring—if intermittent—trope in
African American writing, reappearing in Paule Marshall's work in the
1960s, and in Ishmael Reed's *Reckless Eyeballing* (1986). Boris Max has
been one such figure, though ultimately a distant observer; Rosenberg is a

more humanized version, one who pays a personal price. Max's omniscient characteristics are finally revealed as largely a projection of Bigger Thomas's psychic needs. Rosenberg, conversely, attains transcendent status. What Gordon earlier interpreted as a grotesque feminization is finally understood by him as a protective sympathy. The same physical characteristics that had signified a disgusting inhumanity now mean quite the opposite: "Standing there watching Rosie's fat, frog-shaped body go carefully down the stairs, Lee felt the joy come back into living" (Himes 1986, 375). Acceptance of Rosenberg's appearance implies acceptance of his characteristics of dialogue, negotiation, and compromise as integral to manhood, to the point where Gordon "began seeing Rosie not as a Jew, but as a savior" (376). Even as he clings to communism Rosenberg transcends its materialist limits. While he never sways Gordon to membership in the Party he stands as the key role model in convincing Gordon to make a final stand for the workers. Both Rosenberg and Gordon finally choose a politically aware yet solitary role; the individual may pick a higher social good, yet he does so outside the confines of a defining organization.

The Jew in *Lonely Crusade* stands finally as a beacon of dialogue and reason, of personal choice, offering an alternative to a Black masculinity constricted into rage and self-hatred. A Jewish voice, dialogically inserted into an African American narrative, opens space for an altered sense of self. An alternative means of Black survival is implied, one less dependent on a rigid version of masculinity. The Jewish middle(wo)man begins the painful process of midwifery, of bringing the most marginalized into American society, a process that will at the same time alter masculine roles to favor an increasingly urban, bureaucratic, technological, information-oriented society. *Lonely Crusade* is most important not in its idealistic resolution but in its unrelenting portrayal of the effects of racial ideology on a human mind, its graphic illustration of the interplay between Black self-hatred and anti-Semitism.

IV

The initial reaction to *Lonely Crusade* was intensely negative; Himes laments the book's "terrible reviews" from "the white press, the black press, the Jewish press, reactionary press—*all*" (Williams 1970b, 37). Bluntly tackling racial issues, communism, misogyny, and Black anti-Semitism, the novel managed to offend all segments. The price for Himes's brutal honesty was dismissal. Then too, the novel's sprawling naturalism undoubtedly managed to offend some aesthetic senses; it is difficult to disentangle critique of form from critique of content. When one Jewish critic, Milton Klonsky, describes the novel as a "clumsily written" sensationalist emblem of "American mob culture" (1948, 190) it's unclear how much he is aesthetically dissatisfied and how much he is expressing his revulsion at the novel's blunt portrayal of anti-Semitism. When Klonsky derides "a caricature of a Jewish Communist" and "several vaporous discussions between Negroes and Jews (invariably presented as Communists) on such topics as Negro anti-Semitism and why Jews love money," the reason for his reaction is more obvious and, given the horrible long-term results of anti-Semitic representations, understandable. Subtleties or contradictions within the presentation make little difference; the appearance of anti-Semitism generates a powerful condemnation from Jewish journalists and intellectuals.

The aversion to *Lonely Crusade* suggests unacknowledged pressures for African American self-censorship regarding characterizations of Jews. Even a brief stereotypical image, by leading to hostile reviews and alienating an important part of the reading public, may cause a work's financial failure. This happened in 1927 with Langston Hughes's *Fine Clothes for the Jew*, whose title Hughes regarded "as one of the main reasons for the failure of the book" (Rampersad 1986, 150). A similar condemnation occurred in 1989 with Spike Lee's *Mo' Better Blues*, whose Jewish characters were described as "money-grubbing, envious, ugly stereotypes with sharks' smiles," making of them "misguided artistic failures" (James 1990). Ishmael Reed satirizes such suppression of Black anti-Semitism in *Reckless Eyeballing;* when a Black playwright obsessed by Jews is asked to write about them he exclaims: "Are you kiddin'? Did you see what they did to Chester Himes and Langston Hughes? By the time they finished with Zora Neale she was mopping floors" (1986, 32). Portraits of Black anti-Semitism have been suppressed by media condemnation and its damage to careers. This is not to condemn such condemnations; given the history of anti-Semitism and its tangible results, the impulse to squelch it at its every appearance is understandable. The overall result of social inequality, however, is that Jewish writers have more freely explored a range of Black representations than vice versa, partly because the network of Black stereotypes is so deeply embedded in American society, and so variegated, as to be difficult to pinpoint.

So it is that, at least in mainstream literature, much Black anti-Semitism remained hidden before the late 1960s, while Jewish racial representations are relatively common, if obscured beneath a liberal surface. The reaction to *Lonely Crusade* maintained a pattern in which Jews publicly discussed African American politics, articulating their version of the Black viewpoint, while Blacks withheld criticism of Jews. African American frustration regarding this asymmetrical arrangement would remain dormant for only so long; it would resurface in the Black nationalism of the late 1960s. Until that time Jewish writers felt increasingly free to represent Blacks from multiple (if at times problematic) standpoints: Jewish, American, and universal.

Jewish Assimilationism
White Lies and Black Eyes

*I was what the cabala calls a naked soul—a soul which had
departed one body and awaits another.*
          —Isaac Bashevis Singer, upon coming to America

In the last fifty years Jewish American novels have exhibited a great range
of perspectives, jumping from ethnic explorations to "mainstream" American outlooks and back again. Joseph Heller, Saul Bellow, Allen Ginsberg,
Adrienne Rich, and Grace Paley are only a few of the authors who have
shifted cultural vantage points. John Williams describes how

> Jewish writers moved (or were allowed to move) from writing of the
> "Jewish Experience"—Sholem Asch, Henry Roth, etc.—to the tenuous
> description of the "American Experience," Kantor, early Robbins, even
> early Mailer, back to the now acceptable, though in a different time
> warp, "New Jewish Experience." (Quoted in Muller 1984, 143–44)

While elsewhere Jewish writers and scholars had been proponents of revolutionary social change, or of cultural relativism, by the late 1950s Jewish
American perspectives blended more and more easily into dominant culture.

Prior to this incorporation and recognition, the U.S. Communist Party
had included a vigorous group of Jewish writers who, rather than advo-
cating assimilation into American society, believed in eventual incorporation into an international society free from racial and ethnic hatred. If
the ravages of Stalinism have long discredited these writers, the collapse
of the Soviet Union has further obscured their work. Lamenting this virtual

49

disappearance, Alan Wald catalogs numerous antiracist novels penned by communist, often Jewish, authors. He further characterizes as "partisan and irresponsible" the reduction of "hundreds of poets, fiction writers, and critics drawn to the US Communist movement throughout its seventy-year history to tools, dupes, acolytes, or other mere instruments of 'the Party line'" (1994, 67–68). Wald shows how this body of work is more complex, and often more aesthetically satisfying, then is generally believed. John Sanford's *The People from Heaven* (1943), for instance, combines a folksy American voice with complex modernist interior portraits. Set in the prototypical American town of Warrensburg, the novel collapses centuries of historical brutality into a brief series of events that epitomize a vision of resistance to racism and tyranny. The arrival of America Smith, a symbolically named Black woman, dredges up past brutalities. Her degradation and final rape by the racist Eli Bishop display in microcosm the violence long inflicted upon Blacks and other minorities. The scope of racism is evident in Bishop's planned forced march of humiliation for Smith, along with Warrensburg's only Jew and only two Native Americans. When Smith shoots Bishop dead, she epitomizes violence as the only antidote to virulent racism. With all its psychological complexity, the final message of *The People from Heaven* is a simple one: the need for revolutionary action in the face of repression. Yet the racial/ethnic center of the struggle implies a sensibility at least as sensitive to historical Jewish anxieties as to communist concerns with class.

Although *The People from Heaven*, along with other revolutionary novels, forms an important and neglected strand of Jewish American literature, by the late 1950s such work was eclipsed by a new Jewish voice, one less political, more confident, and quintessentially American. As the Jewish novel evolved and was legitimatized in American literary culture, Jewish authors felt free to portray Blacks from a variety of perspectives. Often they measured themselves as Americans, specifically as White Americans upholding European traditions of rationalism against myths of Black primitivism and emotion. Such a construction, however, is incongruous with the historical Jewish experience of exile and marginalization. The Jewish compromise with American society was often an inclusive version of rationalism. Jewish liberalism, while upholding individualism and democracy for an ever-widening sphere of ethnic groups, tended to adopt Eurocentric ideals of civilization. Contradictions between Jewish history and mainstream American society have often been obscured by universalist beliefs.

The struggle to accommodate Jewish history to American identity is a recurring theme of Jewish literature, with questions of assimilation complicated by the Black presence. In Philip Roth's work, for instance, Blacks are both subjects of historical sympathy and objects against which Jews measure their entry into American society. In moving toward the center, Neil Klugman, the protagonist of "Goodbye Columbus" (1959), balances a past marked by Jewish differentiation and the possibility of an affluent, universalist American future. The agent of the future is his romantic flame, Brenda Patimkin, daughter of a wealthy suburban family marked by the superficialities of American life, by ubiquitous athletics, middlebrow music, and bobbed noses. When Neil describes himself over the telephone as "dark," Brenda asks, "Are you a Negro?" (1989, 7). The question implies in Neil an alienation from the Patimkin family and, for Brenda, the excitement of transgression, one that persists, at least faintly, in Neil's actual status as a Jew just barely removed from the ghetto.

Counterposed to the Patimkin family—to the Jewish future—a Black child explores the public library, the symbolic space of entry into American culture in which Neil works. In his sympathy with the child Klugman identifies with the next generation of ghettoized Americans, and hence with his own Jewish past. Migrating into the Jewish section of Newark, Blacks represent the next—and perhaps the final—sign of Otherness: "Who would come after the Negroes? Who was left? No one, I thought" (91). In the library, gazing upon Paul Gauguin's visions of Tahiti as primitivist paradise, the child can only dream of freedom. The child's rhapsody is threatened by "a very old man . . . white, smelling of Life Savers, his nose and jowls showing erupted veins beneath them" (48). By attempting to check out the Gauguin book this paradigm of White authority in a state of decay threatens the child's fantasies. Neil employs a series of excuses to keep the book available, and further defends the child against a colleague who complains of Blacks, "They're taking over the city" and "You know the way they treat the housing projects we give them" (35). Neil's sardonic rejoinders—"*You* give them"—seem mild, irony as an indirect defense against racism. Given only minor authority, probably still conscious of his outsider status as a Jew, Neil's reaction is ineffective. After the White patron finally gets hold of the Gauguin book, Neil is resigned about the child: "He'd given up on the library and gone back to playing Willie Mays in the streets. He was better off, I thought. No sense carrying dreams of Tahiti in your head, if you can't afford the fare" (120). By the 1960s many Jewish Americans could afford the fare; they could make of Tahitians, and of Blacks, an exoticized Other. As he penetrates the space of goyish possibility so long denied Jews, Neil pauses to identify with those still disenfranchised, with a child darker than his own family. If the Patimkins are in the vanguard of Jews classified as thoroughly White, Neil and his family will eventually join them, while the child remains disenfranchised.

Portnoy's Complaint (1967) satirizes both the superficial nature of the American dream and the claustrophobic Jewish past, displaying attitudes toward Blacks at their most self-serving. Jewish hypocrisy during the process of assimilationism is heightened by the ordinary texture of the Portnoy family's life, including their obliviousness to American racism. Alexander Portnoy's mother, who brags of feeding her Black maid well, nevertheless insists that she sit separately at lunchtime. Mrs. Portnoy then washes the maid's plate and utensils, "running scalding water over the dish from which the cleaning lady has just eaten her lunch, alone like a leper" (1967, 13). The mother displays in only a token way Jewish liberalism, which insists that she treat a member of another marginalized group as an equal. Rather, in adopting the privilege of a society that objectifies the Black maid as a creature sick by definition, Mrs. Portnoy defines herself by contrast as a normal, healthy, naturalized American. To separate himself from his family, to define himself as a different kind of American, both universal and pluralistic, Alexander Portnoy becomes a commissioner defending Black rights. Yet *Portnoy's Complaint* is not primarily about relations with Blacks, who are only a minor factor in the Portnoy family's struggle to construct themselves as Americans. In Roth's fiction representations of Blacks—as opposed to exposition about the status of Blacks—are sparse.

Fictional portrayals show the psychological effects of racial/ethnic status only indirectly, and must be interpreted and teased out. The essay format provides a more explicit means of addressing notions of blackness relative to Jewish American identity. Jewish essayists echo Wright and Baldwin in confessing brutal "truths" about Black-Jewish relations. Norman Podhoretz describes how his personal experiences counteract liberal sympathy with Blacks. Growing up in an urban milieu he found himself terrorized by Blacks until he "hated them with all my heart" (1966, 77). Such feelings may be overcome intellectually but not emotionally, so that, at least to Podhoretz, "all whites—all American whites, that is—are sick in their feelings about Negroes" (86). Imitating Baldwin's unflinching honesty and confessing unspoken truths about racial feelings, Podhoretz projects his own needs onto the racial Other, envying Blacks for their "superior masculinity," for their "physical grace and beauty" (88). The bookish Jew seeks elsewhere that physical release discouraged by his traditional scholarly environment. Podhoretz suffers from a mirror version of the conflict that Himes reveals in Black perceptions of Jews; if Lee Gordon scorns Jews as lacking the masculinity that dominant society both mythologizes in and denies Blacks, Podhoretz envies a Black masculinity he feels lacking in his Jewish self.

Another Jewish literary figure, Norman Mailer, is similarly awed by Black physicality, though with less envy. Writing from a position comfortable enough within American society to allow for deliberate rebellion, Mailer perceives Blacks as role models of physical abandon and psychological freedom. Locating African American society—the Black body, Black movement and sound—as a site of escape from dominant society, he romanticizes and glorifies "the art of the primitive," characterized in music by "infinite variations of joy, lust, languor, growl, cramp, pinch, scream and despair of his [Black] orgasm" (1957, 279). This is, of course, no description of an actual society but a projection, an updated version of the role of the Black minstrel that, according to Nathan Irvin Huggins, historically provided an outlet for "lust and passion and natural freedom (license) which white men carried within themselves and harbored with both fascination and dread" (1971, 254). For Mailer, as for Podhoretz, blackness becomes a hyperreal symbol of the carnivalesque, an escape from the constraints of civilization. If Al Jolson used Black minstrelsy as a means to differentiate himself from the social margins, Mailer employs an updated, ultra-hip minstrel figure in rebelling from the society Jews have worked so hard to enter. Michael Rogin explains of Jolson that "by painting himself black he washes himself white," that blackface "liberates the performer from the fixed, 'racial' identities of African American and Jew" (1996, 102). More secure as an American than Jolson, Mailer feels free to reject dominant society in search of a mythological Black freedom.

Jewish fiction of the 1960s develops currents of racial/ ethnic tension delineated only briefly by Podhoretz and Mailer. Due to the difficulty of separating mimesis from projection, direct representation is especially ambiguous. Many works rely on image, with a sparing use of dialogue and little attempt at entering African American consciousness. Jewish liberalism can penetrate the veil hiding Black society from dominant culture only intermittently. Rather, Jewish writers define their identity both through and against an updated version of blackface wherein the Black figure represents a spectrum of myths, from primitivist freedom to archetypal wisdom to criminality to victimhood. The stance of the individual Jewish writer helps determine his or her depiction of Blacks.

Despite its anxieties and limitations, Jewish fiction is part of a broader social dialogue that alters dominant society, pushing a confrontation with Eurocentric limitations and bringing new voices to American literature. Jewish writers examine both Jewish and American culture through appropriating symbols and voices of blackness. Rather than merely commodification, this appropriation is part of a complex cultural reworking. Of course Jewish sources alone can never accomplish this; a broader acceptance of African American literature and culture is a critical step in creating understanding between communities, in the evolution of a hybrid society.

I

If during the 1950s and '60s Jewish American writers often adopted White perspectives, a sympathy for African Americans persisted. This may be attributed to a multivocal writerly consciousness, to American liberalism, or to lingering memories of Jewish oppression. Countervailing these factors are deeply embedded images of African Americans as primitive, sexual creatures. Saul Bellow's short story "Looking for Mr. Green" (1951) maintains a contradictory spectrum of elements in a short preview of his future representations of Blacks, from the boisterous natives of *Henderson the Rain King* to the noble individualists of *The Dean's December*.

"Looking for Mr. Green" portrays an African American ghetto from the White, specifically non-Jewish, perspective of George Grebe. In scanning a slice of African American society, it prefigures a trope that will be developed, from an explicitly Jewish perspective, by Bernard Malamud and Grace Paley. In Bellow literal memories of Jewish occupation of similar ghettos—indeed, often of the same ghettos at a different time period—are absent, yet ghosts of such memories persist in a sympathy with the Black residents as part of a common humanity. Paradoxically, nearness blurs historical memory, preventing wider contextualization in a time period in which Jews identify strongly with dominant society.

One approach to "Looking for Mr. Green" connects ghetto residents to the myth of blackness as the primitive core of all humans, for which civilization is merely a superficial shell (a trope for which Joseph Conrad's *Heart of Darkness* is paradigmatic). Discussing Bellow's story in 1974 one critic remarks, "The ghetto and its inhabitants become metaphors for man and the dark, incomprehensible world he moves in" (Rodrigues 1974, 389). The story, then, fits into a 1950s literature of existential angst which implicitly contrasts White civilization with the Black libido. Yet Bellow includes bipolar representations of African American characters as either emotional primitives or as sophisticates rising above their condition, making "blackness" a product of individual choice rather than a biological destiny. Embedded in the story, then, are contradictory interpretations of blackness as archetypal Otherness and, alternatively, of African Americans as victims of circumstance essentially no different from other people.

In this non-Jewish protagonist's encounter with Otherness, Jewish consciousness lingers only in an ambiguous fashion. Certainly the protagonist exhibits something of a liberal imagination akin to a 1950s Jewish American sensibility, as Jews struggled simultaneously to enter mainstream society and to remake it in a more inclusive way. Grebe obviously believes that African Americans deserve sympathy, that they should be aided, educated, and eventually incorporated into American society. And if there's a tinge of condescension here, nothing explicit in Grebe's thoughts indicates this. Rather, condescension is structured into a situation in which an educated White man dispenses charity to uneducated Blacks. Grebe's former profession as a classics teacher marks him as special due to the privileging of European culture. He is the cultivated outsider returning to the immigrants' brutish ghetto past. Indeed, his father's career as an English butler marks a family circumvention of this past, not through money but on the higher grounds of character.

Yet the ideal of civilization is problematic in "Looking for Mr. Green," due largely to the troubled historical circumstances in which it occurs. That grand old European civilization which many of Bellow's later protagonists admire is plunged into doubt by the Great Depression, which blurred the line between educated White, poor immigrant, and Black. Reflecting on the vagaries of capitalism, of the monetary system that upholds civilization, Grebe thinks, "what a scheme of a scheme it seemed, how close to an appearance" (Bellow 1977, 105), an observation with devastating implications during a time in which this great scheme had been exposed as illusory. World War II and the Holocaust, too, cast a pall upon notions of European civilization in a story portraying the 1930s from the perspective of the 1950s.

Indeed, "Looking for Mr. Green" often seems to welcome African Americans into (what remains of) civilization. It refutes the myth of Black primitivism by placing it in the mouth of a malicious Italian: "Nobody would get to know even a tenth of what went on among these people. They stabbed and stole, they did every crime and abomination you ever heard of, men and men, women and women, worse than the animals." As a good liberal should, Grebe (in the third-person form of narration) re-coils at this speech as one of "fantasy and passion . . . becoming increas-ingly senseless and terrible" (100). Grebe, furthermore, is acutely aware of himself as an outsider, sensitive that from the Black point of view he is the interlocutor who does not belong: "Among these people Grebe, with his cold-heightened fresh color and his smaller stature, entered like a schoolboy" (91). This complicated passage seems to indicate a separation between Grebe and the Black residents, yet, in expressing his alienation from them, Grebe sympathetically enters their consciousness. In a mo-ment tinged with Bakhtinian awareness of multiple perspectives, he is the stranger and they are the normalizing consciousness.

Faith in capitalist democracy persists, further, in the person of a Black man, Winston Field, whom Grebe encounters early. Like Grebe's butler father, Field, despite his circumstances, establishes himself as a civilized being. He does so first through an obsession with written records marking his social identity in place and time; he fetishistically lays "out his papers: Social Security card, relief certification, letters from the state hospital . . . and a naval discharge" (101). Through the written word, through official documents, he constructs an edifice against the underlying nihilism that wears away at Grebe, the possibility that our society is merely a mutually agreed-upon illusion. Field resists this notion, showing faith in the future of capitalist democracy through a pyramid financial scheme to create Black millionaires: "That's the only sunbeams, money. Nothing is black where it shines, and the only place you see black is where it ain't shining. What we colored have to have is our own rich" (102). If the immediate meta-phor implies that Black is bad, the overall passage displays an acute cyni-cism about the nature of Western civilization as ultimately defined not by moral or aesthetic values, but by cash. Field struggles to transcend his circumstances, mixing a form of rationalist civilization with a bitter hon-esty about the nature of that civilization.

Counterposed to Field is Mr. Green, encountered only in the surro-gate form of an unidentified woman—either his wife or mistress—naked, cursing and drunk. Grebe's brush with naked blackness is a moment of primal emotion: "The contact of her breasts, though they touched only his coat, made him go back against the door with a blind shock" (107). Grebe's status as an agent of civilization, both through his education and his mis-sion into the ghetto, is cast into doubt. The woman enacts an otherness, a bawdiness/bodiness from which the repressed Grebe recoils. Devoid of hope or a future, the woman has little incentive to cover herself with the trappings of civilization. The scene resembles a later Bellow encounter, in *Mr. Sammler's Planet*, with a Black thief, in which the facade of European society is stripped away. In neither is the feeling overtly sexual; the first is characterized by shock, the latter by a lurid mixture of shock and fascination. Throughout Bellow, blackness has an element of the return of the repressed in which educated and yet innocent White observers encounter the primal past.

The bifurcation between the "civilized" Black seeking to elevate himself above his circumstances (Field) and the "primitive" Black, seething in the squalor of circumstances, seeking only the immediate sensations of sex and alcohol (Green) recurs in later Bellow works. And the antiracist theme of "Looking for Mr. Green" is made problematic by Grebe's encounter with the naked Black woman, an encounter that may be read as playing out the Italian's racist oration. This bifurcation of blackness persists throughout Bellow. Are Blacks merely fellow human beings forced by history, by White exploitation, into difficult circumstances? Or are they a symbol of a primitive inner landscape? If liberalism overtly believes the former, old racial images persist covertly, surges of a heart of darkness.

II

The Jewish American position of speaking for and reacting against dominant culture by employing Blacks as symbols of social rebellion is exemplified in *Henderson the Rain King*, which epitomizes 1950s liberalism in its depiction of Africans as noble primitives. Although playful and often admiring of its African characters, the novel nevertheless adopts conventional stereotypes in its quest for American identity. The fictional perspective, neither hipster nor Jewish, is that of a quintessential White Anglo-Saxon Protestant, old-monied and Ivy Leagued, a stance suggesting Jewish comfort within American society. The novel is at least a shade autobiographical in Henderson's multiple wives and restless, probing personality, Bellow trademarks.[1] *Henderson the Rain King*, then, defines one pole of Jewish American identity, a community creating itself as *White* in symbiotic contrast to blackness. Subsequent Jewish American fiction more faithfully contextualizes Blacks, probing African American social history, in an overall movement from flat stereotypes to more complex individualization. The process, however, was diverted by the crisis in Black-Jewish relations that ended the 1960s.

Written prior to the height of the Jewish-Black alliance, prior to widespread acknowledgment of African American writers and thinkers,

Henderson the Rain King displays a certain innocence. The Africa depicted here is a mythic continent ostensibly created from imagination but
actually derived from conventional Western sources in which older depictions of barbarism evolved into countermyths of primal wisdom, and
finally into depictions of exotic traits largely derived from cultural anthropology. Conflicting versions of Otherness are played out upon a fictive
Africa to create a novel that the reader may interpret according to his or her
own background and presuppositions. So one critic, F. Odun Balogun, can
declare *Henderson* as defining "a vision of racial harmony between Black
and White" (1985, 20), while another, Patrick Brantlinger, reads it as continuing "the spirit of Tarzan and Tabu Dick . . . though often reduced to
the level of sophisticated buffoonery" (1986, 218). Neither interpretation
is incorrect; they both derive from a work that replicates the contradictions of the society from which it has emerged. Bellow's liberalism, in its
attempt to atone for past sins, portrays a new "racial understanding," yet
one still infused with myth and implicit hierarchy—at worst, "sophisticated buffoonery"—in which the rationalist learns from an implicitly
"primitivist" wisdom.

Western cultural stereotypes of Africa remained widespread in the
1950s. The image of a dark, savage continent has a long history in the
imperial conquest of Africa. Brantlinger explains how the narrative of a
savage Africa, as played out in boys' adventure novels, reinforced colonial
penetration and conquest. To its explorers Africa was a landscape of primal
danger, "a dark, infernal background where there are no other characters
of equal stature [to Europeans]—only bewitched or demonic savages"
(Brantlinger 1986, 195). Reducing human beings to such images has an
economic end in justifying the exploitation of the African continent. So
the explorer Richard Burton believed in the unalterable savagery of Africans
while defending the need for their raw muscle: "Enormous tropical regions
yet await the clearing and draining operations by the lower races, which
will fit them to become the dwelling-places of civilized men" (quoted in
Brantlinger 1986, 200). As the African continent was colonized, depictions
of savagery intensified, including exaggerated accounts of cannibalism.
Pseudo-Darwinian theories of Black evolutionary inferiority likewise
evolved according to the need for exploitation.

Beyond the economic motive, depictions of Africa reflected social
and psychological needs. Adventure tales undoubtedly serve as an outlet
of imaginative escape from the constrictions of day-to-day "civilized"
life. The outside landscape, metonymic for repressed regions of the psyche,
is a terrain to be explored and ultimately subdued, a mysterious region

brimming with glamour and terror. So Marlow, in *Heart of Darkness*, describes a "civilized" European penetrating an untamed landscape in which

> utter savagery, had closed round him,—all that mysterious life of the wilderness that stirs in the forest, in the jungles, in the hearts of wild men. There's no initiation either into such mysteries. He has to live in the midst of the incomprehensible, which is also detestable. And it has a fascination, too, that goes to work upon him. The fascination of the abomination. (1989, 20)

Novelization is one form—a textual, abstract one—of demarcating and controlling regions of psychic terror. The textual finds its physical analogue in the charting out, naming, and conquering of Africa, whereby the European attempts also to control and administer his own psyche. So Mary Louise Pratt describes the process of exploration, and the attendant travel narratives, as reducing native peoples to "scratches on the face of the country," to parts of a landscape described, dissected, and cataloged so as "to minimize all human presence" (1992, 142). African geography is an emptiness awaiting the European gaze to give it substance through penetration and conquest. The Africa for which explorers set sail was not a real place, but a realm of imagination, at least until they actually landed.[2]

Alongside representations of barbarism, an alternative image grew in reaction, one reversing the civilization/barbarism dichotomy. In this myth the darker, non-European peoples become an antidote to the worries of civilization, with its constant pressure to work, to produce, to advance. The image is of a carefree people living harmoniously with nature. Rousseau, reacting to Enlightenment rationalism, transferred biblical images of Eden onto "primitive" societies unhampered by the knowledge of sin. Knowledge, in an extreme version of this view, has created a dystopia characterized by neurosis, technological killing, and capitalist atomization, while those peoples sheltered from rationalism maintain a harmonious unity with nature, and often an openness regarding sexuality. The image of noble savage is, of course, as much an imposition of psychic needs to define the Other as is the belief in a primitive evil. The psychic map of faraway peoples and places corresponds not with any factual geography but with an imaginary one. Exploration transforms faraway lands to whatever most fulfills European needs, both practical and psychological.

The Edenic countermyth is a crucial, if bifurcated, regulatory principle of *Henderson the Rain King*. Eugene Henderson is a rebellious, larger-

than-life American who, seeking freedom from social constraint, journeys to deepest Africa. Africa exists not as an actual continent, with its
own people and history, but as an empty area that Henderson, in his search
for psychic wholeness, fills in. Bellow makes no attempt whatever (an
attempt that could only be false) to endow his Africa with accurate geography, to people it with actual tribes. He himself explains, "I made up all
those tribes, and the landscape and the languages and the customs. All I
had in my head was the reading I had done twenty years earlier as an
anthropology student, and it all came out of the stacks of the university
library" (quoted in Goldman 1983, 96).[3] The accumulated constructions
of the academy are the raw material for this novel, filtered through an
aesthetic, rather than a historical, consciousness. Or rather the novel is an
inextricable mixture of the two, since the aesthetic and the historical are
intimately connected. In an Africa far from any actual map, Henderson
declares, "geographically speaking I didn't have the remotest idea where
we were, and I didn't care too much. It was not for me to ask, since my
object in coming here was to leave certain things behind" (1976a, 45).
This imaginary land is constructed wholesale for Henderson to encounter
in his flight from civilization.

Bellow's position within a liberal period that perceived Europe and
America as planetary cultural centers is crucial to the novel's genesis.
The Jewish intelligentsia had long been tantalized by the promise of assimilation into an academy supposedly objective and universal, yet created by European societies that had excluded Jews. The classic double
bind repeats itself: how to be a representative, an exemplar, of a tradition
that has hated you for centuries? Or rather, that intermittently hates you,
yet that also declares your (Jewish) tradition as part of its lineage, while
declaring all tradition null and void, superseded by a universal rationalism to which it invites you? If Isaac Bashevis Singer and Bernard Malamud
deal with this challenge largely by upholding the virtues of a Jewish past,
albeit in a modern setting, Bellow portrays the modern intellectual, intensely aware of both Jewish and dominant cultural history yet alienated
from both, constructing an iconoclastic identity, although privileging European sources. The Jewish experience becomes only one facet of intellectual identity, albeit one ideally configured to illustrate the modernist
predicament as isolated, paralyzed, cut off from the romantic past.[4]

Although he differs from most of Bellow's Jewish intellectuals,
Henderson, too, acts the role of alienated modern. Bellow's comfortable
position in America, his status in the literary world, enables him to speak
in the voice of a non-Jewish protagonist, to create a version of universal

man. Ironically, Henderson's status—and indirectly Bellow's—allows a retreat from the very civilization that has produced it. Henderson feels himself as a sore spot on the facade of civilization, an irritation; "I came, a great weight, a huge shadow" (12). His outsider status—in sharp contrast to Jewish marginalization—comes from within, arguably through choice. So he vacations at an elegant resort that "accept[s] no Jews, and then they get me, E. H. Henderson" (7). Like the Jewish hipster, comfortable enough within society to rebel, Henderson rejects the easy condition of his class. Indeed, he rebels also from Jewish law, which is, after all, one root of Western tradition in its monotheism and establishment of law. During World War II, amid the devastation of combat, he discusses his future with a fellow soldier: "So I said, or my demon spoke for me, 'I'm going to start breeding pigs.' And after these words were spoken I knew that if Goldstein had not been a Jew I might have said cattle and not pigs" (20). Henderson employs his insider status as a weapon, simultaneously disdaining Jews as outsiders and as convention-bound. The existence of an ancient tradition is reason enough to break it, not just to taste pork but to breed it (perhaps guiltily signifying Bellow's break from his Jewish identity). Henderson will neither keep Kosher nor conform to society's rules.

To critics who argue that Henderson is merely a Jew in gentiles' clothing, displaying behind his superficial ancestry a particular Jewish moral sense, L. H. Goldman replies that Henderson "does epitomize certain Gentile qualities . . . which are love of personal freedom, a carefree attitude towards the world, a pursuit of the impossible dream, and a tremendous desire for self-indulgence" (1983, 110). Henderson is the figure Jews had long envied: "the big handsome Gentile whom the Jewish kids in the neighborhood look upon with a tinge of admiration. They know they will never become rain kings, but they secretly admire the Hendersons who will" (Goldman 110). I would add that these qualities had become accessible to America's Jews at the time Bellow was writing. Jews increasingly can journey to faraway lands in quest of their "true selves." Rather than being outsiders through imposition, they are now outsiders through declaration, comfortable enough as Americans to reject Americanism (at least intermittently). *Henderson the Rain King* marks a time when Jews could shift onto outside ethnic groups and nations the status of Other, representing them as part of a search for American (Jewish) identity.

While striving to enter American society, however, Jews have often been aware of its hypocrisy and exploitation. An explicit historical experience contributes to a modernist cynicism. In *Henderson the Rain King* such awareness appears only briefly: "My ancestors stole land from the Indians. They got more from the government and cheated other settlers too, so I became heir to a great estate." This subtext *might* lurk behind the entire novel as an ironic commentary undermining the pretext of civiliza- tion . . . except that it doesn't. The matter is immediately dropped: "No, that won't do either. What has that got to do with it?" (Bellow 1976a, 21). The Jewish radical tradition is bracketed. Bellow seems willfully not to write a novel of social consciousness, to spurn the Jewish radical tradi- tion. Instead he writes a purposeful exploration of the American psyche at play in a time of global privilege.[5]

Unable to cope with society's confining expectations, Henderson rebels, embarking upon a modernist quest for identity (resembling that of the hipster). A voice that pleads "I want, I want" impels him to a series of unfulfilled experiences—fighting in World War II, starting a pig farm, playing the violin—culminating in his journey to Africa. This search may be viewed as a version of the colonial spirit driven overseas. As he jour- neys into the unknown he crosses a plain surrounded by mountains, a space "all simplified and splendid, and I felt I was entering the past—the real past, no history or junk like that. The prehuman past" (46). This blank space will soon be filled in, not by savagery but by Edenic innocence. Encountering the Arnewi tribe, Henderson is greeted by "a band of Afri- can kids, naked boys and girls, yelling at the sight of us. Even the tiniest of them, with the big bellies, wrinkled their faces and screeched with the rest" (47). To this picture of childish bliss, taken perhaps from *National Geographic,* is added a Hindu feature—the sacredness of cattle, which must not be touched by the vegetarian Arnewi: "You have to understand that these people love their cattle like brothers and sisters, like children; they have more than fifty terms just to describe the various shapes of the horns" (56). The anthropological platitude that Eskimos have seventeen words for various types of snow is transferred to the shape of animal horns in an attempt to describe a sophisticated culture. In constructing a domain of primeval innocence, Bellow borrows freely, though superfi- cially, from whatever is available to create a decontextualized Africa, slic- ing up and displaying the surfaces of various cultures for Henderson's benefit.

In contrast to the peaceful primitives, Henderson plays the colonial figure, the grand yet blundering interventionist with technological gad- gets who doesn't quite know what he's doing. His arrival is preceded by pestilence, foreshadowing the modernity that plagues him. The frogs that pollute the Arnewi drinking water may be viewed simply enough as a symbolic manifestation of technology's ominous approach, American upheaval entering remotest Africa. Henderson has "little affection for the iron age of technology" (118) that accompanies his approach. Yet his solution to this disaster, this imbalance in nature, is as crude and technological as any Western intervention; he wants to "drive out, exterminate, and crush those frogs" (73)—a desire exhibiting the rationalist will to reshape nature. Henderson simultaneously evades and embodies civilization. At the point where he blows up the Arnewi cistern, destroying their source of water, he has failed in his quest. His encounter with the Arnewi enacts a parable of colonial destructiveness.

Reinforcing the primitive simplicity of the Arnewi beliefs are primitive speech patterns, explicable through lack of familiarity with English yet enhancing the Tarzan-like atmosphere. When the Arnewi drinking water is threatened, their prince can only keep repeating foolishly, "Nevah touch ahnimal in drink wattah" (59). Counterpointing simplicity is another common trope regarding "primitive" societies: an ancient, lost wisdom, primal knowledge obscured by civilization. This comes in the form of "Bitahness," a primitive enlightenment, held by the tribal wise woman, Mtalba. A key feature of "Bitah" is a breaking down of sexual barriers:

> A Bitah was not only a woman but a man at the same time. . . . Some of these people in this courtyard were her [Mtalba's] husbands and others her wives. She had plenty of both. The wives called her husband, and the children called her both father and mother. (75)

Return to an ancient, pregendered society might allow a primal unity of being, a kind of essentialist wholeness. For a society based on gender division of labor, such sexual fluidity transgresses conventional expectations. Andrea Dworkin, among others, explains sexual dualism as creating space for masculine "rape, plunder, violence" (1974, 156), in contrast to a time (itself mythologized) "when people functioned as part of the natural world . . . when men and women, male and female, were whatever they were, not polar opposites" (158). The sundering of conventional gender roles opens a glimpse of a new wisdom, or polymorphous wisdoms, radically transgressive of Western assumptions. Once again, though, Bellow does no more than flirt with radical ideas. He seems afraid to do more than poke at the boundaries of traditional rationalism. Mtalba's role finally is reduced to a generic tribal formula for primal wholeness—"Grun-tu-molani. Man want to live" (Bellow 1976a, 85)—which justifies Henderson's quest. Wisdom here is a definable quantity, possessed by this woman, to be given to Henderson, who asks for a talk "About the wisdom of life. Because I know she's got it and I wouldn't leave without a sample of it" (80). He has received his portion of primal wisdom from the Arnewi.

Equally, however, Henderson's encounter with the Arnewi displays the foolishness of traditional societies. Commenting upon their superstitious fear of the frogs, Henderson lectures the Arnewi:

> Do you know why the Jews were defeated by the Romans? Because they wouldn't fight back on Saturday. And that's how it is with your water situation. Should you preserve yourself, or the cows, or preserve the custom? I would say, yourself. Live . . . to make another custom. (62)

Alongside the portrait of the destructive colonialist is another version of the West as exemplifying common sense uninhibited by tradition. Tradition here is meant to serve the rational human, to create the good society; where it fails, it must be replaced. So assimilationist Jews shed their Judaism. In describing a flexible tradition wedded to rational ends, Henderson contradicts the frog symbolism that associates Western culture with destruction. One can, perhaps, resolve this contradiction by positing a misuse of rationalism at a crude colonial stage, which must be overcome by a more enlightened approach including study of, and respect for, various cultures. Such an interpretation makes the figure of the colonialist merely another tradition, an especially violent one, needing to be overcome by rationalism.

At least two contradictory interpretations, neither quite commensurate with the overall text, apply to Henderson's encounter with the Arnewi. The first considers both Arnewi primitivism and the colonial figure as hackneyed traditions to overcome. This view fails to account for the symbolism of rationalism as the shadow of evil. The alternative interpretation, which regards primitivism as an ur-force opposed to our technocratic society, is insufficiently supported by the development of the tribe, whose superstitions regarding drinking water and whose primitive language come across as naive and self-destructive. Contradictions inherent in 1950s liberalism—which, in various guises, criticized modern technobureaucratic society, stereotyped "primitive" simplicity, and continued the search for rationalist solutions to all problems—permeate *Henderson the Rain King*.

As part of a universalized existential quest, however, Henderson's experience with the Arnewi is only a temporary failure, a necessary part of his personal development (whatever it might mean to the Arnewi, who, when Henderson leaves, cease to exist outside of his narrative glance). He has encountered one archetypal pole: the peaceful. He is now ready for the violent society of the Wariri, through whose rites he confronts a primal aspect of human personality. Their highly ritualized violence resembles not a return to a natural state, but orientalist despotism, another myth of Otherness. One primal myth, that of heightened female sexuality, a capacity denied the heirs of Victorian society, occurs when Henderson experiences "the density of naked women, their volupté (only a French word would do the job here), [which] pressed upon me from all sides. The heat was great and the predominant odor was feminine" (153). This is the orient of sexual exoticism, of harems and exotic dancers—what Edward Said describes as "a place where one could look for sexual experience unavailable in Europe" (1979, 190). The innocent nudity of the Arnewi children evolves into the sexuality of these women, who service the dominant male. Situated between primitivist innocence and orientalist sensuality, the Wariri women exist as primal experience unavailable in Europe or America.

Sexuality and violence are strongly connected in the human psyche. An encounter with primal violence occurs in Henderson's contact with the lioness Atti, whereby he again faces the blunt physicality denied by rationalism. He must "absorb lion qualities" (Bellow 1976a, 254), must conquer his fear, physically experiencing the animal to the point of imitating her crouching, her movement, her roar. Henderson's terror is that of a hunted animal; Atti "sniffed my feet, working her way to the crotch once more and causing my parts to hide in my belly as best they could" (261). This contact creates a profound sensation in the genitals, seat of physicality. Sex and death intertwine as Henderson experiences the terror of the prey, destined to become gruesomely one with the hunting animal in a return to primal violence.

Yet Wariri violence is bound in a network of ceremony and tradition removed from psychic beginnings. Bellow describes a society fitting the myth of the Orient as "static, frozen, fixed eternally. The very possibility of development, transformation, human movement—in the deepest sense of the word—is denied the Orient and the Oriental" (Said 1979, 208). The network of ceremonies is transfixed. Of his people, bound by a series of complex rituals, the Wariri King, Dahfu, points out, "They are living in an old universe. Why not? That is part of my bargain with them, isn't it?" (Bellow 1976a, 292). Dahfu rejects existential self-fashioning; for him tradition creates sufficient purpose for existence. For Henderson tradition is an imprisonment, for he is the product of a society that fosters continuing reinvention of identity. An additional factor behind Henderson's fluidity may be the Jewish diaspora tradition of cultural reinvention, a trace of Bellow's cultural background.

Henderson's education among the Wariri goes beyond a ritualized encounter with the repressed drives of Eros and Thanatos. His discussions with Dahfu continue the path begun by Mtalba, although the wisdom of traditional societies proves insufficient. Only because Dahfu has studied in the West is he able to conduct sophisticated dialogue with Henderson. Western rationalism is cross-pollinated with an essential African wisdom to produce what Henderson calls "a genius of my own mental type" (216), with the word "genius" almost an apology for any reductive primitivism the reader may sense. Dahfu epitomizes Henderson's goal in blending the rational and the primal, including the essence of darkness: "[H]is blackness made him fabulously strange to me. Like all people who have a strong gift of life, he gave off almost an extra shadow—I swear" (209). Henderson must come to grips with the heart of darkness, of Otherness, in supranaturally intensified form. Dahfu's dark nature is akin to Henderson's rebelliousness, his inability to cope with civilization. Dahfu, born in the African primalscape, synthesizes ur-force and rationalist knowledge in a way that Henderson cannot.

Wariri society, though, is based neither on rationalism nor on primitivist impulse, but on tradition. By scrupulously conforming to ritual, Dahfu ends up dead. Deriding the restraints of tradition, the novel glorifies the id as channeled by rationalism, the two working together toward endless reinvention of identity. Vindicated in his continuing refusal to settle down, his abdication of responsibility, Henderson is a modernist nomad at play across a global landscape, living an endless experiment in which traditions may be freely borrowed, exchanged, or ignored in pursuit of a wisdom that increasingly resembles pleasure. If Enlightenment ideals are in doubt, multiculturalism is present only in a superficial sense. In the second half of the twentieth century, a universalist hedonism has become possible for many Jewish Americans. Although an older Bellow would brutally satirize as immature the quest for selfhood exemplified in the revolutionary 1960s, in *Henderson the Rain King* the ambiance of the boys' adventure tale predominates. The soul-searching Jew of Bernard Malamud, concerned with morality, with treating others right, is absent; the adventurous Henderson need never account for his actions. Playfulness is the final thematic note, as Henderson goes "running—leaping, leaping, pounding, and tingling over the pure white lining of the grey

Arctic silence" (Bellow 1976a, 341). Toni Morrison describes this scene as displaying "the frozen whiteness, a new white man in a new found land" (1990, 59). Bellow's hero is lost in the landscape of whiteness, of a dominant culture from whose aspect he surveys the great earth, a blanketing whiteness that subsumes all cultures. So ends a novel otherwise marked by the confusion of a society at a crossroads, torn between worshipping technology and abhorring it, correspondingly torn, in its countermythologizing, between respecting and romanticizing "primitive" peoples. For *Henderson the Rain King*, Bellow took a respite from balancing American individualism with Jewish history. He did not, of course, stop here, but further explored Jewish identity—particularly that of alienated intellectuals—in his subsequent novels.

III

Allen Guttmann describes Jewish writing as essentially diasporic; the source of its power is the experience of passing from one alien culture to another rather than some distinctively "Jewish" essence or vision. So Guttmann posits that "the explanation for the phenomenal creativity of Jewish intellectuals is to be located in their peculiar marginality, in their double alienation from their own heritage and from the culture of the 'host society'" (1971, 226), certainly an apt description for Philip Roth's writing. Cynthia Ozick, in "Towards a New Yiddish," rejects this argument, insisting that only the Jewish writer who draws upon distinctively Jewish experience and values will avoid artistic oblivion. To her literature is tribal, issuing from a particular history, so that "nothing thought or written in Diaspora has ever been able to last unless it has been centrally Jewish" (1983, 169). While such authors as Isaac Bashevis Singer may be historicized within modernism, they, like Ozick, draw upon the continuity of Jewish history, which repeats itself with a difference. Thematically, they lean toward Ozick's definition of an essential Jewish vision. In contrast, such writers as Bellow and Roth, while relentlessly interrogating the meaning of Jewishness, are intensely concerned with assimilation, the process of Americanization and the alienation and moral confusion that it brings. Of writers born in America, Bernard Malamud is probably closest to Singer, finding humanity in Yiddish culture while portraying a Judaism beset by alien values.

Malamud transposes into an American context the Yiddish tradition of colorful dialect voicing the travails of the underdog. Yet he claims also for his stories a universalism consistent with Enlightenment tradition. His famous statement that "Every man is a Jew" (Lasher 1991, 30) refers more to the social predicament of exclusion than to religion. Rather than shrinking humanity to a parochial version of Judaism, Malamud universalizes the Jewish condition of outsiderness as analogous to the existential quest for identity in a hostile world. Such a universalizing philosophy, however, stems from a specific ethnic history. Malamud's three texts overtly depicting Black-Jewish relations—"Angel Levine" (1959—the same year as *Henderson the Rain King*), "Black Is My Favorite Color" (1963), and *The Tenants* (1971)[6]—portray Blacks as embodying an extreme version of Jewish marginalization. Taken together, the three clearly react to contemporaneous developments in Black-Jewish relations, evolving from a hopeful vision of common humanity, to a bewildered misunderstanding, to a final scene of hostility. Granted, each isolated text makes a statement about human character; yet, studied within a historical context, the three dramatize how individual human choices are imbricated by larger social dilemmas.

Contextualizing Malamud in an essay originally published in 1972, Ozick contended that, given the rising hostility between Blacks and Jews, "Angel Levine" "far from being a mythically representative tale about suffering brothers, is now no more than a dated magazine story" (1983, 92). In this rigidly historicized view, the romanticized hope of "Angel Levine" is a fantasy unfulfilled by either history or Malamud's later works. Ozick, as we shall see in chapter 6, simplifies both history and *The Tenants*. Yet her implicit question is crucial: is "Angel Levine" so bound by a naive belief in human brotherhood as to make of itself a simplistic, easily dated sociological tract, so that it "is not merely out of date, it is illusion" (111)?

The story itself begins, in typical Malamud fashion, as a Jewish-inflected fable, an updating of Job. In a New York tenement the tailor Manischevitz suffers a series of misfortunes "in sheer quantity of woe, incomprehensible. It was also ridiculous, unjust, and because he had always been a religious man, an affront to God" (Malamud 1984, 278). The archetypal tale of inexplicable suffering recurs. In universal terms the story questions the meaning of life in a hostile universe; in terms of Jewish tradition, it continues a dialogue with God, an endless questioning of suffering, a chronicle bookended by slavery in Egypt on the one side and the Holocaust on the other.

The differentiating twist setting this tale firmly in contemporary America is the appearance of Angel Levine, a Black Jew, as an answer to

Manischevitz's desperate prayers. This odd event can, again, be interpreted biblically: the extreme test of belief, as when Isaac is asked to sacrifice his only son. Manischevitz's initial refusal to believe that a Black Jew can be a true angel of God can be interpreted as a general refusal of belief, an initial failing of God's test. Alternatively, it can be contextualized within modern America as an early fable about the consequences of rejecting American diversity. This historicized interpretation gains clarity through the ironic reversal of Jewish and Black roles. Not only is a Black angel an anomaly in a Eurocentric religious construction, but a Black intervening on a Jew's behalf subverts expectation (at least in an American setting). So, upon Levine's initial appearance, "Manischevitz guessed he had left his door open and was being visited by a case worker from the Welfare Department" (279), reversing the stereotype of Jewish welfare bureaucrat and Black recipient. This can again be universalized in a variety of ways: being kind to strangers, understanding outsiders, coming to terms with the Other. The universal moves toward a specific social applicability. God's ultimate test of faith is also a test of human brotherhood, one often failed in a racially charged America. A little context enhances the story's richness. Yet a more complex awareness of Jewish and Black relations leads to an even more sophisticated reading. If the Jew has long been a Job figure of archetypal suffering, in America this role belongs to Blacks. Angel Levine thus becomes a metonym for Blacks taking on the inexplicable suffering of Jews. In this symbolic transference the story illuminates a common history, a common humanity.

From a Jewish site increasingly blending into American, Manischevitz enters an ultimate terrain of Otherness. "Angel Levine" moves beyond the usual Malamudian confines of a Yiddish-flavored New York into an exoticized Black terrain, not Henderson's Africa but New York's Harlem, just as alien and much more threatening due to proximity. As is usual in contacts with the Other, the perceiving culture is ultimately enriched in its ability to draw upon a new landscape of images, while the perceived culture is flattened, distorted, and decontextualized, becoming an instrument for the imagination of the perceiving eye. Functioning as a source of darkness and confusion, the classic stereotype of blackness as removal from the good, Harlem is "vast and its lights lit nothing. Everywhere were shadows, often moving" (283). Harlem is hell, or at least purgatory, that underworld into which Manischevitz must descend on a Dantean journey to redeem his lack of faith. Blackness is the terrain of defamiliarization, by contrast with which one comes to terms with selfhood: "In the stores he saw people and everybody was black. It was an amazing thing to observe" (283). Manischevitz's faith is redeemed through an utterly novel vision, an awakening into blackness.

Strangeness and sinfulness characterize Bella's honky-tonk (perhaps named after the Bella in Joyce's *Ulysses,* who also symbolizes carnal imagination), a place "bursting with jazz and the blues" (287), that alien music which has invaded America, initially associated with whorehouses and strip joints. Bella herself is "a big-breasted Negress in a purple evening gown" who "with much laughter through many white teeth, broke into a vigorous shimmy" (284). The image of the happy dancing darky, created to take the edge off the Black presence, to soothe White fears, conjoins with the far more dangerous sexuality: "As Bella's gyrations continued Levine rose, his eyes lit in excitement. She embraced him with vigor, both his hands clasped around her restless buttocks, and they tangoed together across the floor, loudly applauded by the customers" (284). Such a spectacle, a display of sexuality for the benefit of an admiring crowd, is far from the conventional behavior expected of an angel. Levine, rather, exhibits the characteristics associated with Black sexuality, the wanton display of submerged impulses, in a purposefully marginalized space far from the realm of "good" society. Manischevitz, staring "white-faced," reacts according to the dictates of the Victorian superego, unable to accept such spectacle, bound by the constraints of civilization. Repressed lusts unfold before him in this alien terrain. In one reading of the story Manischevitz accepts his own sexuality in accepting Levine as an angel. His initial suffering, then, is metaphorical for his repressed libido; he can never be content until he accepts his sexuality. The Otherness expressed by blackness represents a bifurcated psyche that must be made whole.

Yet ways of reading "Angel Levine" are multiple and interlocking. Manischevitz simultaneously confronts his own lack of faith, his repressed sexuality, and the barrier of racial stereotypes. The story's closure, the psychic healing that occurs on the social and historical levels, is at best incomplete. The Black section of town remains separate from a dominant society that demarcates a repressed zone against which to define itself. More than that, "Angel Levine" portrays the angry reaction of those reified as other without contextualizing that anger: "Beat it, pale puss." / "Exit, Yankel, Semitic trash" (288). Manischevitz encounters a dual prejudice, susceptibility to being Othered as a White and as a Jew. The angry voices clamoring at the end of the Black-Jewish alliance are already represented, a point that Ozick overlooks in dismissing "Angel Levine" as simplistic.

Ultimately, however, the story is one of common humanity. The most powerful symbol of this is the Black Jewish prayer meeting Manischevitz stumbles upon, a scene flavored by both Black dialect and Jewish argumentativeness. Most important is the spiritual dimension, the biblical references, the discussion of soul versus material substance: "'how come we is colored?' 'God put the spirit in all things. He put it in the green leaves and the yellow flowers. He put it with the gold in the fishes and the blue in the sky. That's how come it came to us'" (287). Color may even be read here as an antidote to a spiritually deadening whiteness. The message is antiracist and universalist: the grand variety of colors are physical manifestations of a single spiritual force. So Blacks can worship as Jews with color irrelevant to spirituality, a notion that Manischevitz must accept to be redeemed.

Despite this homage to color, in "Angel Levine" the overriding signifier of universalism, of a common humanity, is finally whiteness (not Malamud's professed Jewishness). The dominant cultural image-system, structured in Manichaean white and black, proves unavoidable. Following his redemption Manischevitz hears "a whirring of wings, and when he strained for a wider view, could have sworn he saw a dark figure born aloft on a pair of strong black wings." Given Manischevitz's acceptance of an America beyond race, the traditional angel figure reconstituted in black seems to transcend the equation of whiteness with goodness. Then "a feather drifted down. Manischevitz gasped as it turned white, but it was only snowing" (289). The conflation of white and black at this time in social history calls for an encompassing whiteness as its final sign, one blanketing out difference, including the Jewishness ostensibly dominant in Malamud. This is the same whiteness in which Henderson frolics, a universal leveling recurrent in American literature. The white implies the black that it smothers; whiteness exists only through opposition to color, which it feels compelled to submerge. Malamud gropingly attempts to undercut this fatal opposition, to arrive at something new, representing the Jew as a third term, one of transition and transcendence signifying a common humanity. So, Manischevitz concludes, "A wonderful thing, Fanny. . . . Believe me, there are Jews everywhere" (289). Such a statement, in displacing the notion of a separate and self-sufficient Judaism, yields a philosophy consistent with Enlightenment Jewry's attempt to weld itself to European universalism. In doing so it implicitly acquiesces to overpowering whiteness—the homogenizing terrain in which Black and Jewish relations occur—which Manischevitz only mistakes for the black angel's feather. The conclusion of "Angel Levine" undercuts the ethnic flavors, both Jewish and Black (even if the Black is compromised by racial symbolism) that it earlier privileges.

Jewish intervention into, and representation of, African American affairs is ambiguously positioned between a dominant universalism and a vision of individual ethnic value, one predicated on the need to build Jewish identity in hostile or indifferent terrain. Jewish philanthropy, often spurred more by the needs of the Jewish community than a deep knowledge of African American society, may be seen as patronizing or hypocritical. A liberalism that blurs ethnic distinctions and ignores economic barriers blinds itself to Black perspectives, a limitation defining Malamud's "Black Is My Favorite Color." The story reverses expected Black and Jewish roles, satirizing the possibility of Jewish oppression, of a continued role as subversive fool, in a context of American privilege. Like Jewish liberals who eagerly signed on to the Civil Rights movement, Nat Lime, the story's narrator, is mystified by African American rebuffs to his friendly overtures. Narrative perspective is crucial here; the single-minded, myopic Lime might fool the unwary reader into duplicating his mistake, into viewing Black behavior as simply inexplicable. So Sidney Richman posits Lime as "a victim amid victims, whose special fate, as a boy and as a man, is to bang his balding head against the facts of blackness" (1986, 98). Richman's interpretation assumes a conventional pattern of victimhood, of repeated, often unexpected rejection. Regarding Black America this interpretation of Jewish history is misplaced, since Jews here are not outsiders but successful Americans. If Jewish liberalism perceives itself as sympathetic, African Americans may understand it as condescending. Evelyn Gross Avery describes how "the well-meaning Malamudian Jew almost begs for victimization through his inability to understand the Negro's emotional conflicts and his incapacity to learn from past experience" (1979, 102). In America the real victims are Blacks: social context reverses the time-honored paradigm of Jews as outsiders. Yet the Jewish protagonist remains oblivious to American context, remains in his mind the eternal victim. Lime fails utterly to grasp the significance of his ownership of a Harlem liquor store. Unwittingly, he fulfills the stereotype of the profiteering Jew who benefits from despair and addiction caused by the society within whose rules he profits. Because Lime individualizes personal relationships, ignoring social and economic context, to him Black intransigence is inexplicable. Lime is a version of the liberal individualist extreme to the point of parody.

The story's framing device, the perspective from which Lime reflects on his relationship with Blacks, sets the stage with a present-tense version of the kind of overtures and rejections he has experienced. Lime's Black cleaning woman, Charity Quietness (one of literature's less subtle names), rebuffs his clumsy attempts at charity and pseudoequality by eating lunch in the bathroom. If the bathroom exists on the margins of the apartment, a kind of shared dirty little secret, Charity Quietness, through her passive resistance, acknowledges her place on society's margins regardless of Lime's token gestures. Black remains separate from White, servant from master, a social and economic relationship that Lime cannot overcome and never quite understands.

Paradoxically, however, social context first attracts Lime to Black America. Although he anticipates libidinal benefits similar to those described by Norman Mailer and sought by Eugene Henderson, he attributes his fascination with Blacks to a charitable heart: "I'm drawn to them. At this time of my life I should have one or two good colored friends, but the fault isn't necessarily mine. If they knew what was in my heart toward them" (1984, 74). Characteristically, Lime immediately contradicts himself, for after admitting that color does make a difference, that he's specifically drawn toward African Americans, he disavows the meaning of race: "[F]or me there's only one human color and that's the color of blood," then contradicts the contradiction: "Who wants everyone to be the same?" (74). Is it ethnic particularism that fascinates him or the ideal of human fraternity? Most likely both, yet he is not quite aware enough to articulate this (apparent) opposition. Lime's convolutions are only a slight parody of the Jewish American dilemma of balancing universalism and ethnicity, a dilemma that often employs Blacks as a measure of identity.

Jewish perceptions of Blacks are themselves torn between identification with a repressed minority and a need to define American identity against the stereotypical freedom associated with blackness. What is it, then, that Lime hopes to achieve through his friendship with Blacks? From the relatively few clues the story gives, it corresponds to Huggins's description of the minstrel image, an outlet for repressed exoticism. The young Lime frequents Black neighborhoods where "the street was full of life" (75). He likes best the "parties at night [where] everybody had a good time. The musicians played their banjos and saxophones and the houses shook with music and laughing" (76). Again, cultural context expands our understanding: the banjo is a traditional African instrument (though now lost to American Blacks),[7] while the saxophone dominates jazz and blues in a way it never did in European classical music. Africanisms predominate here, extroverted and based on principles of group participation, contrary to the passive role of the audience for European "art" music. Such an extroverted community alleviates Jewish Americans' repression and alienation. Lime is exposed to something further: "The young girls, with their pretty dresses and ribbons in their hair, caught me in my throat when I saw them through the windows" (76). Just as the visit to a Black neighborhood is illicit, so are Lime's first, adolescent views of forbidden sexuality. African American society tantalizes, seeming to offer repressed physical pleasures.

Lime's fascination with Black society, however, is not reciprocated. His attempt at friendship with a Black kid, Buster, is stiff and superficial, relying on movies and candy bars as bait. Reflecting on this, the adult Lime shows some awareness of the immediate context for failure: "Maybe because it was a one-way proposition—from me to him" (77). This insight, never expanded upon by Lime to explain his later problems, also applies to the larger shape of Jewish overtures to African Americans, based upon charity that often breeds resentment in a context of economic imbalance. Buster hits Lime in the teeth, explaining, "[Y]ou a Jew bastard. Take your Jew movies and your Jew candy and shove them up your Jew ass" (77). Buster's deeper motivation is left hidden, but certainly he feels humiliated at the notion that his friendship could so easily be bought; as Avery puts it, "to preserve his self-respect Buster must reject Nat's charity" (1979, 102). Upon this personal motivation he easily imposes the framework of traditional anti-Semitism, of Jews as schemers using material goods to their advantage.

In this minifable the Black is an object of guilt and fascination for the Jew, who in turn becomes an object of resentment, of vented frustration. This pattern is repeated by the grown-up Lime regarding love and marriage, practices tied to social heritage. Lime seeks to define himself as an American in a multiethnic context, using a Black woman as a third term to erase his Jewish past. Courting Ornita Harris, Lime again employs material goods as bait. This is, of course, a traditional courtship rite, also based on social and economic imbalance, on a man symbolically demonstrating that he has the means to provide for a woman. Transposed to the context of Black and White, it becomes a transgression. More than Lime, Harris understands society's unwritten law against miscegenation and the difficulties encountered by a biracial couple. She asks, "What about children? Were you looking forward to half-Jewish polka dots?" (Malamud 1984, 81). Mirroring our culture, Harris is a racial/ethnic essentialist, able to comprehend only tidy categories: Black, Jewish, White. Like Bigger Thomas, she has internalized dominant cultural assumptions as a matter of survival; in 1960s terms, she understands rightly the difficulties of mixed marriage.

Indeed, the society surrounding Lime's liquor store is immersed in race and economics, factors that structure its inhabitants' lives in ways to which Lime is oblivious. When hoodlums accost Lime and Harris, their crude ironies display a keener social analysis than does Nat Lime: "'You talk like a Jew landlord' said the green hat. 'Fifty a week for a single room.' 'No charge fo' the rats,' said the half-inch brim" (82). Lime's reply is rather pathetic in its naïveté:

> Believe me, I'm no landlord. My store is Nathan's Liquor's between Hundred Tenth and Eleventh. I also have two colored clerks, Mason and Jimmy, and they will tell you I pay good wages as well as I give discounts to certain customers. (83)

Jewish liberal self-deception regarding participation in an exploitative system could not be more bluntly stated. In considering himself a decent, hardworking businessman concerned with the local neighborhood, Lime fails to understand that his situation is structurally exploitative regardless of how he treats individuals. Like a small-time version of the Dalton family in *Native Son*, he thinks charity and personal humanity can circumvent a social oppression in which he is implicated. The hoodlums understand this, and understand also the unbalanced nature of his relationship with Harris. "No more black pussy for you," they taunt him, and again, "That ain't no lady . . . that's black pussy" (83). Harris is objectified, made into a purchasable good. A material basis underlies Lime's relationship with her, just as it must with his Black clerks, just as it did with Buster. The Jewish schlemiel can no longer be an object of humor or pity when he occupies the dominant position.[8] Nat Lime personifies Jewish liberalism at its most naive, proclaiming a human connection while ignoring his social and economic advantages.

Material imbalance is a key cause of Black and Jewish tension that led to the crumbling of political alliance. From an increasingly secure position in American society, Jews supported Blacks only partly out of benevolence, and partly out of self-interest. The resentment this produces is the crucial subtext motivating "Black Is My Favorite Color." In describing "Angel Levine" as an illusion, and *The Tenants* as depicting the real nature of Black-Jewish relations, Cynthia Ozick ignores Malamud's crucial intermediary story. "Black Is My Favorite Color" satirizes the self-deceiving nature of Jewish assumptions, yet narratorial voice leaves the story's key irony—Lime's utter blindness to the effects of Black social and economic status—to be inferred by the reader. Blacks remain external here, an exotic mystery, silenced, given to seemingly irrational behavior.

This is W. E. B. DuBois's veil, which Whites, including Jews, cannot penetrate. To write "Black Is My Favorite Color" Malamud must have had some awareness of conditions behind the veil, particularly given historical Jewish memory of cultural invisibility. Nevertheless, Malamud does not directly explore African American consciousness, but obliquely satirizes Jewish hypocrisy to undercut the naive belief in Jewish righteousness and African American gratefulness. To be more direct would assume a knowledge of African American consciousness to which Malamud was not privy.

Ambivalent Estrangements
Jewish Role Models and
Black Liberalism

Must I strive toward colorlessness?
　　　　　　—Ralph Ellison, Invisible Man

More so than Jewish literature, African American literature of the 1950s and '60s was torn between protest and an ideology of universalizing liberalism. By the 1960s African American writers including James Baldwin, Lorraine Hansberry, and Paule Marshall were depicting a widening swath of American life. Jewish American writers have traveled a similar path, from works championing ethnic heritage[1] to novels that portray Jews increasingly comfortable within American society. African American works of the 1960s employ Jews as intermediary figures in exploring the tensions between liberalist integration and ethnic heritage. This trend, which appears to suggest a Black experience similar to the Jewish, is misleading, for the two peoples have a quite dissimilar history in America, particularly following World War II. Color is the primary marker of difference in America, an omnipresent reminder of exclusion that, along with historically rooted economic inequity, continues to separate African and Jewish Americans. Even in the works of those Black writers who appear to parallel the Jewish formula, an underlying anxiety is evident behind the integrationist facade. As the 1960s approached, however, the balance between American and Black identities tilted toward the universal.

　　An early African American work employing the "universal" American viewpoint is Willard Motley's *We Fished All Night* (1951). Yet an indirect Black perspective exists in the psychic agonies of the Jewish Aaron

Levin, through whom the reader sees something of the struggle of the Black intellectual isolated from his family and from majority culture. Motley explains Levin's confused, ever changing identity: "[A]s communism, as Christianity had failed him, now too, Judaism failed him" (1951, 429). A position between ideologies, comfortable in no one milieu, is confronted by both Jewish and African American. Rather than being powerfully adaptive to a variety of circumstances, American Jews are portrayed as stateless and shapeless. Prefiguring another 1960s theme, Motley portrays this shapelessness as a temporary condition, a precursor to a struggle destined to change society: "And now the young Negroes, Jews, women, were freeing themselves from themselves. They appeared like strange new flowers, straight in the soil" (229). The isolation of Black America troubles this optimism. On the one hand, the ambiguous relationship of Jews to dominant society is a vehicle for Black characters to glimpse their own dilemma. On the other hand, if Jewish Americans are once removed from dominant American society, Blacks are twice or thrice removed, a situation causing an often unspoken estrangement.

Motley's work only intimates how, following decades of a muted African American voice, the Civil Rights movement would lead to new confidence, spurring Black representations of Jews as political and social allies. Probing Jewish consciousness was a means not only of exploring a people resembling the Black bourgeoisie in their ambiguous status between margins and center(s), but of understanding a bulwark of the progressivism that gave new hope to African Americans. The Jewish diaspora has much in common with the African diaspora: exile in an ambiguous position of cultural hybridity and transnationalism. The drive toward assimilation makes Jewish Americans a role model, but an ambivalent and contested one for a diasporic African community increasingly bent on finding its cultural roots.[2]

I

In *A Raisin in the Sun* (1959) Lorraine Hansberry maintained conventional expectations of African American literature, portraying a working-class Black family, and was rewarded with acclaim. *The Sign in Sidney Brustein's Window* (1965) explores a markedly different part of the social spectrum: a liberal, White intellectual free from immediate financial strain. This broadening of perspective parallels the freedom of twentieth-century Jewish literature to explore multiple consciousnesses; in doing so, it casts new light upon the fragmented, self-deceiving nature of a supposedly unitary American society. Hansberry's diverse chorus of voices fulfills Bakhtin's description of a modern literature that "figures as both the speech of the author and as the speech of another—and at the same time" (1981, 308). *The Sign in Sidney Brustein's Window* extends the process of cultural hybridity paradigmatic of modern literature and of American life.

Nevertheless, as Diane Marre documents, Hansberry's portrayal of a White, Jewish protagonist not only met with far less critical acclaim than *A Raisin in the Sun*, but drew political criticism: "[B]lack nationalists and feminists alike were outraged at her choice of a white male for protagonist" (Marre 1987, 56). To critics searching for strong, independent Blacks and women Marre queries:

> Why should it have been so outrageous and so politically incorrect for a black female playwright to create a white hero figure? The choice seems logical, given Hansberry's interest in the figure of the white liberal and the need for him to be radicalized . . . and her interest in the existentially paralyzed intellectuals she saw all around her. (56–57)

Certainly White liberals have long felt free to depict African Americans in both social and literary works. And certainly White, often Jewish, males have been crucial to progressive movements encompassing African American concerns. Politically and socially Hansberry's choice of topic makes perfect sense, as it does regarding her personal life. Her contact with White intellectuals, her marriage to a "White liberal," must have provided ample material for probing such a figure. Furthermore, Hansberry carries out James Baldwin's project of expanding the boundaries of literature by African Americans.[3] A full representation of American society demands works such as *The Sign in Sidney Brustein's Window* from writers of all backgrounds. An African American sensibility, a cynicism regarding hierarchical social categories, infuses Hansberry's work.

African American society is a rich site for complex portrayals of individuals trapped between cultural traditions. *Sidney Brustein* places a Jewish "patriarch," an articulate intellectual, at the center of the action; no patriarch, however, has ever appeared as so unsure a figure, so lacking a sense of direction, as Sidney Brustein. Outside the clearly demarcated (if artificial) boundaries of nationalism—Black or Zionist or European— uncertainty and alienation preside. Brustein's role as bridge between Jewish immigrant and successful citizen of the New World extends to an array of Othernesses who surround him in bohemian Greenwich Village.

Hansberry portrays convincingly, if briefly, an ambiguous situation that is archetypally American: the struggle of the assimilating second-generation immigrant. Brustein caricatures his mother's reaction to his choice of a non-Jewish mate: "*Not* that I have anything against the *goyim*, Sidney, she's a nice girl, but the rice is too greasy. And *lamb* fat? For the *stomach*? With hominy grits? *Like a lump it sits*" (Hansberry 1987, 235). The intonation and inversion of Yiddish-derived dialect contribute to a worldview of embattled particularism combined with mocking resignation. Displaying contradictions of the Jewish immigrant, Brustein's mother is unable to fully reject the world that Jews are struggling to enter—"*Not* that I have anything against the *goyim*"—although she does reject immersion in this world, at least for her son. To her, as to Portnoy's mother, Jewish pride means a struggle for ethnic particularism, for continuation of Jewish traditions against the unhealthy habits of the outsider. This struggle is inherently Pyrrhic. Those Jews who immigrated to America have largely made their choice; Sidney has already assimilated the language and many of the attitudes of the United States. The Jewish portion of his American identity lies both in maintaining the scholarly inclinations of the "People of the Book" and in a heightened sensitivity to the situation of marginality.

Around this ambivalent figure suspended between cultures, a living metonymy for the assimilating American, clusters an odd, multicultural assortment of characters: an Appalachian woman, a Black ex-Communist, a homosexual playwright. For them Brustein is a link to mainstream American culture. Specifically African American concerns are minimized, subsumed within Bohemia, "the preferred habitat of many who fancy revolt, or at least, detachment from the social order that surrounds us" (211). Sidney Brustein, the Jewish hub around which this motley group spins, is liberal and well-meaning yet also naive and self-centered, and given to intellectual posturing. Isolated from the obligations of the "real" world, he moves from individualistic utopian project (nightclub) to utopian project (newspaper publisher) without the background or commitment to fulfill any plan. In this he is a less headstrong version of Bellow's Eugene Henderson—or a forerunner of the overprivileged, egocentric youth Bellow later portrays—adrift in the world, just barely lacking the talent to fulfill his array of interests, narcissistically seeking to create a "self" guided by no stable goal or tradition. In the world of social alienation he is a sympathetic tourist, not quite fit for the role of intellectual patron to the other characters.

Brustein is particularly patronizing toward his wife, Iris, an American hillbilly, certainly a misplaced figure in Bohemia. Jew as middleman between mainstream America and intellectual circles is a recurring trope from Woody Allen to Philip Roth. Brustein's and Iris's asymmetrical relationship resembles that of Jewish to Black. He has brought Iris into his life and promoted her, assembling his own version of her partly from her actual background and partly from his imagination. Iris is an American "mutt," a mixture of Greek, Irish, and Cherokee romanticized by Brustein as an exotic hillbilly. Yet Iris's artistic ambitions set her apart from her kin; in drawing her away from mainstream, rural, Protestant America, Brustein promises the artistic, cosmopolitan world exemplified by the Jew. To Sidney's romanticization of Iris, Alton Scales remarks dryly that, "If he had his way he'd have her running barefoot in a gingham dress with all that hair flying around" (232). In this bucolic myth Iris participates willingly, making herself into a North American version of the primitives who soothed Eugene Henderson's neuroses; she simplifies her past, portraying her father as a rustic hillbilly. Through participating in Sidney's illusion, she enables him to maintain his encompassing patronage.

Iris's eventual, inevitable revolt, her exclamation "I DON'T WANT TO PLAY APPALACHIAN ANY MORE!" (315), one of several moments stripping away Sidney's illusions, intimates African American discontent with Jewish patronage. Brustein's naïveté is most undermined when Iris's sister Mavis, whom Sidney regards as crude and conventional, as "the Mother Middleclass itself" (267), is revealed in her full complexity. Sidney's misconceptions of Iris's father are exposed when Mavis describes him as an imaginative dreamer whose reenactments of the Greek classics with his children spurred Iris's wish to be an actress (307). Iris's confession that "I just tried to live up to your fantasy about me" (313) exposes the process of mythologization, the mutual lies that people tell each other. The human personality is far more complicated, given to multiple, often contradictory, roles. Mavis's comment—that "There are no squares, Sidney. Believe me when I tell you, everybody is his own hipster" (308)—undermines Sidney's reduction of people into neat bipolar categories.

Just as Sidney configures Iris to fit his preconceived notions, so the Jewish intellectuals and activists who supported the Civil Rights movement had their assumptions about African American attitudes. In a simmering crock-pot of racial, ethnic and sexual difference, themes of alienation, the struggle for acceptance, and the ambiguity of assorted marginal positions continually replay themselves. Alton Scales, the only Black character in *Sidney Brustein*, is no representative of exclusive blackness, but a mongrelized aesthete among a vanguard of outcasts. Able to pass for White, Scales is an ex-Communist disillusioned by the excesses of the Communist bloc, a humanist revolutionary who has had his revolutionary illusions snatched away. His insecurity is more hard-edged than that of Sidney Brustein. Positioned by his racial status, with more at stake than Brustein, he resembles Himes's Lee Gordon minus the anti-Semitism. In warning Brustein of "ostrichism," of the danger of cynicism leading to social disengagement (228), he voices Hansberry's own concern. When Iris derides him, calling him a "white boy playing black boy" (246) because of his refusal to pass for White, he replies, "I *am* a black boy. I didn't make up the game, and as long as a lot of people think there is something wrong with the fact that I *am* a Negro—I am going to make a point out of being one" (246). Rather than fleeing from his racial heritage he accepts its social reality. Quite aware of the artificial nature of racial categories, he nevertheless, like Tidewater in Jay Neugeboren's *Sun's Legacy,* refuses to "pass"; if society forces a choice between meaningless categories, he creates meaning through his willful rejection of hypocrisy.

Yet, like so many Hansberry characters, Alton Scales is contradictory; he is no simplistic exemplar of a cause, or of the humanist Black intellectual. He has his own hypocrisies and his own acceptance of social definitions, most jarringly in his insults hurled at a homosexual playwright: "Turn off, Fag Face!" (268). He again resembles Lee Gordon, whose injured identity leads him to objectify those who threaten his masculinity. Simultaneously Scales has absorbed facets of the Black bourgeois ideology against which he ostensibly revolts. His refusal to marry Iris's sister Gloria when he finds out she's been a prostitute shows an implicit acceptance of dominant ideals. Reduced himself to a stereotype, Scales fails to make the imaginative leap of realizing how others are similarly dehumanized. His rejection of Gloria is complex, involving his personal history and racial pride, which lead him to exclaim: "I don't want white man's leavings, Sidney. I couldn't *marry* her" (302–3). Despite his rhetoric regarding Black identity, Scales accepts crucial precepts of mainstream ideology, notably regarding a pure White woman as a definitive status symbol. A prostitute will neither be respected in White society nor allow Scales to retain his racial pride. His bohemian pretensions are not enough to overcome social assumptions.

Gloria's suicide climaxes a chain of disappointments leading to Brustein's disillusionment. Sidney's idealism is frittered away, dissipated by frustration and defeat, a situation paradigmatic of the modernist antihero. Brustein states it in a cynical monologue, reiterating modernist alienation: "[O]ne does not *smite* evil any more: one holds one's gut, thus—and takes a pill. . . . Oh, but to take up the sword of the Maccabees again!" (297). The warrior Jew is ancient history, and Brustein is no Henderson boldly constructing a new American persona. Upon realizing the failure of his political campaign due to its usurpation by the corrupt "system," Brustein snaps in half a yardstick—"the 'sword of his ancestors'" (317)—a symbolic self-emasculation. Fond of articulating his ennui, he finally experiences it at a full emotional level, actualizing what had been something of an intellectual pose.

Yet *The Sign in Sidney Brustein's Window* is not an admission of defeat, but a call to action on the cusp of the greatest victories of the Civil Rights movement. If Henderson's adventuresome search for fulfillment is actually a retreat from social awareness, Brustein's defeat contains the seeds of a new political covenant. In calling upon Scales to stand firm and to marry Gloria, Brustein employs Black Nationalist rhetoric: "A star has risen over Africa. . . . Over Harlem . . . over the South Side . . . . The new Zionism is raging" (303). This new nationalism is presented as international, a cultural mosaic conjoined with moral humanism for which Jewish and Black histories are a basis. Rather than immovable bedrock, though, they constitute a flexible, usable past. Brustein implicitly equates marrying a White prostitute with an act of rebellion, a refusal to be bound by the racist and sexist assumptions that have hurt his people, too. The play's underdevelopment of Gloria, however, fails to provide a human sensibility that would ground such deconstruction of oppositional social paradigms. Cultural diversity and hybridity are far from recognition. Brustein's energies are dispersed; his plethora of causes amounts to tilting at windmills, making him a Don Quixote ill-prepared for battle, unsure even of what he's fighting. Nevertheless, in Brustein's final vow to fight on in a corrupt world, Hansberry portrays a resolute if weary optimism about the Jewish role in political struggles. Brustein's "tomorrow, we shall make something strong of this sorrow" (340) epitomizes the optimistic spirit of 1964; despite defeats and shortsightedness, the struggle continues. Brustein seems to learn from his mistakes, to be better prepared for future battle. A cross-cultural liberalism, whatever its defects, is the only hope for meaningful social change. The implicit vision, preliminary and ideologically diffuse, is of an America based on principles of individual expression mediated through the prism of multiple ethnicities.

II

The Jewish male as midwife, an ambivalent yet nurturing figure who encourages the development of a Black intellectual class, spans the work of Chester Himes, Lorraine Hansberry, and Paule Marshall. If Wright and Himes portray Jews from a Black perspective, and Hansberry develops a Jewish character as central protagonist, Marshall takes the next step of directly employing Jewish narrative consciousness. This occurs most extensively amid the most extreme upheaval of the 1960s, in *The Chosen Place, the Timeless People* (1969); two works, however, lead up to this portrayal. A sympathy with the Jewish people and awareness of a common history appears intermittently in *Brown Girl, Brownstones* (1959), while "Brooklyn," from Marshall's collection *Soul Clap Hands and Sing* (1964), portrays an utterly different Jewish figure in the lecherous male who projects his social frustrations onto a young Black woman.

Brown Girl, Brownstones portrays an Afro-Caribbean family in an American immigrant tale dramatizing the split between traditional culture and materialism, with the added element of race. Selina Boyce, the protagonist, faces this conflict in her parents, who represent the opposite choices available to her. Her mother's relentless determination to succeed in America enacts a grim parody of the materialistic West Indian community, and simultaneously of the American success story. Conversely, her father is an impractical dreamer who desires only a return to Barbados. Duplicating the course of modernity, of efficiency, of the small-time capitalism that she represents, the mother slowly drives her impractical husband away, and finally has him deported. Boyce rebels against this narrow materialism, befriending disreputable characters, engaging in a rebellious love affair, and copying her father's artistic, impractical nature in her pursuit of dancing. Like that of the fictional Alton Scales and of the actual LeRoi Jones, hers is an artist's derisive vision of the Black middle class.

For the West Indian bourgeoisie, the mythologized figure of the Jew is an important symbol of the New World, of material success. Says one minor character, after griping about exploitation: "Who say I faulting the Jew? I lift my hat to him. He know how to make a dollar. He own all New York!" (Marshall 1981, 38). Jews represent the success to which many

West Indian immigrants in Marshall's world aspire. Financial manipula-
tion, though it may be tinged with moral doubt, is overall admired among
the immigrant community. Jews as vexed symbols of material success,
however, are contradicted by the only actual Jewish character in *Brown
Girl, Brownstones*. Rachel Fine is Selina Boyce's friend and dance mentor, a positive Jewish role model, a "minority" success story embodying
that artistic excellence for which Boyce strives. Still, she engenders contradictory emotions, as in the warning given Boyce: "[B]eware Bohemia.
She's probably some Prog from the village hootenanny set who just loves
Negroes" (251). Bohemia signifies not just artistic possibility but the danger of patronizing tokenism. Jews remain primarily White in the Black
consciousness, and Whites who believe in an abstract version of integration may befriend Blacks merely to relieve their own conscience. Through
inverting American racism they may even continue it, bringing their own
preconceptions about African American identity.

Rachel Fine hardly appears condescending; her relationship with
Boyce seems one of enthusiastic mutual support. Fine confides that her
hair

> used to be very blond and long, and everybody was always saying I was
> like a little *goye* with my blond hair and blue eyes. Except, of course,
> the little *goyim* brats in school. Then, when it started turning dark, ev-
> erybody started commiserating—like it was a tragedy. So I got fed up
> and on my fifteenth birthday I cut it myself and drowned it in black dye.
> (278)

Fine's tale of rebellion provides a warning to Boyce about the pressure to
assimilate. Just as Blacks may favor especially light children, Fine's kin
privilege blonde hair and blue eyes, signs of (White) womanly virtue.
Fine's appearance fools her own people more than the "*goyim* brats"—
only those born into dominant society, the implication is, can truly belong, though outsiders continue to strive for complete assimilation. Similarly Blacks, no matter how light-skinned, no matter how they straighten
their hair, are always prefigured as outsiders. Fine's assimilation is betrayed
by biology, by her darkening hair, and so she completes the betrayal by
hastening the processes of her own body, an act that reverses the intent of
hair straightening. Rebelling against zealously assimilationist kin, she
strikes a blow for her biological and cultural heritage. In placing the mark
upon herself of the outsider she revels in her own difference, much as the
Afro in the late 1960s came to be a source of proud distinction.

Ultimately, common physical differences mean relatively little for relations between Blacks and Jews. After all, there are very few blonde, blue-eyed Blacks. Similarly, common histories of exploitation are belied by differing social status in an America wherein Blacks may never be pronounced "White." Rachel Fine and Selina Boyce's relationship is, in fact, one-sided: Boyce hears much about Rachel's intimate life, yet discloses little of her own (279). In a minor key this duplicates relationships in which Blacks have remained behind a veil, hidden from their Jewish benefactors. When Boyce concludes the novel by returning to Barbados to explore her past, she relies upon Fine to procure the ticket. Her dependence is a symbolic link to Black artists who used Jewish influence for their own exploration of racial, historical, and multicultural identity. Nevertheless, the journey is in the last instance Boyce's own. Fine remains a minor figure in *Brown Girl, Brownstones*.

If Rachel Fine is a direct mentor to an African American artist, in two of Marshall's portrayals Black women stand more ambiguously as heirs to Jewish males, albeit illegitimate ones. Jewish achievements and shortcomings serve as starting points in developing a Black voice. In Marshall's later work *The Chosen Place, the Timeless People* (which I will discuss in chapter 7), Saul Amron, like Max Berman in "Brooklyn," is ultimately unsure of his role, inadequate for his position of authority, ill-equipped to bring Blacks into mainstream society. This task is inherently contradictory, for dominant cultural demands of conformity do not fit the contingencies of cultural innovation demanded by both Black and Jewish history. Rather than integrating into a center, Black culture and literature challenges, reshapes, and interrogates the very idea of center. As Henry Louis Gates Jr. suggests, "the spatial topography of center and margin . . . has started to exhaust its usefulness in describing our own modernity" (1992, 189). A more encompassing vision of hybridity and fluidity is called for than the assimilationist model provides.

A hybrid, multicultural vision is beyond the scope of Marshall's Jewish males, who remain constrained by assimilationism, by a cultural ideal stamped in the image of Western Europe. Given the failure of Jews to come to grips with their own history, their viability as catalysts for Black cultural development is limited. Both Berman and to a lesser extent Amron display ambiguous attitudes regarding their Jewishness, driven by their self-devaluation in a society that rejects their heritage yet that they struggle to join. This is the dilemma of assimilation, of regarding as universal a society quite marked by a specific time and place—by language, physical characteristics, music, literature, all the paraphernalia of culture. A denigrated history confronts many of Marshall's older characters as they struggle for acceptance, from Silla Boyce in *Brown Girl, Brownstones* to Mr. Watford in *Soul Clap Hands and Sing* to Avey Johnson at the start of *Praisesong for the Widow*. From a position of cultural isolation, Marshall's protagonists act to revive historical identity, a task that her work engages by its very existence. As Adam Meyer remarks, "each of these novels concludes with the Black protagonist's return to an ancestral homeland and to the fullness that is embodied in it" (1995, 99). Both Blacks and Jews confront historical memory while constructing a hybrid American identity.

Soul Clap Hands and Sing concentrates not on the reclaiming of identity but on the stasis of lost identity, with each story featuring an emotionally impotent older male. Max Berman, the only non-Black protagonist, shares with these men a rift from his heritage. By featuring a Jewish protagonist, Marshall accentuates commonality of circumstance; the characters in these four stories epitomize the obsolescence of coping with minority estrangement through the lens of dominant culture. In a time demanding a revived cultural identity, the older generation fails as role models.

Using his (slightly) privileged position in an attempted seduction of a young Black woman might make Berman odious, yet the narrative viewpoint creates a sympathetic understanding of the social forces that motivate him. Marshall's surprising narrative choice—to portray the growing, developing character through the consciousness of the stagnant character—illuminates Berman's own broken world and history, leaving the reader to surmise Miss Williams's more obvious, and justified, stance. Denied his career in the McCarthy-ravished 1950s due to a flirtation with communism, Berman situates himself, along with so many Jewish intellectuals, firmly in the Eurocentric academy. Marginalized from his own traditions, he largely blames himself for his unsettled status. He has rejected religion: "[H]is father's face above the radiance of the Sabbath candles haunted him from the shadows reminding him of the certainty he had lost and never found again . . . as on the day [the father] lay dying and moaning into his beard that his only son was a bad Jew" (Marshall 1988, 50). Berman is one of a whole generation of Jews who willfully cast aside the past. Religion is considered a superstition to be discarded upon entry into the modern world, yet repudiating the family's deepest wishes, in a broader sense repudiating a whole culture and tradition, leads to guilt and spiritual emptiness.

Yet secular substitutes for religion fail Berman. Communism, a dream of a universal humanity that drew many secularized Jews, has limited credibility: "[H]e had been middle-aged when he joined [the Party] and his faith, which had been so full as a boy, had grown thin. He had come, by then, to distrust all pieties" (35). The pursuit of literature, another Enlightenment substitute for religion, also proves limited. Great literature—defined as European in origin—is a problematic means of achieving a unified self (since European traditions are less unified than their admirers believe) and becomes increasingly so in a world of multiple, fragmented cultures. Modernist philosophical trends with their incessant questioning of all traditions, including those from which they spring, further splinter literary unity. Exemplifying cultural fragmentation, Berman inspects not only "the usual Rubens nude" but "Gauguin's Aita Parari, her languorous form in the straight-back chair, her dark, sloping breasts, her eyes like the sun under shadow" (39). In a world of far-flung empires the ideal of a singular erotic perfection disappears. The French decadents whom Berman studies further interrogate the human ideal, probing corruption of the soul. Modern literature, with its questioning of idealistic systems and its emphasis on human fallibility, can substitute for neither religion nor traditional culture. Rather than a unified self, Max Berman finds only disconnected beliefs and unfulfilled goals.

Berman's last hope is revealed to him in the guise of his only Black student, Miss Williams, impersonalized by a mental designation as "the girl" and endowed with a complex of semiconscious meanings to Berman by her color, "a very pale mulatto with skin the color of clear, polished amber and a thin, mild face" (38). Though he denies her color's importance, it signifies an inescapable network of meanings. If Gauguin's picture serves as Berman's erotic link to her, his sociohistorical link is a

> discomfort at the thought that although he had been sinned against as a Jew he still shared in the sin against her and suffered from the same vague guilt, irritation that she recalled his own humiliations: the large ones, such as the fact that despite his brilliance he had been unable to get into a medical school as a young man because of the quota on Jews ... the small ones which had worn him thin: an eye widening imperceptibly as he gave his name, the savage glance which sought his Jewishness in his nose, his chin, in the set of his shoulders. (38)

The passage reminds us that prior to the Second World War Jews faced the same kind of legal and social restrictions as Blacks, although to a lesser extent; it makes vivid also the exaggerated awareness and shame of physical difference. Regarding Miss Williams, Berman experiences a provocative mixture of difference and sameness: the difference of her exotic physique, the sameness of the mark of the outsider. He considers her his last hope for a fulfilling connection to life: "She alone was the bridge" (40). In seducing her he hopes to overcome, or at least temporarily tame, his own humiliation. Simultaneously he understands his relationship to her as that of the patriarch, both White and Jewish. He hopes to mend his battered ego in comparison to her: "She seemed to bring not only herself but the host of black women whose bodies had been despoiled to make her. He would not only possess her but them also" (41). Miss Williams's body signifies a historical network through which Berman aspires to the role of conqueror and possessor denied Jews in Europe. She also represents his Jewish history of victimhood. He yearns to repossess history through domination and submission, his White male self nourished through his power over her passive, female, Black body; his Jewish self through the sensual sympathy of victims locked in mutual embrace.

This vision of identity as played out on, into, and through the body of another reverberates through Berman's discussion with Miss Williams regarding Gide's *The Immoralist*. She first articulates herself through an analysis of that novel's protagonist: "[I]n finding out what he is, he destroys his wife. It was as if she had to die in order for him to live and know himself" (44). This quotation illuminates not just Gide's novel but Berman's power over his dead wife and, in anticipation only, over his Black student. Like Rogin's blackface Jew defining his identity against a marginalized people, Berman envisions feeding on a warm young body, on someone else's history and circumstances, to nourish himself, to replenish his lost past.

Though Berman lacks the capacity to realize it (perhaps through disbelief that a Black woman can outwit him), Miss Williams has intimated through her analysis of Gide a will more powerful than Berman's damaged ego. Rather than a passive receptacle, "the girl" turns articulate and vengeful, understanding far better than Berman how he is exploiting her. A White authority figure's transgression—officially forbidden yet unofficially tolerated by dominant society—ignites in Miss Williams a new awareness of her social status, together with the determination to change it. At his cottage she exclaims, "I can do something now! I can begin. . . . Look how I came all the way up here to tell you this to your face. Because how could you harm me? You're so old you're like a cup I could break in my hand" (63). In understanding her role, in facing up to and confronting it, she prepares herself for a future, an as yet amorphous mission that will help her establish a new identity derived through contrast with the ruins of the old. The role of Gide's immoralist is reversed. The young woman

draws life from the dried-up husk of the old man; what he represents will
be flung aside. To Gide's tale is added the complexity of race, of multiple
histories interconnecting. Through Berman's tragedy, Miss Williams has
begun the complex task of voicing her own history. The bridge to knowledge and understanding may be Jewish patronage, but it is a bridge that
stirs anger and contempt, one that Miss Williams must burn.

At least this is her interpretation, as implied in her confrontation with
Berman. Miss Williams, however, is single-minded in her approach. Seething with resentment, she is unable to perceive the tragedy in Berman's
failure. Instead, Berman serves as an intermediary object for her hostility
toward the previous generation of African Americans against whose silence and passivity she rebels. If Berman has simplified Miss Williams,
denied her history and humanity, she, in her youth and anger, remains
blind to his circumstances. Her own dislocation from historical and cultural grounding, which she so eloquently strives to overcome, is not so
different from Berman's. Despite her eloquence, Miss Williams, in her
bitterness, risks continuing a history of estranged isolation; her future remains open. She is an early version of a recurrent Marshall character who,
from the sterile, assimilationist past defined by older generations, must
work toward creating a new cultural identity. Her unresolved anger foreshadows the ascendancy of Black nationalism.

If, by the mid-1960s, Black representations of Jews had proven more
complex and humanizing than the Jewish counterpart, this was soon to
change. The contained anger of Miss Williams was to surface in a critique
of the liberalism of the Civil Rights movement, a critique that employed
raw emotion as its form. This challenge came from both Black nationalism and the New Left. Radical periods tend toward escalation; student
activism led to a relentless critique of American material and social assumptions. The African American counterpart to the New Left, Black
nationalism, is easily understood, given the injustices historically per-
petuated upon Black America and the need for a strong articulation of
identity. In conjunction with an emerging feminism, these movements
shifted oppositional thought and organization from an emphasis on class—
in unionization drives and assaults on poverty—to a politics of difference. For White radicals, a theatrical politics of emotion could act as an
interlude before they moved on to careers and families, but Black America
has always operated with little margin for error. The unalloyed rhetoric of
the late 1960s would act to dislodge liberal coalitions, to splinter the Civil
Rights movement that had created crucial, if incomplete, political breakthroughs.

Burning Bridges
Black Nationalism and Anti-Semitism

In the late 1960s a mask was ripped violently off. This was the face that Black America wore to please dominant society, a tragicomic visage metamorphosing to please the viewer's conception, at times displaying the servile blankness of the slave, at times the gaping smile of the buffoon. Paul Laurence Dunbar initiated the metaphor:

> We wear the mask that grins and lies
> It hides our cheeks and shades our eyes,—
> This debt we pay to human guile;
> With torn and bleeding hearts we smile.

African America had been coerced into putting on a play for the benefit of White America. This was true even for Blacks successful on dominant cultural terms, those performing the role of the responsible Negro proving his worthiness to enter American society.

A Black nationalist critique might take this metaphor to its furthest extent, seeing assimilationism as a series of facades created to serve or impress dominant society: Phyllis Wheatley's sonnets in the European tradition; Booker T. Washington's defense of menial labor as the only tool for Black advancement; Louis Armstrong's grinning and clowning even while creating a unique American music. These are the faces of the Black bourgeoisie: assimilationist, multifaceted, obscured yet ever changing. If Lorraine Hansberry and Paule Marshall are outspoken proponents of Black culture, still they straddle a precarious fence between integration and independence. Reacting against any timidity, Black nationalists struck bluntly, unafraid to name Jews as among those who have failed African Americans. They did so through a purposefully strident rhetorical stance, a dependence on shock tactics, a kind of cathartic purging of the terrors historically inflicted upon Black Americans.

To its critics such blunt, expressivist writing acts as another kind of mask, one reenacting stereotypes of the savage in the updated form of the militant, angry Black, history revising itself as a deadly, earnest farce. This at least is an external view of Black nationalism. Examined within its historical context the picture is more complex. As William Van Deburg acutely phrases it, "Attempting to gain a clear understanding of twentieth century black nationalism is a bit like trying to eat Jell-O with chopsticks" (1997, 1). For instance, the nationalism of the Black Muslims is distinct from that of the Black Arts poets. The former represents the most impoverished and alienated people, and hence persists to this day; the latter expresses the anger of an avant-garde that, nevertheless, is ultimately bound to the larger American society. Various strands of Black and American thought intertwine and overlap over time and across space. Robin M. Williams Jr. explains that "protest movements directed toward essentially integrative changes can coexist with separatist movements of alienation and with tactically hazardous outbursts of expressive violence" (1971, 29). Black nationalist thought and feeling, then, is intertwined with that of integrationism; Malcolm X completes what Martin Luther King Jr. does not say.

Viewed in the context of African American history, Black nationalisms have their own logic and continuity, drawing upon persistent undercurrents, earlier represented by Marcus Garvey's Back to Africa movement (often relegated to the fringes by mainstream historians). In a revision of Booker T. Washington's self-help platform and absent any desire to please White America, Garvey stressed pan-African togetherness, an early form of Black militance. As early as 1924 Garvey included a Jewish presence in his conception of the forces marginalizing Blacks: "[T]he Jew in his political and economic urge is always first a Jew; the white man is first a white man under all circumstances" (1991, 5). The seeds have long been planted for Black skepticism about Jewish intentions.

Resentment of the Jewish role in African American movements also

has a long history. Hence Black nationalist portraits of greedy, hypocritical Jews do not necessarily derive from a metaphysical anti-Semitism,
but mark a break from liberalism and act as a means of psychological
release. At one extreme, African American identity may be defined in
reaction to Jews as overdetermined symbols of historical suffering, capitalist exploitation, and liberal assimilationism (equated with the Black
bourgeois). As a critical part of the liberal establishment, a voice for integration, and a model of assimilation, Jewish Americans were a natural
target of a movement agitating for an independent Black voice.

Tied to an integrationist perspective, the Civil Rights movement was
inseparable from the European-derived liberalism that encouraged it, with
roots in an inclusive, democratic perspective. In traditional liberalism the
ideals upon which the United States was founded, including individual
autonomy, free speech, and, to a more contested degree, free trade, are
held up as goods for which everyone should strive. To liberal critics the
flaw in American democracy has not been in the conception but in an
actualization that granted these rights to only a portion of the population.
Simply extend this franchise, the argument runs, simply allow everyone
the right to chase the American dream, and a society as ideal as possible
within the boundaries of human nature will follow. For Jews the attraction of such a platform is evident, given the American social context; it
frees them from traditional prejudices to pursue a success ensured by the
high level of education Judaism has long fostered. Since Blacks have suffered even more than Jews from discrimination and quotas, any opportu-
nities open to Blacks will be even more secure for Jews, a pragmatic
reason for Jewish participation in the NAACP, in legal advocacy of equal
rights for all citizens, and in the Civil Rights movement. Of course idealism also motivated Jews engaged in the equal rights struggle; a strong
moral sense and self-interest were conjoined. White and often highly educated, Jewish Americans were crucial in articulating the positions of the
Civil Rights movement.

Black nationalism of the 1960s reacted to integration by attacking
any White role in defining African American rights. As Larry Neal expounds, "[T]here are in fact and in spirit two Americas—one black, one
white" (1971, 273) (a statement that renders ironic his own Black nationalism by making apparent its roots in White racist segregation). Rather
than condemning this situation, some Black nationalists proposed their
own form of segregation, a separate nation celebrating the strength of Black
culture. Even in less extreme versions a key Black nationalist platform

supports economic empowerment, including Black control of local neighborhoods, schools, and businesses. Concomitant with this is a call for an
independent social and cultural development: "[W]e shall have to struggle
for the right to create our own terms through which to define ourselves
and our relationship to society" (Carmichael 1968, 119). Such a statement is a de facto challenge to the legitimacy of the NAACP, with its
White liberal—and Jewish—presence.

As part of this self-definition the cultural wing of Black nationalism
declares the necessity of an independent aesthetic derived largely from
Africa. Europe can no longer be considered the center of culture and
thought. An Afrocentric genealogy must be uncovered (or constructed) as
a stable center for Black identity. James Stewart explains:

> The dilemma of the "negro" artist is that he makes assumptions based
> on . . . white models. These assumptions are not only wrong, they are
> even antithetical to his existence. The black artist must construct mod-
> els which correspond to his own reality. (1968, 3)

The notion that no single aesthetic system is universally relevant for judging artistic success radically challenges the liberal humanist project of an
endless cataloging and contemplation of the greatest works of all time.
The Black Arts movement turned to Africa not just in rejecting European
aesthetic standards, but in radically revising the very purpose of art, which
becomes not a timeless (fetishized) object but an evolving element of a
community, inseparable from day-to-day life. Stewart explains the ephemeral nature of much non-Western art as stemming from a different cosmology. In contrast to a Western essentialism, African cultures believe
"that there are no immutable social systems or eternal principles" (8).[1]
Art is organically bound to community, significant only within that context, which defines it and which it defines. Music is the prototypical Black
art, originating in African drumming and dancing.[2]

Black nationalist celebration of African-derived culture occurred primarily in reaction to White hegemony, with Jewishness only an intermediate
term. The relative neglect of Black-Jewish issues occurred in a mainstream
social environment that tended to silence ethnic expression, disallowing
sophistication regarding interethnic issues. Social censorship and self-
censorship have long silenced discussion of Black-Jewish issues, leading
to sudden rhetorical eruptions seemingly devoid of context. A mixture of
admiration and envy is evident in Larry Neal's brief comparison of Black

nationalism and Zionism, his lament that Marcus Garvey "was no Theodor Herzl or Chaim Weizmann, with their kind of skills and resources behind him. Had he been, he might have brought a nation into existence" (1989, 13). Certainly Jewish educational and financial resources in the period leading to the birth of Israel were superior to African American resources prior to the Civil Rights era (itself, however, employing deeply entrenched traditions and institutions, notably Black churches). And Jewish nationalist organizations did not depend on major support from outside groups, as did the Civil Rights movement, for organization and strategic planning. Yet Zionism did need to appeal to Britain, an outside force and a periodically hostile one, in its quest for a nation. Zionism lacked the internationalist freedom attributed to it by believers in Jewish conspiracy.

Between a historical comparison of Black and Jewish status and an implicit anti-Semitism the line is fuzzy, as is illustrated by Neal's contention "that Zionist interests are decidedly pro-Western, and that these interests are neocolonialist in nature and design. In Africa, for instance, a notable amount of the resources of the continent is controlled by Zionist-oriented Jews" (141). Each of these statements contains a certain version of truth depending upon one's historical approach and what one means by such phrasings as "notable amount." Jewish immigration to Palestine and appropriation of land may be considered a desperate necessity—and a historical redemption—by a people who had faced centuries of oppression culminating in genocide. Contrarily, Zionism may be regarded as an extension of a colonial ideology in which Europeans consider the inhabitants of an overseas land as nonhuman and systematically evict them. Only the latter appears in this passage, which moves from a historical interpretation open to debate to a transhistorical paranoia in the immediate juxtaposition of the Middle East and Africa as playgrounds for intrigues "controlled by Zionist-oriented Jews." The international Jewish conspiracy is implicated as the secret force controlling history. The relationship between emulation of a Jewish role model, political disagreement, and traditional anti-Semitism proves subtle and slippery.

I

Key civil rights victories allowed African Americans, no longer in as precarious a social position, to directly question liberal assumptions. Long-simmering resentments erupted in heated rhetoric; Black nationalists attacked

American Jews as alien to Black America, as pursuing their own agenda in the guise of friendship. Given continuing racism and economic diffi-culties, Blacks simply could not afford to consider their story a variation of the Jewish American narrative. This crucial point, which emerges only intermittently in African American literature, is fully articulated in Harold Cruse's *The Crisis of the Black Intellectual:*

> There are far too many Jews from Jewish organizations into whose privy councils Negroes are not admitted, who nevertheless are involved in every civil rights and African-American organization, creating policy and otherwise analyzing the Negro from all possible angles. (1984, 497)

Rather than as common victims, Cruse presents Jews as wedded to domi-nant society, as paternalistically shepherding the Negro flock toward the Jewish definition of Black freedom.

Cruse's larger purpose is to delineate a weakness in Black articula-tion of their situation, and hence in self-understanding. African Ameri-cans, he argues, have failed to examine the importance of their historical role: "[N]ow would be the time for Negro intellectuals to start thinking for themselves as truly independent and original radicals" (195). Instead, Black America remains subservient to a liberal ideology of assimilationism more theoretical than actual. To Cruse, Black intellectuals have simply missed the crucial status of African Americans: "[S]ince the Supreme Court decision of 1954 on public school integration, the Negro-American has been catapulted into the role of being the mover and shaker of modern America while putting the Great American Idea to the most crucial test of its last hundred years" (7). This is certainly compelling analysis; how-ever, in chastising Black intellectuals, Cruse glosses over a significant strand of thinkers who had articulated African American cultural achieve-ments.[3] Cruse's criticism of Black political and economic organization is, I believe, more accurate. Despite their unique historical and cultural role, African Americans have not organized economically as have, for instance, Jews, Irish, and, more recently, Koreans. The ideal of a color- and ethnicity-blind society in which autonomous individuals pursue their own interests is, Cruse argues, an illusion: "In America, the materio-economic condi-tions relate to a societal, multi-group existence in a way never before known in world history" (188–99). While the rhetoric is overblown, Cruse is right to emphasize the need for strong African American economic or-ganizations, as subsequent history has established.

Nevertheless, Cruse exaggerates the power of ethnic particularism.

He regards Jews as enacting the hidden philosophy that has governed American history, winning the competition for group status. To Cruse Jews are simultaneously proto-American, in their understanding of their special ethnic role, and detached from America, free to pursue their own interests. Jewish activists thus allow themselves a strong ethnic identity while subjecting Blacks to idealistic social projects: "Jewish dominance in the Communist Party . . . culminated in the emergence of Herbert Aptheker and other assimilated Jewish communists who assumed the mantle of spokesmanship on Negro affairs" (147). Cruse decries Jewish hypocrisy in upholding assimilation except when it comes to Jews, a hypocrisy most prominently displayed in support of Zionism. Jewish Americans are seen as favoring a dominant cultural agenda for Blacks, while pursuing their own group interests, succeeding in both economic and intellectual terms. His idealization of Jewish accomplishments is evident in his statement that "In America, Jews . . . have no real problems, political, economic or cultural" (168). Jews are fetishized as success objects, a suprahuman group effortlessly achieving all that is denied African Americans, eradicating contradictions between assimilation and group identity, and occupying a position Blacks can only fantasize about. An uneasy combination of emulation, envy, and paranoia is evident in this analysis, which implicitly advances the myth of the conspiratorial Jew, everywhere present, controlling events on numerous levels in a plethora of organizations.

While Cruse's argument is important for its declaration of an independent African American voice, his analysis is inseparable from a personal reaction against Jews. A disgust at Jewishness by definition permeates Cruse's essay "My Jewish Problem: and Theirs," whose title parodies Norman Podhoretz's condescending "My Negro Problem: and Ours." Imitating Podhoretz, Cruse makes gross generalizations on the basis of his personal history. He describes two strangely silent Jewish boys, foreigners, who stole some candy almonds from him, leading to a childhood impression of the "Jewish type," "bad foreigners of a special kind . . . that special kind of Jewish nose, the Jewish face" (145). Such fetishistic physical differentiation is a common characteristic of racism. Both Jean-Paul Sartre and Sander Gilman establish the obsession with physical difference as characteristic of a metaphysical anti-Semitism making of Jews the outsider, a vehicle for hatred and paranoia. So Cruse describes a teacher whose "alleged Jewishness colored the whole pedagogical relationship. Very early I began to relate classroom troubles with foreigners and Jewishness" (147). Rather than ascribing one's difficulties to an individual teacher, to systemic problems with the schools, or to personal shortcomings, anti-Semitism blames an immutable external source. Stereotypes of Jews operate at a highly personal level in the evolution of Cruse's political philosophy. He uses personal incidents—his teacher's accusation that he smelled, the "racial arrogance" of a Jewish shopkeeper (156)—as a starting point for explicating the development of his attitudes regarding Jews. His description of some friendly Jews, together with his argument "that Jewish race prejudice was no more than a reflection of the general American ideology" (162), alleviates the negative descriptions, making the essay appear as painfully honest. Like Podhoretz he cloaks the overall thrust of his essay behind an acknowledgment of the contradictions that issues of race and religion always engender. His essay attempts to have it both ways, to explicate the odious Jewish nature while escaping charges of anti-Semitism through token mention of larger social factors. This trajectory leads to the verge of excusing Nazi atrocities:

> [T]he blood cult of racial superiority concocted by the German Nazis allowed them to attack the Jews on the basis of "blood purity," but the real basis of the expulsion was economic, political, and cultural. Jews were simply too powerful in Germany to suit certain German nationalists. (172)

Denying the validity of biological racism—an ideological category that includes anti-Black racism—Cruse explains Nazi attacks on Jews as based on cultural and social grounds. In Germany, as in America, he perceives an almost transcendent Jewish power.

Cruse's writings exemplify how a study of African American political and social divergences can shift gears to adopt a paranoid anti-Semitism. His stress on a strong awareness of African American history is crucial, with an important corollary the need for a declaration of independence from Jewish patronage. However, Cruse's obsession with the Jewish role in the downfall of the black intellectual is excessive. Surely the larger White society, with its deliberate erasure of Black cultural achievements, bears the greatest responsibility for any African American failures. Blacks have faced a plethora of problems unknown to many American ethnic groups: racism, poverty, lack of education, amputation from a historical homeland, broken family structures, and still more racism. In Jews, Cruse finds a unified explanation of Black paralysis, circumventing the need to analyze deeper social and historical causes. Cruse's obsession adapts European anti-Semitism to the African American situation in a perverse form of cultural hybridity.

II

Harold Cruse's work, though not as overtly anti-Semitic as that of certain other Black nationalists, is more comprehensively so. Poets associated with the Black Arts movement—notably Amiri Baraka and Nikki Giovanni—made more blatantly anti-Semitic statements; however offensive, these are symbolic and intermittent. The revival of anti-Semitic slogans served a rhetorical, politically contingent purpose, protesting exploitation, as well as marking a break from liberalism. These poets portray Jews as metonymic for dominant exploitation, but not as the singular cause of Black underdevelopment. They develop from, and react against, an African American literary establishment that has displayed a maze of contradictory opinions regarding Jews, complicated by extraordinarily close ties to Jewish institutions and cultural figures. Beyond the Jewish role in publishing such authors as James Baldwin, many Black writers have had Jewish spouses, among them Richard Wright, Lorraine Hansberry, John Edgar Wideman, Alice Walker, LeRoi Jones (Friedman 1995, 121) and Ishmael Reed (T. Reed 1997, 113). Not surprisingly, given such ties, Black anti-Semitism has been only an intermittent theme of African American literature. In sharp contrast, the Black Arts movement erupted with overt attacks upon Jewish landlords and shopkeepers. These strongly voice Black pain, while implying deeper problems of Black identity as it measures itself through and against Jews. Despite its overt stance, Black nationalist literature did not develop a united or continuous portrait of Jews and their relationships with Blacks. The Jewish role as one measure of Black identity—as aliens in a strange land who nevertheless intimate success and acceptance—is touched upon only intermittently, if violently, in Black nationalist literature.

LeRoi Jones's development from a beatnik poet with modernist inclinations into the Afrocentric Amiri Baraka is best understood within the context of a Black professional and artistic class that feels empowered, after years of suppression, to express terrible frustration. His anti-Semitic proclamations are inseparable from his rebellion against this class, against an integrationist need to conform to the assumptions of White society. The young Jones might have been a model for Lorraine Hansberry's Alton Scales, who identifies strongly with the beatnik counterculture yet remains aware of the social meaning of his blackness, Scales is a character torn between worlds, ripe for the kind of extreme swings that characterize Jones's/Baraka's career. Growing up in a bourgeois black family, struggling to be a poet, Jones had scant institutional outlets for his rebellion aside from the countercultural beatniks. Scales's claim that "as a lot of people think there is something wrong with the fact that I *am* a Negro—I am going to make a point out of being one" (Hansberry 1987, 246) culminates in LeRoi Jones's metamorphosis into the confrontational Amiri Baraka. In his autobiography Baraka explains this shift, describing his European education as the imbibing of "White people's words," which may be profound and beautiful but which generate "a non-self creation where you become other than you as you" (1984, 120). Such a demarcation of White and Black provokes an extreme countermyth, one that neglects the tangled, hybrid influences inherent in all Americans (influences obscured, however, by America's physical segregation). In the beatnik world Baraka felt isolated, felt he was "smother[ing] the brown consciousness tied irrevocably to the black mass soul" (162).

An early intimation of Black Arts anti-Semitism occurs in LeRoi Jones's *The System of Dante's Hell* (1963), which applies modernist techniques, reconfiguring classic literature onto African American life. The splendidly organized system of Dante's *Divine Comedy* is transposed to the Newark ghetto, with the ironic reversal that the victims suffer for where they have been born rather than through sins they have committed. Lloyd Brown argues convincingly that Jones "rejects the West's Christian image of hell and the total eschatology in which that system is rooted" (1973, 133). The novel is therefore a bitter satire in which hell is not a place of punishment, but a state inflicted by one group of humans upon another.

In applying a hierarchical system to 1960s America, *The System of Dante's Hell* briefly includes a place for Jews, lifted from classical anti-Semitism. In a gin joint paradigmatic of ghostly lust and degeneracy, a Jew sits "with checks and money at the table . . . [while] a line of shouting woogies waved their pay & waited for that bogus christ to give them the currency of the place" (Baraka 1963, 128–29). A more conventional anti-Semitic image cannot be found. As a "bogus christ," this Jew reveals the real American religion to be money. Yet Jones portrays the Jew as a front for something else: "Two tremendous muthafuckers with stale white teeth grinned in back of the jew and sat with baseball bats to protect the western world" (129). A larger power structure—ideology backed up by raw force—exists behind the Jew, who acts as the visible face of exploitation, but not as its source.

The Jew as metonym, as middleman- (but not necessarily as source) of brutal exploitation, exists early in Jones's writing, but only attains fruition following his transformation to Amiri Baraka. More than a poem, "Black Art" is a manifesto dramatizing the need to move art away from an isolated aesthetic stance: "Poems are bullshit unless they are / teeth or trees or lemons piled / on a step. Or black ladies dying. . . ." Poetry, rhetoric, and life become inseparable; poetry is written to promote acute awareness and social action. In combination with a conscious adaptation of the language of the street, this philosophy leads to repeated attacks upon Whites, as well as anti-Semitism: "[W]e want poems like fists beating niggers out of Jocks/ or dagger poems in the slimy bellies/ of the owner-jews" (Baraka 1991, 219). The language may be metaphorical, but the pain it voices is very real toward a people who often seem to be allies, yet who also participate in the economic exploitation of Blacks. Such references are particularly disquieting from a poet who had been part of the Jewish-inflected beatnik movement, who had been friends with Allen Ginsberg and had married a Jewish woman. A closer study of Baraka's career, however, shows that he lacks the obsessive, paranoid quality of a genuine anti-Semite, one who makes of Jews a transhistorical enemy. Rather, his anti-Semitic assertions are a means of articulating problems faced by African Americans, particularly professionals and intellectuals, regarding their participation in a society that has so brutally oppressed their people. Of course, whatever the context such assertions are dangerous, having repeatedly led to actual attacks upon Jews.

For both Blacks and Whites, the late 1960s was a time of unrepressed expression. If White youth adopted a new radicalism—spurred largely by the threat of being sent to Vietnam—the increasing acceptance of extreme rhetoric allowed Blacks to articulate old hurts in new ways. For Earl Raab such rhetoric is defensible when arising from desperate social circumstances, as a discharge of excess through symbolic invocation: "When a demand is made, or an act committed primarily to vent anger or frustration, then we enter the realm of expressive behavior" (1969, 30). Whatever its psychological connotations, Black anti-Semitism distorts cause-effect relations: anger finds a surrogate object. The Jew acts as a tangible representative of an abstract social system. Baraka's extremism expresses a declaration of independence: the old rules of discourse within the Civil Rights movement are over; Black nationalism must make its own rules. Shlomo Katz's argument that attacking Jews was a way for Black radicals to attack traditional Black leadership (1967, 125) suggests Baraka's immediate motivation. Baraka's anti-Semitic utterances express his generalized anger at American society, breaking its rules of "politeness" (or of silence) by using the Jew as a generalized symbol for the worst aspects of White capitalism. Baraka's pronouncement of "another bad poem cracking / steel knuckles in a jewlady's mouth" (1991, 219) further expresses the Black Arts privileging of raw emotion over aesthetic perfection. This is, however, an evasion, since the White society that Baraka attacks has traditionally denounced Jews to deflect rage from economic and social oppression.

Nevertheless, Baraka's anti-Semitism was an intermittent part of one phase in a career marked by drastic change. Even within this time period his poetry is contradictory, at times displaying an anguished identification with Jews. In Baraka, as in so many texts, African American perceptions of Jews are torn between identification and rebellion. Images of Jews as biblical heroes, Holocaust victims, urbane Americans, hypocritical patrons, and greedy usurers form a multilayered strata. If Lorraine Hansberry and Paule Marshall foreground identification with Jews, with criticism a submerged yet insistent impulse, in Black Arts poets the axis shifts toward rebellion. Baraka contrasts his philosophy with an aestheticized poetics akin to "the Liberal / spokesman for the jews [who] clutch[es] his throat and puke[s] himself into eternity" (219). An atomized individualism becomes a kind of verbal masturbation, serving only to disconnect people, to rob art of its communitarian nature. Through parodic overstatement Baraka attacks academic poetry and liberal discourse as contributing to endlessly delayed justice. The Jewish role here shifts somewhat, from standing in for capitalism to standing in for the Black bourgeoisie, simultaneously apologists for, and psychological victims of, capitalist ideology.

Ensuing from Baraka's complex relations with Jews during his wrenching life changes, Jews attain multiple meanings in his poems, often through the use of dominant cultural stereotypes reinscribed into Black Arts rhetoric. Jews may be represented as agents of oppression, or just as easily as silent victims of a terrible historical crime akin to American treatment of Blacks. The two are related in their acquiescence to dominant society and assimilation (even where it equals death). In an implicit comparison between the self-destructive impulses of the Black and Jewish bourgeoisie, Baraka writes of "the ugly silent deaths of jews under / the surgeon's knife. (To awake on 69th street with money and a hip nose)" (1991, 71). To Werner Sollors, this poem reveals "a self-deceptive acceptance of the beauty ideal of the oppressive culture, a middle-class gesture of ethnic betrayal. At this point, Baraka sees other ethnic groups, and especially Jews, as a metaphoric extension of Blacks" (1978, 91). Rather than metaphoric, the parallel is literal; both peoples, in their assimilationist zeal, will rewrite the narrative of their values, their history and culture, to conform to the ideals of a dominant society that scorns them. An assimilationist Black may manifest this compulsion to conform to dominant society through hair-straightening, a physical disruption of biological character-istics. Similarly a Jew may rewrite her self-image not only internally but externally by literally having her nose broken and restructured, subjecting the text written upon her body to drastic editorial revisions imposed by an alien consciousness (a process reversed by Paule Marshall's Rachel Fine). The ultimate exemplar of this phenomenon is Michael Jackson with his repeated skin-lightening treatments and plastic surgeries.

Even in the heat of his Black nationalism, Baraka continues a para-doxical, angst-filled identification with the Jewish role of archetypal vic-tim. "Citizen Cain" conveys terror of lynching and castration, a repeated fate (both metaphoric and literal) of young Blacks denied their manhood. Fearing he hasn't the guts for resistance or suicide, Baraka imagines being "herded off like a common jew, and roasted in my teary denuncia-tions." If America's Blacks lack the courage to speak up, if they replay the silence of Germany's assimilated Jews, they might suffer the same fate: ghettoization and incessant pogroms, a Kafkaesque vulnerability to being denounced, punished, and finally killed for a crime defined by in-scrutable outside forces. If the Middle Passage began the Black American journey, might not a Holocaust end it, bookends of genocidal terror defin-ing African American history? The fear is of duplicating the passivity of Jewish victims through millennia of persecution culminating in the Holo-caust. Rather than a linear history leading to transcendence, both Blacks and Jews have faced a nihilistic dystopian history. Such fears lead among Jews to Zionism, among Black nationalists to the need for action, at the very least for a scream to break the apathy of middle America.

For Baraka, then, the Jew stands as a symbol of both middle-class passivity and ultimate victim, both of which stem from a denial of histori-cal identity. Given that Baraka considers the American system inherently corrupt and exploitative, a liberal stance becomes a stand-in for acquies-cence, a means of selling out. All other activities are essentialized into a singular retrogression. "The People Burning" employs the Jewish figure not as a helpless victim but as a sellout, sarcastically enjoining, "Become a Jew, and join the union, / forget about Russia or any radicalism past a hooked grin." A worthy activist past is implied here, from which Jews have lapsed. The contradictory figure of the Jew—both radical and capi-talist—has lost its duality, its radicalism gone, its capitalism conjoined with White society. The Jew is now a warning of the dangers of assimila-tion, of forgetting one's history. Despite his bourgeois childhood—indeed, arising in contradistinction to the Black middle-class struggle to create themselves as mainstream Americans—for Baraka a history of oppression and suffering leads to uncompromisingly struggle; the only alternative is participation in an exploitative system. Baraka reduces unionism, Jewish liberalism, and integration to versions of materialist assimilationism, to the "hooked grin" of a Shylock obsessed with money. American materialism soothes and corrupts. Jews are metonymic for capitalism not only in their immediate dilution of radical, nationalist strength into a bland liberalism, but in their archetypal, mythologized construction: "[O]ur nation is kneeling in the snow bleeding through 6 layers/ of jewish enterprise" (Baraka 1979, 190). Two gross American dangers conjoin and crystalize in this image: assimilation and materialism. America threatens to steal ethnic identity while creating a desperate zero-sum game, a survival-of-the-fittest contest squelching all communitarian—and hence Africanist—values.

Baraka's anti-Jewish sloganeering, then, is really a metaphorical warning against assimilation. Yet such a metaphor invites misreading. As Earl Raab points out, "[T]he ideology of political anti-Semitism has precisely always been poetic excess, which has not prevented it from becoming murderous" (1969, 32). Extending this kind of argument to other groups, Sollors complains of Baraka's "blatant anti-Semitism, illiberal antihomosexual agitation, reactionary antifeminism, and expedient antileftism" (1978, 177–78). The reduction of groups of people to stereotypes—whatever the cause, whatever the justification—is invariably dangerous. An academic reading of Baraka, however important in contextualizing the African American struggle, does not remove the possibility that others may read him differently. Certainly the oppression Blacks face in America has been, and continues to be, far worse than that faced by Jews. Yet anti-Semitism, an ideology as murderous as any in history, may have disastrous results if revived. Some of those who read Baraka may take him literally.

III

Baraka's anti-Jewish sloganeering legitimized a trend. Nikki Giovanni, during the Black nationalist phase that launched her career, issued mixed, often hostile proclamations regarding Jews. She accelerates an evolution of historical parallels from a means of identification to one of rivalry for the status of Chosen People: "America has called itself the promised land—and themselves God's chosen people. This is where we come in, Black people. God's chosen people have always had to suffer—to endure—to overcome" (Giovanni 1968, 54). In America biblical roles are displaced:

Blacks take the place of the Hebrews, Jews side with the Egyptians. America, in secular mythology the promised land toward which dispossessed peoples flock, is also to African Americans the land of slavery, a schizophrenic version of both Egypt and Promised Land. The superficial adulation of material success—the misplaced values of White society— belies any claim to "chosenness"; only Blacks, who came to America as slaves, have replicated the suffering of the Israelites; only they, this passage implies, shall receive redemption. Giovanni foreshadows later claims of Blacks as the real Jews, of White Jews as usurpers of the Israelite tradition.

Both biblical and modern history provide material for Black identification with Jews, an identification spurring emotions from sympathy to admiration to revulsion. Giovanni invokes a modern parallel between Black oppression and the Jewish Holocaust. Her "Poem *(No Name No. 3),*" warns oppressed Blacks that "Anne Frank didn't put cheese and bread away for you / Because she knew it would be different this time" (24). While employing parallels between European Jews and American Blacks as a means of defining Black history, Giovanni rejects these parallels. Rather than a massive Holocaust, the poem implies a slow genocide, a continued violence intermittently physical, incessantly psychological, slowly draining the life from Black communities. Anne Frank's provisions will do no good; more dynamic resistance is called for. Only *if* Black consciousness can be mobilized, Giovanni warns (echoing Cruse), can racist patterns, the repeated cycles of "whi-te reaction," be ended. Reflecting the concerns of 1960s activism, Giovanni posits this reaction in larger historical patterns, the deaths of Indians and Vietnamese children, the exposure of Arab women to "isrealijews." Not only is the Holocaust inapplicable to the African American situation, but Jews are now among the oppressors, and perhaps have always been when Giovanni's designations for Israelis are disassembled. "Is real I Jews" or "is really Jews" questions the verity of those claiming biblical inheritance, or perhaps intimates that this inheritance, which drove off the inhabitants of Palestine, exhibits the colonizing nature of both biblical Israelites and modern Jewry.

As in Baraka's nationalist phase, *Black Feeling, Black Talk, Black Judgement* often reduces Jews to physical symbols of capitalist exploitation. Giovanni's notorious "The True Import of Present Dialogue, Black vs. Negro" places, near the center of its maelstrom of angry images, the Jew. "Can you stab-a-Jew / Can you kill huh? nigger" replicates Baraka's anguished calls to action. Such questions as whether "a nigger [can] kill a honkie" and whether he can "piss on a blond head" are largely rhetorical; in the poem's context the Jew is only one of a network of enemies. The killing is probably symbolic, a crushing of the mental structures that have kept the oppressors inviolable while they send African Americans off to die for their causes. In what are often political tracts compacted into coiled poetic forms, Giovanni critiques Jewish influence, sarcastically complaining about the dependence on "our Jewish friends" (1970, 17). Though couched in bitter terms, such a statement extends Black complaints regarding Jewish patronage rather than invoking traditional anti-Semitism.

Most blatant, and most enigmatic, is Giovanni's contention in "Love Poem," that "it's impossible to love / a Jew." Certainly the line was intended not only for the African American audience targeted by the Black Arts movement but to jar Jewish liberals out of any complacency. In its entirety the poem places Jews in a strange middle position, both a part of and apart from dominant society. The opening, "it's so hard to love / people / who will die soon," recalls the Holocaust, the Jewish victims one cannot love, as an implicit warning against complacency regarding poor Blacks. Near the conclusion the poem returns to the theme of victims: "it's so easy to love / Black Men / they must not die anymore." It is difficult to love history's victims, those who die and disappear. Yet simultaneously, paradoxically, they must be loved. The silent victims of the Holocaust become a metaphor for young Blacks, one that implicitly connects silence and self-hatred. What happened to Europe's Jews, the poem exhorts, must not happen to America's Blacks. As potential murder victims, young Black men maintain a vulnerability demanding love. Only power, political and economic but also discursive—the ability to designate one's status through literature—can protect them: "it's a question of power / which we must wield." Ironically, America's Jews, like those of prewar Germany, lack this power "cause there isn't one Jew . . . in the cabinet." Running against the thrust of Giovanni's poetry, this statement highlights the multiplicity of Black attitudes regarding the Jewish role in America. Despite stereotypes of Jewish influence, neither Jews nor Blacks are represented at the highest level of decision making. The implication is that, unlike the Jews in Germany, African Americans must gain real political power by whatever means necessary. Although the statement that "it's impossible to love / a Jew" appears next to the characterization of Nixon's cabinet as Jew-free, it floats free of a definite speaker; it appears as a voice from above, a transcendent signifier. Jews are left in an odd limbo, a symbol of minority vulnerability, yet still an object of hostility. Toward such a hated symbol, one whom it is "impossible to love," the Black nationalist attitude remains strangely inconclusive.

Such radical ambivalence recurs in the prose of Don L. Lee (now

Haki Madhabuti), a Black Arts practitioner whose poems largely ignore Jews, but whose introduction to *We Walk the Way of the New World* (1970) discusses, as if out of nowhere, the Black-Jewish parallel. Like an iceberg, the submerged meaning of the Jewish presence is, for African Americans, larger than the visible surface. Lee juxtaposes Black silence with the silence inflicted upon pre-Holocaust Jews, drawing the same lesson found by Giovanni in "Love Poem": that "when it comes down to the deathwalk, no one will save a people but the people themselves" (Lee 1970, 15). The only means of survival for a hated people, a means forgotten by the Jews in Europe yet remembered all too well in America, is to

> become a nation within a nation. You create and sustain your own identity. In effect, Jewish teachers teach Jewish children . . . Jewish doctors administer aid to Jewish patients (and others); the Jewish business world services the Jewish community; and each sector continually draws on one another to build that community. (15)

For developing Black nationalist identity and community, America's Jews provide an ideal model, while the eradication of Europe's Jews serves as a dire warning. Like Cruse, Lee stresses the need for Black nation building. In one foreboding sentence, he extends Cruse's paranoia: "If a Jew hates you, you'll never know it; if he plans to kill you, you know even less: Sophistication" (15). The Jews, made tough and clever by history, just might be the worst enemies faced by Blacks. At one moment Jews are fellow sufferers with Blacks; at the next a role model; at the next an invisible, deadly enemy.

A revision of classical Jew-hatred, of paranoia regarding an omnipresent, deadly enemy, is one extreme of Black nationalist belief. Yet even though it defines itself largely against Jewish liberalism, Black nationalism is not inherently anti-Semitic, even where it appears to be. An essentialist anti-Semitism, though sometimes difficult to distinguish from a specific, contextual critique of Jewish politics, is a far different phenomenon. Indeed, implicit critiques of Jewish liberalism are common to Richard Wright, Nikki Giovanni, Amiri Baraka, Paule Marshall, and Lorraine Hansberry, all of whom represent Jewish Americans as potential ethnic role models, despite their alleged assimilationism and materialism. For Black nationalists the recurring theme is the need to duplicate the political cohesion of American Jews while avoiding an assimilationist enfeeblement of Black identity. And whatever the excesses and potential misreadings of this rhetoric, it has served a potent historical purpose as a declaration of identity.

IV

In defining the complexities of African American life, with its multiple subject positions, Black nationalism has built-in limitations. So Larry Neal, in his brief writing life, moved from an unadulterated nationalism to a complex historical awareness. He comes to understand Ralph Ellison's work, earlier denounced by Black Arts theorists, as a synthesis drawing on the total African American experience, simultaneously employing and subverting the conventions of the Western novel. Similarly such musicians as John Coltrane and Sun Ra

> indicate a synthesis and a rejection of Western musical theory at the same time, just as aspects of Louis Armstrong's trumpet playing indicate, in its time, a respect for the traditional uses of the instrument on the one hand, and on the other, to the squares, it indicated a "gross defilement" of the instrument.

The Black musician "can take the other dude's instruments and play like your Uncle Rufus's hog callings" (Neal 1989, 53), imposing an alien sensibility, blowing an Africanist assortment of calls and rhythms through a technology used, in its European setting, for relatively pure melodies within a limited range. No better example exists than jazz of Homi Bhabha's process, whereby "the other 'denied' knowledges enter upon the dominant discourse and estrange the basis of its authority—its rules of recognition" (Bhabha 1994, 175). The trumpet growls its African inflections fused with European technique and musical ideas to create a new art form. Contrary to Audre Lorde's powerful mythologizing, the master's tools can indeed blow down the master's fortress, or at least infiltrate and alter it. The musician rearranges elements of European and African sensibility to "create another world view, another cosmology springing from your [the musician's] own specific grounds, but transcending them as your new world realizes itself." Neal draws conclusions far removed from those of the earlier Black Arts movement, explaining that "we have to . . . understand our role as synthesizers: the creators of new and exciting visions out of the accumulated weight of our Western experience" (1989, 53). Once he analyzes the specifically American content of his favorite art, Neal is impelled toward a version of cultural fusion.

Political realities, too, worked to marginalize Afrocenticism and Black separatism, which in practice meant isolation from friends and allies. For Amiri Baraka the journey away from a confined nationalism meant a turn to communism, a universalist ideology that shared his bitter denunciation of exploitation while shifting blame away from Whites as Whites, toward abstract social forces and a vision of a universal redemption that transcends race. The African American situation encourages a search for an ideology that will heal the bifurcated consciousness, soothing the rage created by exploitation and rejection. Yet African American life is too complex to be encompassed by any ideology; communism slights its unique features while Black nationalism neglects the fluidity of American cultural identity. Baraka's search, marked by the intensity and desperation of a religious convert, requires the hardness of purpose to engage in incessant battle with society, with the oppression his people face; perhaps only a unified ideology, such as communism, can supply this?

Most African American art and literature, however, turned to a mixture of beliefs and cultures more ambiguous than either nationalism or communism. Yet some form of nationalism remains latent in the work of many Black writers, if only as a lingering response to the ideology of whiteness. Nationalism, after all, is the central stage in a recurring colonial/postcolonial pattern from dominant myth to countermyth to hybridity (all three stages of which are simultaneously present, to some extent, in any piece of postcolonial literature). Indeed, after a post-1960s latency period a hybrid African American literature has flowered. Reflecting upon Black nationalism in 1993, Amiri Baraka's daughter, Lisa Jones, claims: "[T]he works and protests of the nationalists 'made us possible. . . . Though we make fun of them, if it weren't for . . . Larry Neal and my father, we wouldn't have the freedom now to be so nonchalant'" (quoted in Ellis 1989, 236–37).[4] By the 1990s Black nationalism could be contextualized as a necessary leap toward a burgeoning, and increasingly complex, African American voice. For contemporaneous observers lacking such context, it was often interpreted as merely hostile. Rather than reflecting upon the complexities and contradictions of Black-Jewish relations, Jewish writers were spurred to an alarmist response, as the next chapter will show.

Black nationalism breached issues hidden in African American writing shaped by liberalism. References to the Jewish Holocaust in both Baraka and Giovanni complete a cycle of identification beginning with the biblical Hebrews. Yet these poets construct identity not through sympathy, but against the failure and passivity of Jews anxious to assimilate—

most dramatically, through their silence prior to the Holocaust—and through the blurring of cultural difference under a blanketing universalism. However, the boundary between social critique and anti-Semitism was often unclear. When this boundary was crossed, Jewish shock and abhorrence followed.

6

Jewish Backlash
The Return of the Black Primitive

Black anti-Semitism produced Jewish responses from repugnance to tortured attempts at understanding, emotions evident in fiction of the late 1960s. Jewish leadership had emphasized the idealistic side of their participation in the Civil Rights movement; their role as spokespeople for another race seemed to them natural. The denial of this assumption surprised Jewish intellectuals and leaders who, amid an array of contradictory statements, reacted with overall hostility. Writing in *Commentary* in 1969, Milton Himmelfarb complained that "in the Black rhetoric the Negro seems to have only two external enemies in the United States, whites generally and Jews specifically." Blaming Jews for the exploitation of Blacks is, to Himmelfarb, a grievous fallacy that implicitly continues dominant cultural scapegoating of Jews: "What is it they say we are doing to Negroes? Genocide, emasculation, rape. Black Panther types say that; and also black teachers, professors, intellectuals, community leaders—in print, on the radio, on television . . ." (1969, 34). While this statement might capture the nature of some Black anti-Semitism, the extent is exaggerated. Clayborne Carson asserts that in 1967, "Actual incidents of publicly expressed anti-Semitism were few in number, and none involved persons who still identified themselves as civil rights leaders" (1992, 44). By 1969 Black anti-Semitism had been explicitly voiced, although not as widely as Himmelfarb claims. Still, the unspoken fear persists of a kind of miniature Nazism, an attack on Jews for their mere existence that might spread to the White community. From an African American point of view, such worries may seem unwarranted among a politically and economically secure people; from a Jewish point of view, a mere twenty-five years after the Holocaust, anything seemed possible. That anti-Semitism occurred among African Americans, a group whose rights large numbers of Jews were defending, further distressed the Jewish community.

Liberal rationalists might expect African Americans to act in their own best interests, to continue good relations with a group that has supported Black interests, perhaps with carefully reasoned arguments explaining disagreements with Jewish leadership. Yet attempting to understand Black anti-Semitism from the framework of traditional liberalism is a virtual impossibility, given liberal faith in the ability of reason to transcend ancient conflicts. Belief in objectivity is naive regarding racial relations, which have always been based on fear and misunderstanding. Liberal universalists—including many Jews—also ignore the sense of inclusion ethnic identity provides in an otherwise alienating environment, and so have often neglected the importance of African American cultural identity. History cannot be instantly junked by the offer of assimilation. African Americans cannot be expected to accommodate effortlessly to demands of universality in an American society that has long oppressed them and refused to acknowledge their history.

If traditional liberalism offers one extreme in dealing with Black nationalism, radicalism offers another. Jewish radical activists avoided facing the historical dangers of anti-Semitic rhetoric by accepting Black nationalism as the singular, authentic voice of the repressed. Writing about the Student Nonviolent Coordinating Committee, Carson links Jewish and Black radicals as promoting a "tactical and rhetorical militancy that was rooted in the shared African American-Jewish radical culture that was centered in New York" (1992, 37). Since much of the rhetoric of Black Power emerged from a milieu with extensive Jewish participation, it is not surprising that Jewish radicals continued to support this rhetoric even when it turned hostile. Following Himmelfarb's essay, Nathan Glazer complains of how, influenced by "the sycophantic association with young blacks . . . young white radicals, mostly Jewish, accepted without argument anti-Zionist and anti-Semitic resolutions" (1969, 35). Caught between traditional liberalism and radicalism, the Jewish community lacked a historically nuanced means of reacting. Largely, this was the result of the long suppression of Black voices, so that African American critiques of liberalism were never really heard.

I

The response of Jewish writers to Black nationalism was as divided as that of the larger Jewish community. Struggling with mixed success to overcome historical racism, Jewish fiction writers by 1970 faced a new twist in constructions of blackness, this time emanating from the African American community itself. Although conceptions of a natural Black separation from White America were far from new, the source was. Employing countermyths of a special Black aesthetic, Black nationalism risks reinforcing primitivist stereotypes. Wittingly or not, Jewish writers tended to fold contemporaneous images of Blacks as angry revolutionaries into conventional stereotypes. As traditional Jewish fears of anti-Semitism lessened, dominant cultural anxieties regarding social disorder were accentuated; stereotypes of Black primitivism and criminality infiltrated Jewish literature. So Mariann Russell lumps Bernard Malamud's *The Tenants* and Saul Bellow's *Mr. Sammler's Planet* together with John Updike's *Rabbit Redux* as reducing Blacks to "a convenient metaphor for the disturbing elements in white society . . . in the last analysis, not an image of black culture, but a mirror image of the prevailing white culture" (1973, 93). White anxieties concerning dissension, social breakdown, and sexual freedom—particularly during a period of upheaval—are projected onto the figure of the Black. If these fictions "do not go beyond the portrayal of the black man as the 'other'" (100), then what has happened to the Jewish history of marginalization? Have these authors so melted into dominant society as to be indistinguishable from John Updike? Yet both Malamud and Bellow filter representations of Blacks through a lingering Jewish perspective. Both display a concern with the outcast—an implied historical parallel—that leads to a cry for sympathy even in the midst of conflict, even in scenes of brutal violence.

It is difficult to find a work that is more a mirror of prevailing events, a reaction to immediate circumstance, than *The Tenants* (1971). In this tale a Jewish writer, Harry Lesser, provides intellectual guidance to an aspiring Black writer, Willie Spearmint, who responds with increasing resentment and, finally, brutal anti-Semitism. *The Tenants* led to charges of racism. Addison Gayle, for instance, comments that Spearmint "is a black man as seen through the eyes of a white man: crude, coarse, insulting" (quoted in Harap 1987, 27). The discourse of the text may be read as implicitly racist: Lesser's designation as "the writer" contrasted with Spearmint's as "the black" makes clear the basic opposition of the intellectual and the physical that the two represent. The common referent of

the last name for the Jewish character ("Lesser") and the nickname for the
Black ("Willie") further emphasizes social status as engraved in language:
an implied "Mr." versus a "boy."[1] Cynthia Ozick asks the crucial question
of why Malamud chose such a duo—an educated Jew, a successful writer,
matched against an unpolished, unpublished ex-convict: "The balance was
unequal, the antagonists unfairly matched" (1983, 102); "Suppose
Malamud had given us Ellison instead of Willie—then what?" (103). Such
an approach would have allowed for a sophisticated intellectual exchange,
a novel of ideas (rather like the Howe-Ellison exchange on the role of
Black literature). Ozick argues that the difference between Lesser and
Spearmint enhances the novel's dramatic conflict, yet concludes that the
primary reason for Malamud's choice comes from immediate history:
"Malamud did not make Willie. He borrowed him—he mimicked him—
from the literature and the politics of the black movement. Willie is the
black dream that is current in our world. Blacks made him" (108). Black
nationalism, not Malamud, is seen as responsible for reconfiguring old
stereotypes. In this reading, Willie is an archetypal figure of the Black
Arts movement, one dramatizing Black attacks upon Jews.

Ozick simplifies the historical background. The Willie Spearmint that
Malamud has constructed enacts, in both his life and art, a paradigmatic
stretch of African American literary history, from Black naturalism to Black
Arts, from Richard Wright to Amiri Baraka, a blurring of history for the
sake of parabolic completeness. Dramatically, Spearmint synthesizes and
intensifies, while losing historical specificity. And the relationship between
Spearmint and Lesser replays in microcosm the Jewish role of patron and
the Black rebellion from this relationship. Lesser's initial reading of
Spearmint's work replays the experience of the Jewish intellectual first
reading African American literature, seeing displayed a world he's been
only vaguely aware of, has experienced only tangentially in both life and
art: "The book was mainly naturalistic confessional, Willie's adventures
simply narrated, the style varying from Standard English to black lingo,
both the writing and psychology more sophisticated than Lesser would
have guessed" (60). Such a work is a necessary step in the African American project of narrating one's own story, of identity formation, in Lesser's
words of "writing as power" (66). The literature that inspired Malamud's
conception of Spearmint is clearly spelled out: "[I]t's been written before,
and better, by Richard Wright, Claude Brown, Malcolm X, and in his
way, Eldridge Cleaver" (66). The power of such works to reveal a brutal
truth beneath the facade of American opportunity is magnified in a time
when there was little acknowledged African American literature. Spear-

mint as parable of Black literature is severely limited not only by the exclusion of Ellison, but by the neglect of such figures as W. E. B. DuBois and Zora Neale Hurston. And writers such as Ishmael Reed, Toni Morrison, Gloria Naylor, and Charles Johnson had not yet expanded—in a rich variety of ways—the Ellisonian project of cultural hybridity, of simultaneously foregrounding both European and Africanist traditions (often through mischievous parody). To the Jewish reader in 1971, the African American literary tradition may very well have looked like the angry, barren landscape exemplified by Willie Spearmint and earlier spelled out by Irving Howe.[2]

The Jewish eye remains the perceiving one in *The Tenants*, interrupted by the snatches of literary fragments purportedly from Spearmint's pen, Malamud's reforging of the only window on Black life available to many Jews. The novel quite literally enacts this perception. Simultaneously, the intellectualized Jew pitted against the primitivist Black enacts a far older, more deeply ingrained myth. Much drama arises from this archetypal conflict, which is, however, eroded by the novel's modernist experimentation, its fragmented narrative and sudden turns from naturalist to poetic language. Irregularities in style and form are integral to the novel's metafictional uncertainty, with works contained within works. The sense is conveyed not only of Spearmint and Lesser struggling to find the proper means to express their condition, but simultaneously of a larger authorial consciousness undertaking the same struggle, failing along with his characters to create closure. The ideal of a godlike author imposing form and meaning is revealed as problematic, if not to aesthetic experiments, then certainly to a novel entwined with social history.

Alvin Kernan places the novel's metafictional setting within a larger (theoretically monocultural) history: "The Imaginary Library built by print, the House of Fiction built by Flaubert and Henry James, has degenerated in *The Tenants* into a squalid New York City tenement. . . . The House of Fiction has been invaded by the world and has degenerated into a fearsome place of decay and terror" (1986, 197).[3] Absent from Kernan's discussion, as from many discussions of modernist decay, is the multiethnic nature of the incursion into "civilization": Jew and Black inhabit this desolate tenement, struggling to create a literature, a cultural narrative, from their fragmented positions on the margins. They must build their own "house of literature" from the skeletal structure of the tenement building, of European form, giving it flesh through the artistic labors of besieged minority experience. Whether this amounts to a unified project or an unresolved collection of separate literatures remains an open question, and a crucial source of conflict in *The Tenants*. Lesser's positioning of his own work as part of a European-derived evolution further confounds this question. The building materials for this problematic literature, which may or may not be the start of multiculturalism, are presented as archetypal simplifications, crude and dichotomous. The intellectual Jew posited against the physical Black, aesthetics against raw emotion, is an effective device for portraying an artistic dialectic, effective also at building dramatic tension, but painfully inadequate at portraying human and social complexity. Among other themes, *The Tenants* enacts the Jewish writer's struggle to balance European notions of form with the demands of multiethnic America, of a Black culture as filtered through a Jewish perspective. In Lesser, European assumptions of universal aesthetic standards are clearly dominant. In this scheme Spearmint stands for pure ethnicity, for the Jewishness that Lesser has himself rejected. No wonder that Ellison, with his penchant for folding European influences into the aesthetic mix, could not be represented in *The Tenants*; Lesser already represents this position in purer form, submerging his ethnicity to European ideals far more than does Ellison, with his subversive use of European source material.

Lesser's Europeanized nature makes of him the universal, humanistic figure of Malamud's claim that "all men are Jews." Since Judaism defines itself as exclusive—both genealogically and as a religion—such a claim is as much European as it is Jewish, or rather it inscribes European universalism within the narrative of Jewish suffering. Universalism becomes a means not of exploiting other peoples but of inviting them into a larger cultural project, though with European culture implicitly atop the hierarchy. Meek, incapable of giving offense, Lesser overflows with sympathy (or insecurity masked as sympathy?) for the injured Spearmint, sheltering him and critiquing his work at intensifying risk and personal pain. Extending this saintly picture of himself, Lesser's novel is about the aesthetic struggle for love. Willie, by contrast, is driven by a hatred of Whites that intensifies throughout the novel, transmuting into a hatred of Jews (a transference similar to that of Lee Gordon in *Lonely Crusade*). While such hatred may be unavoidable, it risks a self-justifying, self-perpetuating cycle.[4]

Each writer's predicament is reflected in his work. Willie Spearmint has a powerful tale yet lacks the tools to tell it. The circumstances that provide the narrative—poverty, abuse, hatred—preclude the education to convey his story in a form acceptable to dominant culture. Spearmint's emotions are not the primitive joys of the exotic Other that Lesser seeks, but the pain of the oppressed. From Spearmint's writing Lesser gleans a loathing of White society: "[H]is first major insight into his life is how much he hates *them* for maiming the blacks who maim him" (Malamud 1971, 60). Initially, however, Spearmint asks for Lesser's help (an occurrence at variance with the history of Jewish-Black relations). According to Lesser, "Willie has good ideas for stories but doesn't always build them well; in the end they fall short of effective form" (67). The role of teacher assumes a craft to be mastered, a singular notion of form, an assumption rejected by the Black Arts movement. Willie's reaction to Lesser's critique is twofold: an increased devotion to writing and a protest against Lesser's status as arbiter of form. Increasingly Willie broods, developing into an obsessive personality replicating Lesser's neurosis. Black artistic development imitates Jewish in turn imitating European, suggesting the future path of African American literature, at least regarding form. Yet this synthesis never coalesces; Spearmint cannot assume the Ellisonian role of "creating the consciousness of his race." Whether this is due to his lack of education or to an essential lack in his nature, the novel's parabolic form does not address.

Given repeated failure to meet Lesser's standards (which Lesser cannot meet for his own work), Spearmint becomes bitter. Increasingly believing that White/Jewish literature is insufficient for capturing the Black essence, he develops an expressivist attack on aestheticized ideals of form: "Art can kiss my juicy ass. You want to know what's really art? *I* am art. Willie Spearmint, *black man*. My form is *myself*" (75). He has evolved from practitioner of the protest novel to exemplar of the Black Arts movement proclaiming an intertwining of life and art, enacting himself as a version of the primitive exotic. Spearmint's rhetorical exaggeration is close to satire, except that the Black Arts movement itself relied on excessive dramatization. This virtual self-parody is the rhetorical point; to Spearmint the truth of Black existence, the hatred Blacks have borne and now bare, is itself beyond parody: simply the survival of Blacks upon this continent, under these conditions, is an artistic statement. Black literature, according to this philosophy of artistic essence, cannot replicate the tenets of White literature (or of Jewish literature replicating White). At the crucial point of juncture, Black style and Black anger (the interaction between the two is indeterminable) causes a veering away. To the Black nationalist, the Jewish benefactor increasingly becomes a promoter of rationalist myth.

Spearmint's intensifying obsession with Jews is best captured in a pair of his short stories. Early on, he portrays a Black man driven "to murder a white and taste a piece of his heart" (65). By *The Tenant*'s end he is writing of Goldberg, a Jewish slumlord stabbed to death, of whom one attacker suggests "Let's cut a piece off of him and taste what it tastes like" (203). White is transformed to Jew; in both cases, the assaulting Blacks feel an urge to consume the dead corpse of White society, to symbolically incorporate the power of that society into themselves. In both cases, such consummation fails; in the first tale, the heart is lost among the mass of organs, implying a dormant structure, a White society lacking heart, not worth consuming or imitating despite the morbid assimilationist compulsion to do so. In the second story, ingestion is barely attempted, since "He [the corpse] tastes Jewtaste, that don't taste like nothin good" (203). More so than the White body, the Jewish body is depicted as always already repulsive, just as the anti-Semite considers anything Jewish repulsive by definition. On top of the oppressive characteristics of White society that it has taken on, the Jewish body is saturated also with traditional anti-Semitic characteristics, is untouchable. In incorporating characteristics of their oppressor, Jews betray their own history—and their commitment to civil rights—becoming an intensified symbol of dominant social hypocrisy.

Malamud's version of Black nationalism, then, entails movement from a psychologically necessary acknowledgment of hatred for Whites, to a wallowing in that hatred, to a transference onto the Jewish object, an all-consuming abhorrence that has too often been the final destination of anti-Semitism. Yet as a representative of Black Arts literature Spearmint is atypical; he is less educated and less self-conscious than many in the movement. Much Black nationalist anti-Semitism was expressive, symbolic, and sporadic, quite unlike the omnipotent anti-Semitism of Spearmint's final writings, which climax with a description of an American pogrom in which Jews are dragged out of their stores, lined up, and shot (219–20). This is the scene of European rather than Black anti-Semitism, of the pogroms and death camps to which traditional anti-Semitism has led. In *The Tenants* Black anti-Semitism intimates genocide, the greatest Jewish fear.

A corollary to this fear is a foreshadowing of the Black Muslim belief that African Americans are the true Jews, that America's White Jews are usurpers. Spearmint's last story ends when Goldberg's killers "go to a synagogue late at night, put on yarmulkes and make Yid noises, praying. / In an alternate ending the synagogue is taken over and turned into a mosque. The blacks dance hasidically" (203). This scene illuminates, in grotesque juxtaposition, both a rich cultural hybridity and a death struggle. The immediate motive driving this story seems to be Spearmint's desire to take Lesser's place, to become a substitute Jew, a success story in America. The larger context is that of Jewish economic success in conjunction with an (apparent) ability to maintain their traditions. In "dancing hasidically," the killers unite Black and Jewish versions of soulful spirituality, creating through destruction the harmony that Spearmint and Lesser never achieve. Behind this grotesque cultural appropriation is the ideal of a displaced yet divinely chosen people, a status for which Blacks and Jews continue to vie. In this extreme scenario, only with the destruction of the Jews can Blacks take their proper role as America's true minority, creating the American spiritual center from the margins.

Anti-Semitism in *The Tenants* occurs parabolically as a metahistorical struggle, but stems directly from the personal situation of the two protagonists. Spearmint is threatened in the two arenas that Freud defines as crucial to any human being, love and work: work in Lesser's repeated criticism of Spearmint's writing, the art by which he struggles to define himself; love in Lesser's wooing of Irene Bell, Spearmint's girlfriend. In this sphere, too, racial perceptions are critical. Like Nat Lime, Lesser is curious about the myth of Black sexuality and hopes "Willie would bring along a lady friend or two. He had never slept with a black girl" (37). If superficially the relationship between Lesser and Spearmint is one-sided, in an unspoken exchange Spearmint offers Lesser access to (perceived) African American primitivism, an exotic Otherness, an unrestrained sexuality. When he consummates this fantasy, however, his expectations are greatly disappointed. The woman, Mary Kettlesmith, explains, "My doctor said I am built a little small. You have to go easy not to hurt me at first" (127). Instead of a type, the Sexual Black Woman, Lesser finds himself involved with an individual, one member of the human species, in this case a frail one, who explains afterward, "The bed is not my most favorite place" (129). If the expectation is for erotic novelty the actuality is disappointing: a skinny, frigid human being rather than an exotic plaything open to exploration and penetration by the White adventurer. The Black essentialism perceptible elsewhere in *The Tenants* is here subverted.

Although Lesser is subjected to a reprisal for his incursion into Black society, Kettlesmith's defenders seem more concerned with her value as a social symbol—with protecting their rights over a Black woman—than with her worth as a human being. Racial fiction is enacted as reality. In subjecting Lesser to a game of the "Dozens," the men render his aesthetic ineffectuality painfully evident. To an array of vulgarities, all he can manage is such statements as "your mouth is a place of excrement" (132). Even his obscenity is aestheticized and latinized, a symbolic impotence.

Like Henderson among the Arnewi he has blundered, misunderstood the customs; unlike Henderson—unlike adventurers on faraway continents—he cannot simply pack up and leave. He is called "a fartn shiteater faggot whore kike apeshit thievin Jew" (134). "Jew," the climactic term in the series, designates absolute outsider status, removal from both dominant and minority societies.

Like Mary Kettlesmith, though to a lesser extent, Irene Bell is perceived largely as female terrain marking the boundaries of Jewish-Black and Black-White relations. Spearmint's affair with Bell is normalized by avant-garde posturing, which either pretends not to recognize race or crosses racial lines as an act of defiance. Though Bell is an underdeveloped character—Ozick complains that she "exists to accommodate neither Willie nor Lesser, but the exigencies of a made fiction" (1983, 106)—her movement from a Black to a Jewish lover is clearly delineated, as is its significance for her identity. While one can scarcely comprehend why, as a human being, she would tolerate the treatment inflicted by both Spearmint and Lesser, each obsessed with his own work, as a symbol she effectively plays the part relegated her. Her destiny is to move from artistic assimilationism back to her Jewish past, to an affirmation of ethnic identity. As a blond actress, Bell is a symbol of entry into American society, with "blond" an emblem of glamour, and "actress" signifying an ever-shifting America, the ability to play many parts. In Spearmint, Bell seeks a transgressive version of American identity, remarking on the thrill associated with his color: "The blackness of him scared and excited me" (Malamud 1971, 118). Like Lesser she explores the emotional freedom associated with African American society, largely through the mystery of Black sexuality. While wearing the guise of American icon, she explores one of dominant society's most extreme transgressions (simultaneously accepting dominant assumptions of its transgressive nature).

Lesser discerns in Bell uprootedness and unhappiness at her attachment to an alien society, with "alien" encompassing both White and Black gentiles: "He was sure her discontent was with herself. / 'What's the true color of your hair?' / 'Black,' she mocked, in a low voice. 'And my name is Belinsky, not Bell'" (52). Lesser woos her with the word "Shalom" (139), a signifier that among the truly assimilated would mean little, but that maintains an illocutionary power, a magic word awakening her underlying Jewish nature. Her growing love coincides with a physical characteristic associated with Jewishness, the sprouting blackness she chooses for her hair. In pushing the blond surface, approved by dominant culture, ever further, this blackness intimates Jewish self, a look and attitude that "redeemed her face, and perhaps something inside her, for she seemed kinder to herself" (154). Like Rachel Fine in Marshall's *Browngirl, Brownstones*, in achieving her maturation Irene Bell emphasizes the black growing under her blond hair. Her blondness signifies an evasion of ethnicity, an entry into the assimilationist avant-garde that paradoxically allows her romance with a Black man. Blond is surface, a patina of acceptability; black represents the "inner" Jewish self, though this self remains undefined. The confusion stems from Malamud's contradictory definition of Jewishness—are all men Jews, or are Jews a specific ethnicity? Is Jewishness a universal or a particular? In Malamud, it seems to be a universal, a humbleness combined with sympathy, an ideal toward which outsiders can migrate, as does Frank Alpine in *The Assistant*. The leveling universalism of Eurocentricism is redefined according to a different set of criteria. Paradoxically, this Jewishness has a specific style and history, which Bell acknowledges in accepting her Jewish (black hair) roots, and finally consummates through Lesser.

Irene Bell, Jewish by birth, moves toward a Malamudian Jewishness—Jewish by virtue of one's humanity—through the sympathy that her relationship with Spearmint engenders. In a strange reversal—the Jew in blackface—a Black here acts as middleman on a journey from assimilationism to Jewish identity, becoming a tool in the construction of someone else. Sympathy for Spearmint becomes a test case in the building of a Malamudian Jewishness. Irene says that "Willie's struggle to be a writer . . . is one of the most affecting things I know about anybody's life. It moves me an awful lot. He has to go on" (Malamud 1971, 147). This welling compassion endows her with the Jewish humanitarianism that, in the Malamud cosmology, makes her a deserving partner for Lesser. Yet, rather than being exclusively Jewish, Bell's sympathy for Spearmint observes Toni Morrison's description of an American literature that uses Blacks "as a means of meditation—both safe and risky—on one's own humanity" (1990, 53). While her guilt accords with the role of empathetic Jew, she worries that she is merely replicating dominant cultural oppression: "I have this awful feeling as though you and I are a couple of Charlies giving a nigger a boot in the ass" (Malamud 1971, 148). As an exchange, the relationship between Spearmint and the couple of Irene and Lesser works to the couple's advantage. Spearmint has supplied them with a cultural experience, a visit into a world of Otherness, of expressive language and sexuality. Though this journey may be rocky and unfulfilling, alongside it occurs a voyage toward a new humanitarianism. Irene and Lesser construct a fuller version of Jewish American identity. The outcome of the Jewish foray into Black society is an emergent humanitarianism, one strangely positioned between a moral triumph and a kind of high-minded slumming.

Lesser's response to Irene outlines a far different interpretation: "All this amounts to is two people—you and Willie—finally agreeing to end an affair. If you aren't betraying him as a man you aren't betraying his color" (149). This statement of universality, of colorblindness, belies the circumstances of Spearmint's life and of Irene's attachment to him, both of which are predicated largely on his blackness. Lesser's stance toward Spearmint ignores the manner in which race has affected relations between the three of them. His criticism of Spearmint's book coincides with the revelation of his affair with Irene, a relentless truth-telling destined to incite the violence that had been symbolically staged in the earlier game of the "Dozens." In complaining that Lesser is "trying to steal my manhood" (50) and later that Irene "hurt his blackness" (171), Spearmint articulates the fragility of both his racial and his masculine identity. Cobbs and Grier's analysis of Black emasculation through internalizing dominant cultural hatred underscores the threat that Spearmint has faced all his life and that climaxes in Lesser's actions. Lesser's subsequent remark that "I treated him like a man" (191) suggests a view of universal autonomy oblivious to Spearmint's condition. Rather like the decolonizing states cut off from the imperial centers on which they had been kept artificially dependent, Spearmint is asked to accept too much all at once. The demand that Spearmint accept his responsibilities "like a man" assumes an atomistic individual free from the demands of history, enacting in miniature the kind of universal leveling that Black Arts thinkers protest against.

As a parable of extreme difference written within an unresolved historical moment, *The Tenants* dramatizes its own lack of closure by including three contradictory endings. This postmodern trope is not just a metafictional aesthetic experiment within a bounded text, but is generated by the larger "text" of contemporaneous events. Just as Malamud writes the characters Lesser and Spearmint, whose inconclusive states mirror Malamud's own confusion, so society—the author behind the author—plays a critical part in constructing *The Tenants*, a work that not surprisingly mirrors unresolved social contradictions. In the first ending the tenement burns down, ravaged by either Levenspiel or Spearmint. The House of Art, with its Old World civilization, its complex network of rooms, of structure and facade, does not survive in the New World. The intransigent attitudes, the extreme characteristics of warring minorities, inhibit a pluralistic modern literature. This apocalyptic ending, suggested only briefly, is a product of deep despair.

Malamud's second ending is utopian: an interracial wedding in a mythic African setting presided over by a tribal chief and a rabbi. The fantastical nature of this reconciliation between Black and Jew is evident in the lack of narrative buildup, of any attempt to present it as a realistic possibility. Rather it occurs in the consciousness of some disembodied author—"Here's this double wedding going on, that's settled in his mind" (206)—a version of Lesser's long-searched for ending intertwined and confounded with Malamud's ending. The African scene is familiar to readers of *Henderson;* it is one of mythic grace, of "girls of the clan, oiled and ornamented" (207); of drums, spears, and dancing; of the tribal voice announcing harmony: "The bride price, you bring ten cows, do be paid and we make acceptance" (210). This tropical scene of primitive tradition stages an unchanging ceremonial innocence. The marriage of Black and Jew, oddly enough, revives tradition through mixing a wholesale (if invented) African ceremony with the ministrations of a rabbi, a duality of cultures rather than a mosaic or melting pot. In 1970 this is perhaps the closest that could be envisioned to a multicultural hybridity. Yet even as fantasy the wedding ceremony is disturbed by ominous warnings of racial strife. The rabbi proclaims, "Oh, what a hard thing is marriage in the best of circumstances. On top of this what if one is black and the other white?" (215). Similarly the African chief intones a warning from the Tiv of West Africa (quoted in more formal translation at the start of Marshall's *The Chosen Place, the Timeless People*): "If somebody do bad it do not die. It live in the hut, the yard, and the village. The ceremony of reconciliation is useless. Men say the words of peace but they do not forgive the other" (212). Even fantasy is disturbed by reminders of hatred.

Such tribalist hatred overwhelms the final, and most prominent, conclusion of *The Tenants*, which repeats and intensifies the earlier scene of violence between Lesser and Spearmint. Lesser precipitates this final battle by destroying Spearmint's typewriter (227), both a silencing and an act of symbolic castration with the typewriter substituted for the traditionally phallic pen. The (Euro-American) House of Art has restricted access. As Levenspiel systematically nails shut the tenement's doors (228), the Black author is squeezed out, denied voice and space. Jewish Americans have occupied the European site of culture, declaring it their own and continuing its exclusionist traditions. Jew and Black meet in a final scene of violence, locked in bitter, seemingly unending struggle: "Lesser felt his jagged ax sink through bone and brain as the groaning black's razor-sharp saber, in a single boiling stabbing slash, cut the white's balls from the rest of him" (230). Each reduces the other to essentialist stereotype: Lesser cuts out the brain, the site of abstract reasoning, of writerliness, leaving only body, only the physical; Spearmint slices out Lesser's sexuality, the site of physical pleasures absent in the mythic Jew. In their ideological fervor, perhaps they are really slicing away their own humanity, their complex artistry, reducing themselves to stereotypes. No integrated personage remains. This scene will be replayed in Jay Neugeboren's "Elijah," in which a rabbi fights a Black minister. In *The Tenants,* moreover, there's no youthful figure, no Elijah, to prefigure a better future in which youth overturns racist tradition.

At the greatest extreme of violence, however, there is still sympathy: "Each, thought the writer, feels the anguish of the other" (230). Violence occurs through a too-close identification, a kind of brotherly understanding that yields great bitterness. Paul Berman outlines a theory of "the Almost the Same," for those "neither 'other' nor 'brother'" who alternate feelings of intense similarity and intense difference (1994, 5). Given historical parallels and protests of mutual goodwill, when Black and Jew diverge each is prone to personalize differences. Lesser's sympathy for Spearmint is clearly delineated; whether Spearmint sympathizes with Lesser remains unanswered in a text centered on Jewish consciousness. We see only Spearmint's reaction, which remains opaque to Lesser. We cannot know if Spearmint feels "the anguish of the other," only that his hatred appears extreme beyond reason. In a passage applicable to *The Tenants,* Berman describes the contemporary Black-Jewish situation as "Separate beds, separate rooms; the same house. Love, hatred; a wobbling back and forth. . . . An intensity that never quite evaporates—all of it destined to go on as long as polyglot America goes on" (28). If America is a family it is a highly dysfunctional one. Written at a time of visible hatred, the novel ends with a cry for "mercymercymercymercy," a desperate cry with little chance of an answer. James McPherson describes how, "even after the 115th plea for mercy by Levenspiel, there is no period and there is no peace" (1989, 15). Malamud's artistry lacks closure because the American society upon which it draws is itself torn and incomplete, unwilling to fully acknowledge its bloody history, unable to incorporate its many ethnic groups. America's Jews are implicated in the history of oppression, at least in the economic hierarchies that this history has created. By 1970 the liberal dream of (Eurocentric) equality seemed bankrupt, while no multidimensional vision of America as a plentitude of ethnicities had arisen to replace it. The erasure of cultural diversity had led not to unity but to an ethnic particularism of hostile stereotypes and incessant conflict.

II

If *The Tenants* portrays an America wounded by ethnic conflict, Saul Bellow's *Mr. Sammler's Planet* dramatizes a full-scale assault on Western civilization by a primitivist hedonism. In *The Tenants* Black primitivism may be interpreted as a mark of racial anxiety in conjunction with class difference. In *Mr. Sammler's Planet* blackness is an organic force, a contamination, an overarching sign of difference. In both novels, Jewishness is portrayed in a relatively new alignment with dominant society: in conflict with blackness, at least partly as a reaction to Black nationalism. In *Mr. Sammler's Planet*, the conflating of Jewish and dominant cultural anxieties goes further, at least initially, with blackness clearly an alien force. Representations of blackness as dangerous, primitive, and highly sexualized find their most notorious expression in Jewish literature in Bellow's Black thief. With anxieties regarding social breakdown especially acute at the end of the tumultuous 1960s, *Mr. Sammler's Planet* presents an implicit parallel between the failures of European civilization and a mongrelized, pleasure-seeking version of contemporary America. Yet by the novel's conclusion a revisited Jewish past throws the protagonist briefly into sympathy with the figure of the Black. If Lesser's identification with Willie Spearmint remains problematic, emanating as it does from an Enlightenment universalism, in *Mr. Sammler's Planet*, lacking as it is in any explicit identification with Blacks, the protagonist's final sympathy derives from the Jewish history of marginalization.

Contradictions within *Mr. Sammler's Planet*, together with the controversial subject matter, lead the novel—like *Henderson the Rain King*— to be interpreted in radically different ways. Stanley Crouch emphasizes the novel's portrait of America's increasing self-indulgence and irresponsibility: "When it arrived, the deeper meanings of *Mr. Sammler's Planet* were missed by those who were afraid that Bellow had become a racist and a fuddy-duddy" (1996, xi). Certainly the novel is at least as harsh toward White youth as toward the Black thief. Yet the portrait of the thief is more distanced, more that of an external observer than a fellow human being. So Brent Staples criticizes the thief's dehumanized facade, feeling great disappointment in a writer he admires as a sharp chronicler of human character: "I expected more of a man who could see into the soul. I expected a portrait of myself, not as the beast I'd been made out to be, but as who I was at heart" (1994, 220). While a single character should not be expected to stand in for larger social groups, a metonymic use of the Black male recurs in much American literature, and in a variety of media. Lacking greater context regarding African Americans, Artur Sammler's perceptions mirror deeply ingrained social beliefs.

Placing Bellow's novel in an immediate context of social disruption and Black anti-Semitism, L. H. Goldman claims that "because this work lacks the detailing of events that led to this disruption in [Black and Jewish] relations, the statement that is preserved for posterity is a racist one" (1983, 187). Goldman assumes that Bellow's depiction of Black primitivism and violence is a reaction to Black nationalist rhetoric, especially as directed against the figure of the Jew. Certainly the portrayal of youth rebellion and ethnic struggle in 1960s New York City is closely related to contemporaneous social events; yet Black nationalism and the breakdown of the Black-Jewish alliance, though likely triggering events for the writing of *Mr. Sammler's Planet*, are irrelevant to its plot. Rather the Black thief is a direct symbol of anxiety about crime, more generally rooted in a larger ideology that renders blackness as the antithesis of civilization. Goldman is right in perceiving the Black figure as an allegorical presence symptomatic of social breakdown, but wrong in implying that a Jewish perspective explains the thief's symbolic nature. The thief is a compact, dramatic version of a recurring European and EuroAmerican mythologization: blackness as the primitive, the carnal, the return of the repressed. Any Jewish perspective, at least in the novel's initial thematic development, is eclipsed by that of dominant society.

If, however, *Mr. Sammler's Planet* symbolically reduces Blacks to icons of primitivist energy, its portrayal of Jewish history undermines this mythologized sign of Otherness, revealing the arbitrariness of racial distinctions. Since the Nazis represent both White purity and a barbaric force that eclipsed European civilization, the sign of blackness as applied in the novel virtually deconstructs itself. The implicit alignment of White with civilization and Black with primitivism conflicts with Nazism and with the historical Jewish role of racial Otherness. By exploring Sammler's personal history as embedded in a larger Jewish history, the novel gradually unveils a counternarrative of terror inflicted upon marginalized peoples, culminating in a moment of identification between Jew and Black.

The story of Artur Sammler's life is absurd, a literally psychotic record of events featuring wild swings—from cultivated European to Holocaust victim to materially secure American—that eradicate social boundaries along with notions of a stable civilization. Through the course of the novel, an alternative emerges to the dehumanizing reductions of the thief: an unfolding sympathy, although only in muted form, since the contradiction between Black as frozen symbol and Black as historical subject is never resolved. The irrational fluctuations of Jewish history elicit an anguished search for meaning, a submerged guilt never explicitly analyzed by Sammler (despite his incessant social analysis). By the conclusion a Jewish concern with the outcast, an increasing disgust at the terror of violence, leads to a cry for sympathy, for an end to the brute violence that dominant ideology once brought to Sammler and now brings (albeit indirectly) to the thief.

The novel's thematic structure is unwieldy; it is based upon an interplay between civilization and barbarism, opposing concepts between which Artur Sammler is precariously balanced. To Sammler civilization emanates from the European Enlightenment while barbarism, symbolized by blackness is epitomized by the twin events of Holocaust and 1960s upheaval. Yet Nazism, the antithesis of civilization, originated far from Africa on Europe's fertile ground. The Holocaust depended upon mind, bureaucratic planning, control of every detail of its victims' bodies to the point of obliteration. Conversely 1960s radicalism, as depicted by Bellow, emphasizes freedom of the body, a playing out of all physical and sexual impulses, an invasion of the physical, the dark Other, into the substance of the New World.

Although Sammler is a product of a cultural philosophy that rejects Jewish particularism in favor of European civilization, his Holocaust experience obstructs such a position. Europe may just as easily be the source of a new, and terrifyingly efficient, kind of barbarism. Drawing upon Max Horkheimer and Theodor Adorno's characterization of the Enlightenment's incessant drive toward total mastery, Kurt Dittmar argues that

> The Holocaust, the system of the German concentration camps, was based on the ultimate self-sufficiency of purely rational organization *(Mind)* and at the same time on the ultimate reduction of existence into mere corporeality *(Body)*, thus presenting itself—and this indeed is Bellow's perspective—as the final result, the *ultima ratio* of the Enlightenment. (1991, 79)

An arrangement privileging mind over body, driven to organize, classify, dissect, and control, is unbalanced, out of harmony with the human state in relation to its environment. Prior to the Holocaust, Sammler supported Enlightenment idealism in a specific form championed by H. G. Wells, as he explains in a speech at Columbia University:

> [T]he project was based on the propagation of the sciences of biology, history, and sociology and the effective application of scientific principles to the enlargement of human life; the building of a planned, orderly, and beautiful world society: abolishing national sovereignty, outlawing war . . . a service society based on a rational scientific attitude toward life. (Bellow 1970, 41)

Sammler can no longer countenance this utopian dream. Hyperrationalism—organization, bureaucracy, centralized planning—was twice a failure in extreme opposite versions, the Nazi one of absolute racial hierarchy and the communist one, which gave all power to a small elite that claimed for itself primary control over history. The status of such intermediate solutions as the (pseudo)socialist bureaucracy that extends over Western Europe is of no concern to Sammler, who dismisses the entire rationalist project as "a kind-hearted, ingenuous, stupid scheme" (41). In rejecting his prewar optimism, Sammler follows the only path possible after his encounter with the Nazis, after his rising from the mass grave they dug for him and his kin. Wells's manuscript lies buried here, as does Sammler's conception of European civilization.

Europe is the origin-point of this failed civilization and of its antithesis, Nazism. America, too, is defined by a barbaric opposition to civilization, a liberalism taken to nihilistic excess, an extreme represented by the Black thief. Yet the parallel implied between Nazism and 1960s radicalism is exaggerated, at the very least. Ignoring the enormous gap in the results of the two movements, they are irreconcilable in basic intent and character. Nazism's starting point is exclusion, clear demarcation followed by escalating marginalization of the Other. Sixties radicalism, while it may have led to an excess of (sometimes violent) rhetoric, defined itself through inclusion, through acceptance and (at least partial) incorporation of an increasing array of Others, most notably of the Black Other.

The assumptions against which 1960s radicalism revolted are defined in Sammler's initial cosmology, wherein Europe is the source of the highest ideals of civilization while Africa represents an opposition against which Europe may be defined. African traits of primal contact with emotional and sexual pleasures are extended to America's callow, uninformed youth. Bellow's America is a site of metaphysical struggle between opposed worldviews, with European civilization losing its authority to primal Africanism. New York City is the result, an archetypal scene of cultural hybridization defined amid struggle: "like an Asian, an African town. . . . You opened a jeweled door into degradation, from hypercivilized Byzantine luxury straight into the state of nature, the barbarous world of color erupting from beneath" (7). Hybridization is portrayed here not as the creation of new artistic forms and aesthetic sensibilities, but a mishmash of misplaced societies, a surface decadence covering primitive emotionalism. Sammler continues to be informed by his European rationalist roots; from his perspective no "real" civilization is possible; in place of European culture one finds a "hypercivilization," which should be read as "pseudocivilization," as glittering facade, orientalism hopelessly entangled with African barbarism.

New York's radical decadence, which privileges body, sensation, physical experience, seems puny after the horrific destruction of the Holocaust. Yet the novel is incessant in its attacks upon the cult of youth, portrayed as hedonistic, narcissistic, ignorant, and—a crystallizing symbol for all of these—sexually wanton. Sammler's Columbia speech draws the ire of a young radical who declaims to the crowd, "Why do you listen to this effete old shit? What has he got to tell you? His balls are dry. He's dead. He can't come" (42). Sixties radicalism is represented as a barbaric carnival, intolerant of those who might question its premises; youth has no wish to hear the arguments of this civilized and justly cynical old man. Freud's reduction of the human experience to sexuality, as popularized by Reich, is taken literally here: one *is* one's sexuality. Physical pleasure is the common denominator of our hedonistic society channeled, though Sammler ignores this point, by capitalism to the most basic of pleasures, bought and sold or otherwise exchanged. America's radical youth, despite their radicalism, are products of the very society they critique; the sexual revolution is a consumerist utopia, the search for ultimate individual fulfillment, one end result of Enlightenment's privileging of the self.

Sammler's critique of 1960s radicalism is directed against a youthful culture that partakes of only a latter-day debasement of European philosophy. Psychosexual urges, instant gratification, arrested development: this is the philosophy of the youth movement. Sammler judges this debasement of the Western heritage the legacy of the 1960s counterculture, America's contribution to world culture.[5] The youthful characters in *Mr. Sammler's Planet* are all, to one extent or another, versions of this debased creature in a perpetual state of immaturity. So Sammler's niece Margotte engages in pseudointellectual discussion beyond her understanding; his daughter Shula steals a manuscript on H. G. Wells's *The Future of the Moon* (symbolically stealing the rationalist inheritance); his nephew Wallace floods his house searching for hidden money; Wallace's friend Feffer generates wild aerial photography schemes; Sammler's niece Angela follows a debauched path of sexual experimentation ending in divorce and insists upon divulging every detail to Sammler. This host of straw figures is perfectly happy to dispense blame upon themselves: "I'm a different generation," says Wallace; "I never had any dignity to start with" (241); "I was a dirty little bitch," admits Angela (153). There's something conniving even about these confessions, as though by admitting their weaknesses Wallace and Angela have abrogated responsibility and can continue their self-indulgences. They place themselves within an array of little Others, self-caricatures nibbling away at the foundations of Western society as represented by Sammler.

The overarching symbol of Otherness—the Mother Other—is blackness, the African darkness transposed to America. Besides its sexual connotations, an extrarational force already awakened by femininity, blackness conveys the threat of violence. Sexuality endangers self-control, destabilizing the neat categories that order the world. Marriage is the institution that controls sexuality, places it in its proper category, and allows the ordered propagation of society. In *Mr. Sammler's Planet*, 1960s disruption of institutional controls over sexuality is linked to blackness. Angela's orgiastic behavior, her flaunting of propriety, exemplifies "a sexual madness . . . overwhelming the Western world" (66), a madness typified by the dark, primitive peoples with their assumed violations of Western marriage norms. Shula's theft of the manuscript on H. G. Wells signifies a rejection of Western norms:

> [S]uddenly she too was like the Negro pickpocket. From the black side, strong currents were sweeping over everyone. Child, black, redskin— the unspoiled Seminole against the horrible Whiteman. Millions of civilized people wanted oceanic, boundless, primitive, neckfree nobility, experienced a strange release of galloping impulses, and acquired the peculiar aim of sexual niggerhood for everyone. (162)

The symbolic meaning of blackness, presented here as overblown satire, could not be more explicit: the primitive, the rawest physical urges, absolute sexual abandon. The repressed returns not in a brief eruption, but in an oceanic gushing, the heart of darkness unleashed in the putative heart of civilization. The passage makes sarcastic use of the "radical" point of view, which considers "the unspoiled Seminole" as the archetype of inno-cence, of freedom prior to the constraints of civilization, of the "horrible Whiteman." That vast terrain of the primitive, the ocean of the precon-scious, which awaited Henderson's investigation as well as his play, takes on an utterly different character transposed outside Africa's boundaries. Only Africa is sufficient to contain the danger represented by the African: only there can he be a prince, a symbol of freedom and primal wisdom to be enjoyed by the White male explorer. Displaced to America the African threatens the boundaries of civilization.

Blackness as oppositional to civilization is, of course, a myth, having nothing to do with any biological or cultural characteristics or with African American society in its day-to-day functioning. Black culture, diffused into White society, loses its social and communal meanings and becomes a decontextualized symbol of rebellion. In twentieth-century America the evolving adaptations of Black music by flappers, hipsters, and hippies employ blackness as transgression.[6] The equation of blackness with for-bidden sexuality, with taboo forays, with a dangerous mixture of sex and violence, is a creation of White society to account for its own suppressed desires and anxieties. When Blacks provide such services, in an underground economy of prostitution and drug dealing, it is under duress from a system that provides them with few options. Similarly, the range of Black styles adapted by White society, especially as they move from the fringes to the mainstream, are transformed into a consumer-culture version of rebellion, a product draped upon the bodies and emanating from the stereos and mouths of White youths. And yet in *Mr. Sammler's Planet* the archetypal symbol of the blatant hedonism created by this wealth is a Black man, the mythic meaning of blackness condensed into a physical—and by definition de-humanized—object.

As a hypermythologized symbol, the Black thief may seem active, dynamic, larger than life, yet spied upon by Sammler he is reduced to an object of spectacle and gossip, the exemplar of primitivism under the scru-tinizing gaze. Observing the criminal activities on a barbaric New York City bus, Sammler imagines himself imagined as "a tall old white man (passing as blind?)" observing "the minutest details of his crimes. Staring down. As if watching open-heart surgery" (5). Sammler constructs his own gaze as that of the scientist, the physician engaged in the minute details of biology, engrossed in veins and blood and pumping muscle, the diagrammer of scientific rationalism as it grasps the living heart, the cen-ter of life. Yet having survived the Holocaust, Sammler, as symbolized by his blindness in one eye, can no longer idealize such a version of civilization, such detached observation. His awareness of the limitations of his own gaze parallels an increasing distrust of its infallibility. The day of the privileged unidirectional gaze is over; the exemplar of European civilization becomes gradually conscious that the Other is in fact sentient, is bitterly watching his own objectification. The Black Other gazes back, analyzes Sammler, and plots a response.

Sammler's perspective on the Black thief—the perspective of the narratorial consciousness—is limited to two seemingly opposite stereotypes, the criminal and the African Prince. I say "seemingly," because the criminal is merely an aberrant version of the prince due to displacement from his African environment. The Black appears to Sammler gorgeously attired with stately bearing, an Americanized gangster version of the prince:

> The dark glasses, the original design by Christian Dior, a powerful throat banded by a tab collar and a cherry silk necktie spouting out. Under the African nose, a cropped mustache. Ever so slightly inclining toward him, Sammler believed he could smell French perfume. (10)

This is an orientalized version of the African characterized by an exoticized facade, a corruption displayed with the stately demeanor of civilization: meticulous grooming, a Europeanized scent, a designer label. From these orientalized trappings of "civilization" his African power threatens to burst forth, as repeatedly conveyed through animal imagery, beginning with his first appearance, displaying "the effrontery of a big animal" (5)—a primitive power barely contained, indeed paradoxically enhanced, by his designer suit. Stolen from Africa the prince is utterly misplaced; he is reduced to picking pockets, the pettiest of crimes (while still exuding his royal aura).[7] A displaced figure alienated from his surroundings, he is recreated as something new, a discordant bricolage adapted to its new environment yet somehow not adapted.

If Sammler draws one set of conclusions from this figure, his younger, more Americanized relatives draw another, one consistent with the rationalist gaze yet also with the naïveté of a youthful liberalism. Margotte's reaction is of incessant analysis:

> To Margotte it was fascinating. Anything fascinating she was prepared to discuss all day, from every point of view with full German pedantry. Who was this black? What were his origins, his class or racial attitudes, his psychological views, his true emotions, his aesthetic, his political ideas. Was he a revolutionary? Would he be for black guerrilla warfare? (14–15)

Margotte epitomizes the worst rationalist excess of "German pedantry" mixed with the superficiality of the radical left youth movement. Although she ostensibly delves more deeply and sympathetically into the Black's point of view than would a European, she undercuts this by a childish disregard for consequences. Like Sammler on the bus, she slices and analyzes this figure, verbally dissecting him and reducing him to a specimen upon a table. Her easy mention of guerrilla warfare displays the irreverence of the New Left. Several times removed from any reality of blood and bullets, she is free to explore violence through rhetorical explorations that enact a reductive caricature of Enlightenment rationalism.

Sammler, unlike Margotte, faces the reality of the criminal as their confrontations intensify. The criminal's forceful display of his genitals is effective as a symbolic device of the primitive state, the "sexual niggerhood" overtaking America, though quite absurd as a plausible response to Sammler's intrusiveness. Black male sexuality threatens the edifice of "civilization" signified by the abstract phallus, the ideological construction of a monolithic civilization naturalized as the only rational social order. The phallic order is neuter, mental, removed from any actual sexuality. In opposition to this abstract construct is the myth of blackness, whereby, according to Frantz Fanon, "in relation to the Negro, everything takes place on the genital level" (1967, 157). The repressed physical returns projected onto the Black so that "one is no longer aware of the Negro but only of a penis; the Negro is eclipsed. He is turned into a penis" (170).

This extreme dehumanization, the reduction of a human being to a part, is undergone by the thief as he moves toward cornering Sammler. In the application of Black-as-penis animal metaphors abound: the genitals emanate an otherworldly aura and exist as a mysterious organism, huge and alien: "It was displayed to Sammler with great oval testicles, a large tan-and-purple uncircumcised thing—a tube, a snake; metallic hairs bristled at the thick base and the tip curled . . . suggesting the fleshly mobility of an elephant's trunk" (Bellow 1970, 49). This fantastical description is of nothing real but emanates from the imagination, from a simultaneous fear and fascination with sexuality—that submerged mystery released in modern America—from a terror of the Black Other, of one's own exaggerated, all-consuming sexuality objectified as an alien, uncontrollable thing. Blackness represents also the youthful libido, the sexual revolution, a love fest denied Sammler, earlier repressed by that civilization he so admires, now represented by an organ with which he cannot compete. The taboo sexuality displayed here represents a disturbance in the symbolic order, a threat to the hierarchy of power. The organ's uncircumcised state flaunts the safe and clean and known, establishing an identity alien both to Jewish tradition and to rationalistic Western medicine, for Sammler the twin pillars of civilization.

Within Bellow's version of the debased ideology of the 1960s, the thief's organ goes well beyond its biological functions, threatening the demarcations of the symbolic order. To Sammler it appears as "a prominent and separate object intended to communicate authority. As, within the sex ideology of these days, it well might. It was a symbol of super-legitimacy or sovereignty. It was a mystery" (55). It is Slavoj Žižek's Thing, "*das Ding*, the impossible-real object of desire. The sublime object is [to Lacan] 'an object elevated to the level of *das Ding*'" (1989, 194). It is, to Sammler, "the transcending, ultimate, and silencing proof" (Bellow 1970, 55). This transcendence cannot itself be defined or given form. To Žižek, "what the object is masking, dissimulating, by its massive, fascinating presence, is not some other positivity but *its own place*, the void, the lack that it is filling in by its presence" (1989, 195). The fetishized, religious object—here the thief's penis—stands in for an emptiness, takes on an imagined meaning whose dimensions it in no way bears or resembles (of a mystery so undefined that even the idea of resemblance is impossible). Added to this is the historical weight given its Black alienness, its representation of a history and meaning marked by a vast divide between the dominant cultural gaze and the actual subjects of that history.

The penis, then, transgresses conventional structures and repressions, subverting the dominant order. If on the bus the thief breaks the invisible contract of property rights which rules daily interaction, what he represents is hugely disproportionate to this minor transgression. Sammler's relatives, in discussing the thief's penis, glamorize its size and power. Through seeking meanings appropriate to their voyeuristic version of rationalist curiosity, they participate vicariously in transgression (though the novel, in its initial description of the organ, has already fetishized and mythologized it far more than do the relatives). Told about the incident Feffer exclaims, "'Stupendous! . . . What the devil was it like?' He was also laughing . . . 'How big a thing was it? You didn't say. I can imagine'" (Bellow 1970, 121). Any danger inherent in Sammler's forced voyeurism is overlooked; the thief becomes a novelty act. Wallace, too, interrogates Sammler: "Was it sixteen, eighteen inches? . . . Would you guess it weighed two pounds, three pounds, four?" (185). The penis becomes an object of bizarre exaggeration regarding the nature of the Other. The satiric edge is obvious, pointed not at the thief but at Wallace. The humor derives super-ficially from the speculative fantasies of youth culture, but this is merely the innocuous-seeming tip of an enormous iceberg, the barely hidden sub-stratum of racial fantasies that themselves mask dominant cultural anxi-eties. African Americans are reduced from a complex group with its own history and culture to mythic icons.

African American society, then, is notable by its absence in *Mr. Sammler's Planet*, which sets up a myth of blackness lightly deconstructed by humor satirizing White youth. To Sammler, though, blackness remains threatening; when the thief pins him it is certainly not a comic moment but a crystallized representation of Western civilization's besiegement. Yet the novel's climax undermines the primal power of blackness, creat-ing an instant of cathartic sympathy with the criminal. Blacks remain marginalized, to Sammler a recurrent object of mystery, yet they are finally revealed as contained by the repressive forces—both mental and physi-cal—of dominant society. The youth upon which the novel heaps such scorn appear right to trivialize the thief's power; the real power remains in the service of the privileged.

By 1970 the Jewish image had shifted to the point where a Jew could be represented as brutally enforcing the dominant order, a dramatic change when one remembers that *Mr. Sammler's Planet* was written a mere twenty-five years after the Holocaust. No longer the abject victim, the Jew takes on a new role in the person of Eisen, policing the society that has so long oppressed Jews. Given no first name, Eisen, whose name means "iron" and who forges artworks out of bronze metals commemorating Israel's 1967 victory, is described by Sander Gilman as one who "like Israel, has strengthened himself, has become a 'muscle Jew'" (1986, 373). The Is-raeli warrior is both a reaction to centuries of oppression and humiliation and a return to the narrative of the biblical Hebrews who fled from sla-very and, through military valor, claimed the Promised Land. Eisen en-acts the figure of the Jew as no longer a sickly, stunted bookworm but as a prime physical specimen triumphantly reclaiming Israel not only as sol-dier but as farmer draining swamps, making the desert bloom.[8]

The surprisingly critical attitude apparent in *Mr. Sammler's Planet* toward the muscle Jew is bound up with the protagonist's Holocaust ex-perience. As an exemplar of European civilization, Sammler had his Jew-ish awareness forced upon him by the rise of the Nazis. The meaning of his heritage is determined entirely by external forces. His birth heritage is as a highly assimilated Jew eagerly adopting a version of liberal rational-ism that believes in dialogue rather than violence. The tradition of talk rather than action, of refusing violence when possible, is also integral to European Jewry, to the shtetl culture. In escaping the Nazis and becoming a partisan warrior, Sammler is forced to adopt a new identity removed from his prior beliefs. He abandons all compassion for the enemy. When a German prisoner pleads, "Don't kill me. Take the things. . . . I have children" (Bellow 1970, 139) Sammler shoots unhesitatingly. The detailed portrayal of the prisoner—the description of his physical characteristics, of his fear—creates sympathy by humanizing this component of the Nazi war machine. The situation justifies Sammler's killing yet also brings him closer to the level of the oppressor, not just in his actions but emotionally. War may preclude mercy, yet Sammler moves far beyond killing through necessity. Reconstructing the act, he remembers he learned "to kill the man and to kill him without pity, for he was dispensed from pity" (141). Such amoral nihilism echoes the Nazis in puny microcosm and derives from the regularized efficiency of their slaughter. Beyond nihilism the act is one of revenge; beyond revenge it is an act of barbaric pleasure once Sammler "knew how it felt to take a life. Found it could be an ecstasy" (141). This is the ecstasy of complete domination over another, the climax of the will to power.

Sammler's transformation is compelled by an extreme situation that demands complete remaking of self. Marked for extermination first by the Nazis and then by the advancing Russian forces, Sammler becomes "one of the doomed who had lasted it all out" (140). He joins Bigger Thomas in a state of existential deprivation from which the only salvation is murder: "And now the idea that one could recover, or establish, one's identity by killing, becoming equal thus to any, equal to the greatest. A man among men knows how to murder. A patrician" (145). Bigger Thomas murders from a state of absolute deprivation, both material and intellectual. That Sammler, the epitome of privilege and education, could be reduced to such a condition forces a recasting of definitions. "Civilization" becomes a problematic term; its constructed nature is unveiled through the dissolution of differences between Jew and Black and between Black and White. At least to an extent, we are what society makes us, following a script written externally. Civilization is not an innate quality; once acquired it is not always retainable. We are creatures of circumstance. In his astonishing plunge from the civilized elite planning a utopian future to the outcast Other considered fit only for extermination, Sammler exemplifies Jewish vulnerability to external definition.

If Europe is the site of Sammler's plunge to a condition of absolute nihilism and America is the site of a hybrid corruption of misplaced cultures,

Israel, the remaining great hope for world Jewry, fares little better. Discussing Bellow's depiction of Israeli military power, Andrew Furman remarks that, "ultimately, Bellow uses Sammler's sensitive perspective toward Eisen's violence and the violence of the Six-Day War to illustrate the very real moral costs of Israeli might" (1996, 53). Sammler's later reflection over his own acts of violence, as in his ironic comment that one establishes "one's identity by killing," act in concert with his reactions to Israeli violence, leaving little room for faith in Jewish redemption through military triumph. Visiting the Sinai battlefield in 1967, Sammler reflects sardonically that "it was a real war. Everyone respected killing" (Bellow 1970, 251). The ideal of the noble warrior-Jew is derided by the Arab corpses Sammler witnesses: "The clothes of the dead, greenish-brown sweaters, tunics, shirts were strained by the swelling, the gases, the fluids. Swollen gigantic arms, legs, roasted in the sun. The dogs ate human roast" (250). The only comparable carnage in *Mr. Sammler's Planet* occurs at the Nazi mass grave site, replicated in miniature through Sammler's act of killing. Violence begets violence; the Holocaust begets, but also justifies, Sammler's killing; the persecution of the Jews and their continuing danger excuses Israel's wars. The focus on the Sinai carnage should not be interpreted as a simple condemnation of Israel, for its urgent situation is dramatized. Sammler, though described as "no Zionist," hurries to Israel when "for the second time in twenty-five years the same people were threatened by extermination" (142). Self-preservation is the final determinant of Jewish action.[9]

Israel is a scene of Jewish angst, of wrenchingly contradictory attitudes regarding that country's critical role in Jewish survival and the fierce new image it provides for a people long characterized as nonviolent. Eisen, like Sammler a crippled Holocaust survivor, finds his identity among the muscle Jews. If Sammler's blinded eye forces an increase in the perceptiveness of his remaining good eye, and an awareness of its limitations, Eisen's crippled leg is a symbol of stunted emotions. Sammler considers that "Eisen certainly deserved to be cared for, and that was one of the uses of Israel, to gather in these cripples" (155). In fleeing to Israel Eisen establishes the manhood denied him by history through reclaiming a singular, mythic image, a warrior redemption. His journey to America is motivated by a similarly simplistic goal: material success (155). He strives to become the postwar international Jew, using his newfound mobility to build identity through whatever means is most convenient. Sammler, by contrast, flees to America to reestablish his intellectual moorings in a new context; though demoralized and besieged from all sides, he attempts to reshape some moral ideal. The utterly different reactions of Eisen and Sammler to similar histories seem to suggest a role for individual agency. In New York City the two characters, their life stories so parallel, their characters so different, meet under the sign of the Black Other. Although the thief is portrayed as powerful, dynamic, as everything the ghetto Jew is not, he in fact occupies the position to which the Jew was relegated in Europe: ghettoized, immobile, an object of dominant societal projections.

Now characterized by geographic and intellectual mobility, both Sammler and Eisen have taken on the freedom of the international post-Enlightenment elite. Emotionally this freedom reaches a new level in the hands of Sammler's youthful relatives; devoid of notions of history or responsibility, for them the Other has lost its taboo status. Their thrill-seeking, voyeuristic attitude propels a confrontation with the thief. Feffer, through his photography, focuses the scientific eye on the thief not out of rationalist investigation but for his own material benefit and self-aggrandizement, the final extension of the privileging of self characteristic of the Enlightenment, intensified and externalized in capitalist, consumer-oriented America. The thief becomes a commodity to be framed, packaged, and sold to *Look*, the magazine for the curious eyes of the masses. The naive Feffer ignores the lesson of his own contemporary history—which has witnessed Civil Rights marches and Black nationalism—that African Americans are not passive objects, a reality that emerges in the thief's assault on Feffer.

Yet Black power proves stronger in rhetoric than in fact. Despite the Civil Rights movement African Americans remain largely segregated, disadvantaged, at the mercy of dominant culture. Finally the Other, whose mysterious strength seems to increase until the novel's climax, is revealed as helpless before the forces that created it. If commercial media control the commodity of blackness in its various, mythologized versions, so state power physically controls Black people through intimidation and, when necessary, violence. The scene of violence between Black and Jew, in *The Tenants* one of ceaseless conflict between equal adversaries, here is mediated by the watching crowd, by a larger society prepared to intervene. The Black thief is revealed from the beginning as outnumbered, an object of the public gaze, which stares in fascination at the violence of the primitive. This is a violence that the larger American public has created through systematic oppression, and in which it voyeuristically participates. At the scene of assault the state, though well equipped to prevent and punish violence, doesn't need to intervene. Eisen, once an object of the ultimate state terror, now himself undertakes the job of legitimized violence, of containing the Other. Sammler, by contrast, feels helpless: "extremely foreign—voice, accent, syntax, manner, face, mind, everything, foreign" (287). Psychologically he returns to the outsiderhood that the Nazis had imposed upon him, sharing with the Black the status of victim. The conscience of the diaspora Jew contests the muscle Jew. When he realizes the coming brutality Sammler intervenes:, "Don't hit him Eisen. I never said that. I tell you no!" (291). More than the helpless diaspora Jew, Sammler chooses—from a position offering real choice—against violence. As the pickpocket lies bleeding on the asphalt, Eisen replies to Sammler's objections, "You can't hit a man like this just once. When you hit him you must really hit him. Otherwise he'll kill you. You know. We both fought in the war" (291). The warrior Jew, the Jew remade as violent enforcer, is compelled to savagery. Sammler, who exhibited the warrior mentality when fighting the Nazis, proves unwilling to do so as an agent of majority power. If in the Holocaust Jews are devoid of choice regarding their dehumanization—able to choose only passive death or, in a few cases, brutal violence—Eisen and Sammler are now able to make a broader moral choice. By actively opposing Eisen Sammler renounces his wartime self, the partisan of the Polish forest who joyfully slaughtered a German soldier. He has chosen the inheritance of the diaspora Jew: nonviolence when possible.

In the America of *Mr. Sammler's Planet*, Jews no longer occupy the position of outsider; it is African Americans who are the marginalized, victimized presence. As Feffer and the thief, Jew and Black, battle for power, the outsiders watching and debating are largely Jewish. Jews are now the privileged, observing the spectacle of the Dark Other, deciding his fate. Jewish thoughts, emotions, and motivations are the focus here. The primitive Black figure begets violence by the Israeli Eisen, the warrior Jew. Only in defeat is the Black humanized, displayed for the watching crowd as an object of sympathy as he "bled thickly on the asphalt" (291). A flicker of the common past emerges in the figure of the Other surrounded and bleeding, the Other who was once the Jew.

Eisen's speech—"When you hit him you must really hit him"—reveals the dilemma of Israel, of national conflict driven by desperation, resulting in cycles of brutality. The Jewish situation relative to African Americans provides an oblique commentary on that of Israel. On the one hand, guilt generated by the Arab-Israeli conflict becomes a mechanism of humanization that applies toward the Black thief. On the other hand, the thief remains exteriorized, a mechanism, an object for reflecting Jewish concerns. The absence of African American society in *Mr. Sammler's*

Planet leaves the thief an empty sign of blackness, a symbol that can only preserve conventional stereotypes. Though humanized by his final vulnerability he is, throughout the novel, an emblem of exotic excitement, of primeval fear, and finally of Jewish guilt. Jewish history, the mechanism driving Sammler to nonviolence and pity, provides only a brief, problematic connection to the thief. The meaning of Jewish suffering and marginalization as it relates to moral choice, to American identity, remains unresolved. The American Jewish community, poised between a history of ghettoization and comfortable assimilation, a hitherto almost unimaginable fulfillment of the American dream, seems to face diminishing reason to care about another ghettoized people. Although the Jewish past continues to shape Jewish perceptions and reactions, almost imperceptibly history fades and so too, perhaps, does the meaning of the term "Jewish American," now not just physically but culturally difficult to separate from "White" America.

III

Ideals of progress, both social and literary, are belied by the tribal divisions in both *The Tenants* and *Mr. Sammler's Planet*. If one considers literary dialogism as a process evolving toward increased understanding and respect, Black and Jewish literature of the late 1960s and early '70s is a step backwards. Rather than incorporating other voices in a dynamic, interactive language, these texts seem to reincorporate old stereotypes. Reinscribed within the framework of ethnic American history, however, these images take on subtle new meanings; they grapple with understanding one's own past through the lens of another ethnic group. Further, they mark the end of an artificial universalism that ignores real historical and economic differences. They are an unpleasant, but probably necessary and certainly fascinating, stage in uncovering suppressed anxieties. Trauma and ancient tribal hatreds seem more deeply engraved in the human psyche than a simple version of dialectic progress can account for. Black nationalist eruptions and the reaction against them mark a violent closure to a period of somewhat illusory idealism. The dire warnings inherent in these works simultaneously plead for understanding and change.

    Whatever hopefulness may have remained, the rhetorical excess of Baraka and Giovanni, and the symbolically heightened reactions of Malamud and Bellow, stem from a perception of previously unacknowledged differences. For Jews this divergence has meant a questioning, and inevitable compromise, with an idealistic picture of American pluralism. As Jews incorporate comfortably into America, historical memory increasingly conflicts with social and economic status. The differences come to overpower the similarities, making affinities with Blacks seem increasingly unaccountable. A flattened version of Black nationalist assertiveness may serve as a new container for old stereotypes. At the same time blackness is a persistent reminder of past Jewish marginalization. The Jewish model of American minorities working together in harmony, equal yet distinctive (though perhaps with Jews first among equals), is disrupted by the continued existence of a Black underclass. Racial stereotypes linger in the collective (un)conscious, waiting to be revived by Blacks frustrated by continuing oppression, and by Jews anxious to define themselves as mainstream Americans. The mutual sting of racism and anti-Semitism is especially hurtful to minorities who have been repeatedly maligned and who now hear these slanders from the lips and pens of a group with whom they had felt kinship. Hence the decade of the 1960s, which began with shared struggle and visions of harmony, ended in bitter acrimony.

Aftermaths

*Nationalism, Internationalism,
and Diversity*

The simplistic images associated with Black nationalism and the reaction against it provide a crude, if necessary, framework to begin examining literature in the aftermath of the 1960s. The range of responses to this framework, however, was complex and variegated. Certainly, Black nationalism was a palliative against self-hatred, against a vision of Blacks as an unformed people waiting to be swallowed up by a greater civilization. However, ethnic pride does not preclude a larger imagination, a conglomeration of many particularities, including an identification as American—as part of a rich polyglot culture—as well as a global awareness. Many proponents of Black nationalism moved toward believing in "third world" solidarity, in socialism, in multiculturalism, in new versions of democracy—in a variety of movements neither particular nor local. Isolationism may be one manifestation of Black nationalism, yet it is often temporary and contingent. So Joyce Ladner argues that "Black nationalism is *not* a racist ideology with separatist overtones . . . but simply a move toward independence from the dominant group" (1971, 206). Black nationalism is a necessary phenomenon, but one connected to other movements and identities. If history propelled African Americans toward a separatist consciousness, history has also placed them in a situation in which isolationism is impossible, in which they are inextricably bound up in a larger society and culture. A complex archaeology defines the history of

African American literature, much of which combines rich portraits of Black society with a multicultural, internationalist sense. And nowhere has this been more true than in the aftermath of the 1960s.

An identification as one of several connected ethnic groups has been true, to varying degrees, throughout African American history. During the 1960s a number of Black poets explicitly identified with Jews. James A. Randall Jr. gazes at a Jewish figure with an oppressive history clinging to him: "One would think that the will/ To be free had never lodged / In his bones" (1971, 278). In this figure Randall "saw myself," saw the psychological slavery weighing down both Jew and Black, sapping their humanity. Robert Hayden, too, explores parallels between Blacks and Jews, including an elegy to a concentration camp in "Belsen, Day of Liberation" and a memory of Jewish friends in "The Rabbi." The latter, though, ends on a note of alienation with the words, "The rabbi bore my friends off / in his prayer shawl" (1985, 9). "Witch Doctor" features a Black church deeply inflected with Jewish symbolism, including "ragtime allegros of a 'Song of Zion'" where the sermon preaches to "Israelites, true Jews, O found lost tribe" (35). Cultural hybridity is implicit here, yet so is Black self-identification as the "true Jews," prefiguring Black Muslim claims. Hayden cannot help but be tinged with a Black nationalism in many ways alien to his sensibilities. Identification with various groups, from Jews to pan-Africans to "third world" peoples, refers back to personal and social histories, to the experience of blackness. History, tough and tangled, twists like a vine through and around these writers; history connects them to other peoples, and roots them in ancestral experience. The identity articulated by Black nationalism runs, to varying extents, through virtually all African American writers. In the aftermath of the 1960s, this identity was ubiquitous.

I

Paule Marshall's work implicitly critiques White supremacy and the psychological dilemma it poses for Blacks. In her fiction elements of Black nationalism interact and compete with a lingering liberalism decentered from Europe. In *The Chosen Place, the Timeless People* (1969) this friction provides a powerful basis for portrayal of a Jewish character in full, human complexity against a backdrop of suppressed Africanist identity. If Selina Boyce in *Brown Girl, Brownstones* uses a Jewish role model to spur her search for identity, and Miss Williams in "Brooklyn" defines herself against the retrograde Max Berman, *The Chosen Place, the Timeless People* consolidates these figures. The Jewish anthropologist Saul Amron serves as intermediary for a Black woman, Merle Kinbona, to develop and articulate her historical consciousness. Amron, like Berman, is an ambivalent, isolated character; unlike Berman he persists stubbornly in working toward his vision of a better humanity. Saul Amron is resilient, aware of his past and of historical parallels between Jews and Blacks. On a small Caribbean island he leads a modernization project humanitarian in its attempt to alleviate poverty yet moribund in its dependence on Western institutional assumptions. After a major career failure Amron, in contrast to Berman, has returned to try again. It is as though in the charged atmosphere of the late 1960s Marshall sees new hope for Black-Jewish cooperation.

Positioned between an enslaved past and an attempt at modernization under difficult circumstances, Bourne Island remains frozen in strict social hierarchy. The Middle Passage, the traumatic origin of history for the African diaspora, provides the ur-event for this milieu. Saul Amron and Merle Kinbona gaze over the Atlantic at "the nine million and more, it is said, who in their enforced exile, their Diaspora, had gone down between this point and the homeland lying out of sight to the east" (Marshall 1992, 106). The Holocaust parallel is implicit as Jew and Black stare at the watery grave. The Atlantic becomes a memorial to the dead, to the vanished African past scarcely mentioned, but always present, in the novel. What is left is the Middle Passage: "chains—like those to an anchor— rattling in the deep holds of ships, and exile in an unknown inhospitable land—an exile bitter and irreversible in which all memory of the former life and of the self as it had once been had been destroyed" (282). If the Jewish communities of Europe were literally burned up in the Holocaust, a host of artists and institutions have kept their memory alive. African American remembrance of Africa is more tenuous, more distanced, while the Middle Passage lacks the institutional structure that has been developed to memorialize the Holocaust.[1] In connecting the Holocaust and the Middle Passage, Marshall strives to augment historical memory of the latter.

Colonial oppression continues to define the present through Bourne Island's rigid social and racial hierarchy. Whites based overseas have highest status; they have the leisure, education, and most of all the capital to come and go, to extend charity to Bourne Island as they please. Next on the hierarchy are the largely light-skinned wealthier classes who form the island's government; and finally there are the poor Blacks in the impoverished

Bournehills. For the people of Bournehills White men remain distant and invisible sources of power. Their discontented agent is Saul Amron, the Jewish middleman, dislocated from his own history, striving to balance their aims, his own, and those of Bournehills's people.

Bournehills appears as a postcolonial zone devoid of history, a timeless place that seems anything but chosen. Symbolically Bournehills is either a haven or a retreat from the great outside world, either a cosmic center or an isolated backwater. Although its people seem distant from the biblical Chosen People, like the Jews they preserve their traditional ways under harsh circumstances and look to a heroic past memorializing an old slave revolt led by a Moses figure who (due to insurmountable odds) failed to lead his people to freedom. Still, the people of Bournehills romanticize this revolt: "We was a people then, man; and it was beautiful to see" (139). This memory is more ephemeral, and hence more desperate, than is Jewish identity with its stable, central source. From historical fragments an idyllic past is formulated, a protonationalist legend blending elements of tribal and "third world" socialist myths. The tale is biblical in a grand sense: there has been a redemption and a fall; Bournehills seems timeless in its apathetic squalor, yet its people envision an Edenic future.

Such a future seems improbable on an island stubbornly unchanging. Modernization programs supported by American philanthropy repeatedly fail, due partly to the shortsightedness of the programs' organizers and partly to the inflexibility of a people set in their ways. Black resistance to outside (postcolonial) patronage is inherent in this situation. The need for national identity and the need for modernization seem to converge via the person of Saul Amron. To the timeless traditions of Bourne Island, Saul appears as an irritant, a Jewish professor seemingly atop the hierarchy yet strangely outside of it, more responsive than most outsiders to the islanders' need for autonomy, for a say in their economic future. Saul's sensitivity, the novel implies, is largely due to his status as a Jew, a people also persecuted, also caught between tradition and assimilation.[2] Saul himself explains: "I didn't choose anthropology simply as an escape hatch, even though that's often said of us [Jews]. But then we're not only the butt of many a joke but a convenient symbol, it seems, of Western man's alienation and disaffection" (321). Jews, linked to the West and the Enlightenment, are also perennial outsiders, a people "fleeting, mobilized, emigrating, and turned into nomads" (Deleuze and Guattari 1986, 25), a diasporic status shared by the international African community. Saul Amron's role as a middleman, as the articulator of diasporic identity, is passed on to

Merle Kinbona. In a century marked by cries of alienation, of existential aloneness, Jewishness and Africanness stand as fulcrums between radically different societies.

Saul's family history enacts this nomadic middle position. Sephardic blood links him to the Jews of Spain and North Africa with their darker coloring, and hence symbolically to the people of Bournehills with their African ancestry. His mother claims a literal link, telling of an ancient family odyssey through South America and the Caribbean, and makes the unsubstantiated claim that there are "tombstones bearing the family name on the island of Jamaica" (Marshall 1992, 164).[3] Saul's international roots/ routes seem to connect him to Bournehills, yet the link remains problematic. The travels and travails of his family are symptomatic of the Jewish experience of a three-thousand-year exile leading to the Nazis. In a century of massive death, of two world wars and the advent of nuclear weapons, Saul binds himself to the Holocaust at a visit to the death camps, where he meets his first wife. At the site of death he encounters love, hope for the future, for regeneration of a lost people. If Saul in his personal life never resolves this terrible history, Merle Kinbona faces a similar situation with her failed marriage. Like Saul she returns to the site of her previous failure. Her concluding journey to Africa is an attempt to reclaim not only her husband and child but herself from historical oblivion; the outcome, however, is left unresolved.

For both Saul and Merle the encounter with history produces a struggle to balance ancestral memory with contemporary political disenfranchisement. While avoiding the faults of previous attempts to impose modern technological solutions, Saul alters a pattern of dependency on outside sources and revitalizes the spirit of the old slave revolt (405). Saul tells Merle that history, both the good and the bad, must be transmuted; people "who've truly been wronged—like yours, like mine all those thousands of years—must at some point, if they mean to come into their own, start using their history to their advantage" (315). The past, including all its suffering, becomes a usable resource to build toward a future. Saul Amron's historical philosophy, together with his attention to local culture, prefigures current theories of multiculturalism.

This philosophy, despite its glimmer of hopefulness, ends in at least momentary failure. Dominant hegemony proves too powerful, particularly given Saul's historical and psychological ambivalence. Saul has already failed in his early anthropological work and in his marriage. The young Saul is another version of Max Berman, torn between cultures and places, shorn of identity. Both are called upon, despite their own ambivalence, to act as authority figures, as those anointed to lead, judge, and guide; yet both prove unfit for reconstituting the White male patriarchy according to a new idealism. The ideal of Westernization, of a final, modern, techno-logical society in which everyone is clean and safe and happy, cannot be devised by these psychically divided human beings, particularly in the face of a postcolonial capitalism that undermines its own promises. In his ambition to resuscitate stagnant cultures, Saul Amron worries "that I'm out to play God on a minor scale by thinking I can come into a place and do so much" (321). He is underprepared for the role of rebuilding amidst a postcolonial mental struggle. Just as Saul is finally unable to link West with South, first world with third, European with African, modern with traditional, so Jews in *The Chosen Place, the Timeless People* are ulti-mately problematic in their role as sympathetic facilitators.

The strangely unresolved role of the Jew, the position of the in-be-tween, is passed on to the character of Merle Kinbona, described by John McCluskey Jr. as "the bridge between the West, symbolized by the Amrons, and Africa, represented by the peasants of Bournehills" (1984, 327). Merle and Saul are sympathetic doubles, both poised between dominant and minority cultures, both struggling to use their position to aid the oppressed, both doomed to impotence in this effort. Their love affair parallels the Jewish-Black alliance; they are fated to split, to pursue their own roles and histories. Merle, the mixed-blood child of a wealthy white landowner, despite her elite English education has not acceded to dominant cultural myths. She is the strongest voice for Bourne Island itself. Like Merle the island is a multicultural entity, a product of international motion and cross-pollination. Merle's tangled history parallels Saul's, that of the wandering international figure; after long journeys both have come to Bournehills. Merle wears a wild pastiche of fashion choices, costumes and jewelry from myriad societies (Marshall 1992, 4); her multitextured history is ostentatiously displayed upon her body. Europe, Africa, and the West Indies meet in her person, though whether she wears them or is bound by them—a slave of historical and personal circumstance—is unclear. Her costume is drenched in postcolonial ambivalence, with "each item . . . opposed to, at war even, with the other, to express a diversity and disunity within herself" (5). Her life philosophy similarly is a bricolage, a "third world" socialism, an internationalist nationalism attempting to unify a mass of peoples while maintaining their unique ethnic identities. Like her cos-tume her opinions are overt, pouring forth in an unending flow. She speaks for the poor of Bournehills through the voice of the educated. Her status and its relationship to Saul is most evident when she exclaims "I'm a Jew too" (317). She explains this as metaphorical, as identification with all peoples and religions (317), yet it reflects also their parallel wandering, their tangled histories, their disarrayed psyches. More than this her philosophy, like Saul's, is to take matters into one's own hands. She belongs to an educated elite wedded to a specific culture and tradition yet also transcending it. Given Saul's ultimate failure, she takes on the role of the cosmopolitan international Jew, albeit for a territory more appropriate to her heritage.

Merle's affair with Saul, in glaring contrast to Miss Williams's rejection of Berman, consummates their historical resemblance, engendering a new phase in the fight of those characterized as Other. The imperative for universal (implicitly Eurocentric) standards gives way to a struggle for cultural recognition. To Saul, Merle is perhaps an exotic Other but certainly a political ally. In both his disastrous marriages Saul proves unfit for the role of guiding Jewish patriarch. He has not resolved the intricate challenge of maintaining the past in a postcolonial world that demands constant innovation. *The Chosen Place, the Timeless People* concludes with resignation. "After Bournehills," Saul muses, "there aren't any places left for me to go" (467). Under the shadow of assimilation, Jewish liberalism has exhausted itself. Yet unlike Max Berman, Saul Amron consummates his relation with a Black woman and does so in a situation of relatively equal status, their brief affair intimating a common purpose. It is up to the educated, articulate Merle Kinbona to carry on: "I'll be coming back to Bournehills. This is home" (468). As the 1960s wanes so does the Jewish voice, leaving a pan-Africanist, and internationalist, voice as vanguard of expression for the marginalized and exploited.

II

An author difficult to classify, who combines a sympathy for Jewish Americans with Black nationalist inclinations, is John A. Williams. His connection to Africa (Muller 1984, 32–33) and his critique of Martin Luther King's philosophy of nonviolence, particularly in the book *The King God Didn't Save*, link him to Black nationalism. Yet Williams differs from Black Arts writers in his open affinity for Jewish Americans, in his long-standing concern with Israel, and in his awareness of African Americans as quintessentially American. So he states that Blacks and Whites are "intertwined here and now. The challenge is to really look and see how much" (1964, 161). Williams adds that "I have been to Africa and know that it is not my home. America is; it is my country too, and has been for generations" (169). Despite Williams's cynicism, a cry for a harmonious multicultural America emerges in much of his work.

Williams's deep split between a bitter cynicism regarding what America has been and a desperate hope for what its multicultural richness suggest it might become is evident in two of his novels dealing with relations between Blacks and Jews. In the Jewish experience of assimilation and divided consciousness, and in the cultural enrichment that Jews have brought to America, Williams reflects upon the Black experience. *The Man Who Cried I Am* (1967) briefly depicts the aid and friendship of a Jewish literary critic for a Black writer, and reflects upon parallels between the Holocaust and the African American situation. *!Click Song*, written in 1982, is in part a reflection upon the 1960s, an emotional time remembered in a kind of bitter tranquility. Largely autobiographical, yet including flourishes of morbid hyperfictional excess, these works reflect the turbulence of the 1960s and the wrenching changes in Black-Jewish relations.

The protagonist of *The Man Who Cried I Am*, Max Reddick, benefits from the Jewish intellectual and literary critic Bernard Zutkin.[4] Zutkin emphasizes the mutual dangers faced by Jews and Blacks: "We need each other," he tells Reddick (294). The connection is both spiritual and practical, for White supremacy threatens both peoples, necessitating an alliance for which the ultimate symbol of danger is the Holocaust. Like Merle Kinbona, Reddick uses Jewish patronage as a stepping-stone in developing his own hard-edged identity and historical perspective. Still, he must fight incessantly the tokenism inflicted upon his writing.

The marginalization of Black writers may be increased by the need to prove one's ability against the backdrop of European tradition in which White skin and literary talent have long been implicitly linked. Writing in a period in which there was often only one widely recognized African American writer, Williams has decried the limitations of tokenism. *The Man Who Cried I Am* extends this complaint, depicting Black literary success as decided not by talent but circumstance, as a matter of having the right patron. The patrons depicted come from two groups often shunned by mainstream society, yet positioned to take advantage of Whiteskin privilege: Jews and homosexuals. Reddick constructs an absolute dichotomy: "one was either in the Bryant camp or the Zutkin camp" (Williams 1967, 39). Similarly, in *Reckless Eyeballing* (1986), Ishmael Reed posits Black literary success as a result of position and patronage, though Reed's binary patronage groups are Jews and White feminists. Tellingly, both Williams and Reed portray Jews as ultimately sympathetic, honorable allies, while reducing homosexuals and White feminists, respectively, to the hypocritical, self-serving role often ascribed to Jews.

In Williams, Black and Jewish identifications occur through the medium of the Holocaust, associated with the horrors of African American slavery and foreboding the possibility of a future genocide. At the personal level the Holocaust is dramatized in the person of Reddick's friend and occasional lover:

> Regina Galbraith (formerly Goldberg) had been the sole member of her family spirited out of Nazi Germany. The rest were dead. Gassed and cooked, most likely. From what she'd told him, they were nice people, willing to please everyone, more German than Jewish. (1967, 161)

The latter statement parallels Baraka's concern with assimilation, the danger of losing one's identity—and one's life—amid an alien soil. Galbraith's suicidal depression is the result of trauma, of a history continually relived in the individual psyche. The past haunts the present; Black America maintains the psychological heritage of slavery and racism. Painting a larger historical panorama, Williams recounts a history of blood and slaughter wherein Reddick, "whether in America, Europe, or Africa . . . is haunted by 'faces out of nightmares,' as Bernard Zutkin terms them, by a civilization capable of genocide" (Muller 1984, 82). In a nightmare reflection upon history, Williams further connects the Armenian genocide, Hebrew slavery, the Crusades, the African slave trade, the war on communism, and Hiroshima, climaxing with "human lampshades, Zyklon B, cakes of soap made from human fats" (1967, 68). This passage begins and ends with the Holocaust, making of it the central symbol in a single history of oppression and slaughter.

Williams evidently felt his naturalistic, partially autobiographic writing to be insufficient in portraying the incessant repetition of historical disaster. In its conclusion, *The Man Who Cried I Am* connects past genocide with a potential future by leaping into another genre, a horrendous version of escapist thrillers, depicting a secret government plan to subdue Black America in the event of widespread rioting. Ending in a ghoulish suggestion of "vaporization techniques" (376) this blueprint serves as a dire warning of a future Holocaust visited upon Black Americans (a possibility also explored by Black Arts poets). The only protection from this threat may lie in a militant nationalism. In the Williams cosmology African Americans must be vocal, vigilant, and well armed to prevent a new Holocaust on American soil.

If, in Williams, the Holocaust acts as the ultimate symbol of minority vulnerability, and hence connects Blacks and Jews, adoption of dominant stereotypes may conversely serve to drive oppressed groups apart. Psychologically emasculated Black men may make Jews, women, and/or homosexuals objects of a hatred employed to mask pain and vulnerability. Such projections occur, in varying manifestations and to varying degrees, in writers including Chester Himes, John Williams, Amiri Baraka, and Ishmael Reed. In *The Man Who Cried I Am* one object of scorn and frustration is the homosexual literary agent Granville Bryant. The homosexual here takes on the recurrent Jewish role of scapegoat. Yet, like many Jews in African American fiction, Bryant is an ambiguous figure, given a degree of sympathy through narrative identification.

In an extended description, through the mouthpiece of Granville Bryant, Williams makes of homosexuals the ultimate aliens, stranded on earth after a spaceship crash:

> Looking very much like humans, they mixed with the populace without attracting attention to themselves. Being of superior natures, they soon mastered the skills of the earthmen, then went on to become their betters. They could tell their own from an arch of the brow, a vocal inflection, a bend of the wrist, the pelvic walk. (189)

Bryant attempts to wrest the narrative of homosexuals away from a heterocentric society that has narrated them as dysfunctional, as misfits and perverts. He does so through the medium of science fiction, a strand of American popular culture that normalizes the alien and exotic. Simultaneously he speaks to the outsider status of Blacks, to a shared mistreatment. As with Jews, homosexual exclusion leads to the role of intermediary between Blacks and dominant society, to an appeal for solidarity. Indeed, much of Bryant's description fits Jewish stereotypes: "Slowly, over the centuries, they came to control many of man's efforts on earth, but they did it secretly. They were laughed at, hated, legislated against, harassed, made vulnerable" (189). For the mythic Jewish conspiracy is substituted a homosexual conspiracy. Yet this description is at least partly applicable to assimilating Jews, whose status may lead to secrecy in public, an unmentionable shame within mainstream America yet also a kind of secret club, a solidarity characterized by group success in business and the arts.

Paradoxically, the thrust of *The Man Who Cried I Am* ignores the implications of this passage. If Bryant appeals to a shared alienation, Reddick's reaction to his narrative is scorn: "You don't understand *nuthin'* Max was thinking" (190). Bryant has always slighted Max, instead supporting a homosexual Black writer, a thinly veiled version of James Baldwin, whom the novel treats with scorn as a backbiting opportunist (217). Homosexual outreach to African Americans, like Jewish patronage, often spurs resentment, particularly among those unsure of their masculinity. The defensiveness of Chester Himes regarding Jewish effeminacy is apparent also in Reddick's reaction to the homosexual Bryant. The threat to African American masculinity enters the inner psyche, a state symbolized by Reddick's rectal cancer. Like a homosexual he is anally penetrated, eaten away. In many African Americans a history of hatred is internalized. The question is to what extent, and what combination of forms it will take: hatred of Whites, of women, of Jews, of Blacks, of homosexuals, and almost always of self.

While hatred and paranoia continue to eat away at the characters in John Williams's *!Click Song* (1982), they are tempered by a spirit of reconciliation. The role of the ethnic American writer is represented by two contrasting characters: Cato Douglass, the African American protagonist, and his foil, Paul Cummings, who reprises and intensifies the character of the ambivalent Jew adrift between cultures. An additional pair of characters enact binary roles: the protagonist's wife, Allis, is the compassionate, nurturing Jew, while her father personifies the racist Jew. Significantly, the younger generation Jew is the sympathetic one, a portrayal that reflects both the spirit of the 1960s, which the novel recalls, and Williams's overall identification with Jewish Americans.

The driving force behind Douglass and Cummings's changing relationship is the tumult of the 1960s, particularly regarding ethnic and racial identity. Working on a television documentary on Civil Rights movement protests, Douglass travels South with a Jewish cameraman, who "remember[s] a Germany of shattered glass and night visitors, of populations that later claimed not to know what went on in those camps outside their towns" (Williams 1982, 127). The turmoil of Nazi Germany is replayed in the violence of the racist South. By contrast with Germany, however, these oppressed people actively fight victimization. To avoid a repeat of the horrors that were visited upon a passive and scared minority group, Jewish volunteers stand beside African Americans.

If the need for action is a recurring theme in Williams, in *!Click Song* the opposite is embodied in Paul Cummings, who initially displays the silent, desperate need to fit into society earlier characteristic of German Jews. His drive to assimilate dominates any need for ethnic identity. As in

The Man Who Cried I Am ethnic writers—such as Cummings and Douglass—succeed or fail not due to talent, but to the vicissitudes of the literary establishment. *!Click Song* emphasizes the restrictions long placed upon Black authors: the lack of opportunity; the restriction to protest literature; the tokenism that admits only one predominant Black author at a time, and compares Black authors only with each other. Douglass reflects, "[W]e all knew this and talked about it among ourselves, compared idiocies and idiots, when we could gather without the hostility such knowledge engenders. Yet none of us dared say it aloud" (180).

Compared to Blacks, Jewish American writers have had great freedom of opportunity. They may be judged simply as White, or may display their ethnic background; they may employ a variety of voices and postures. Williams himself explains Cummings's ability to move effortlessly between societies (Muller 1984, 143–44). Although Cummings capitalizes upon this mobility, his freedom is somewhat illusory, for his career is channeled by external social forces. Rather than a universal man able to leap identities—to transcend place and time—Cummings acts as cipher reacting to social expectations. It is ideology, rather than Cummings, that is particularly flexible for a Jewish American writer of the 1960s. Given Cummings's internal emptiness, it is not so surprising that, despite his literary success, he commits suicide. Unlike Cato Douglass—whether due to individual strength or the adoption of a strong Black identity—Cummings is unable to survive dominant expectations during a time of radical change, to create a consciousness and independence that maintains some psychological integrity.

Cummings begins the novel as a repressed Jew ashamed of his background. Douglass states, "[S]ometimes Paul puzzled me: Was he for or against Jews? There was much news about the death camps in Europe" (Williams 1982, 19). Rather than supporting his fellow Jews, Cummings maintains an embarrassed silence, a common immediate reaction for American Jews, as though hiding their status will save them from the fate of Europe's Jews. Cummings later explains: "Other kids played ball on Saturdays; not us. I tried to hide my yarmulka; our parents spoke Yiddish and English with an accent" (184). Unlike a dark skin, a Jewish background may be camouflaged. Yet camouflage tempts avoidance of social issues, while a blatant racial status may forge psychological strength. About Cummings's attitude Douglass reflects: "I had never supposed that the bigotry in the United States was devastating enough to make a Jew want to pass forever as a Gentile" (182). Cummings is a plastic figure, anxious to bend to the demands of dominant society, an ultimate version of a subject who has lost his subjectivity and been reduced to a shifting intersection of social expectations. His Jewishness is determined from without, from the evolving status of Jews in American society.

Although his malleability, his chameleon identity, may begin from vulnerability and proceed through cowardice, it acts as de facto opportunism. Cummings passes for White when it suits him, and metamorphoses into a Jew when Jewish literature becomes popular. As Douglass's wife ironically remarks, "Maybe it's a smart thing to be a Jewish writer these days, darling" (187). The reviewers of Cummings's breakthrough Jewish novel praise "his fine sensibilities, his courage in baring his soul" (205), missing the fact that the novel could easily be explained as jumping on a bandwagon, choosing the path of least resistance. The book is marketed and criticized as an ethnic, not an aesthetic, product. Paradoxically, the Cummings who denies his Jewishness marries two Jewish women, while the explicitly Jewish Cummings marries a gentile. Yet this is not so paradoxical, for a White, gentile wife is a status symbol, and Jewishness has become a symbol of literary success. The fact of Cummings's Jewishness finally allows his escape from the marginalization traditionally associated with Jewishness.

!Click Song is sprinkled liberally with references to Jewish literary figures—Bellow and Mailer and Malamud—which act as both symbols of successful ethnic writers and bitter tokens of the exclusion of Black writers. The flip side to Cummings's success is Douglass's crash, coinciding with the changing marketability of his race. Unlike Cummings, Douglass has acknowledged his background from the start, writing passionately of the African American experience (while positing this as a window on universal themes). To Cummings's success as a Jewish writer is added another ironic, painful contrast to Douglass: Cummings's commercial and critical success in writing about African American life. Douglass reflects that Cummings, despite his friendship with Black authors, "had missed our essences, capturing instead, unlike some of the others, the Mau-Mau, the Panther, the militant, the revolutionary, the supercock" (280). Besides appropriating and profiting from the Black experience, Cummings has gotten it wrong, resorting to stereotypes. Both art and personal friendship have failed to nullify assumptions rooted deep within the collective social and psychological consciousness. African American life is reduced to an arena for exploring White fantasies of primal adventure. Douglass criticizes "White writers [who] were always running off to Africa, literally and fictionally, to mine for gold" (280), a reference at least partially to Bellow's *Henderson the Rain King*. When a

privileged existence offers ennui, which becomes a tiresome literary theme, Black exoticism is called upon to add voyeuristic excitement.

In the frivolous, apolitical 1980s, Douglass is repeatedly told to avoid Black literature, that serious social themes no longer sell. Rising and falling in popularity, appropriating each other's themes, Black and Jewish literature have performed an intricate dance. Cummings's popularity depends upon cultivating a colorful, uplifting version of ethnicity that skirts the horrors of racial marginalization:

> [I]llusion could only persist, *insist*, if one caused the reality to be absent.
>   I was Paul's reality, finally, and who ever wants much to do with that?
>   And he, goddamn it, was mine. (332)

Black and Jewish literature reinforce each other in projecting a simulacrum of ethnicity onto American life. Yet intermixed with phantasmic constructions are actualities; a Black revolutionary or a basketball player both produce a myth and live it, inspiring future generations, as does a Jewish intellectual or businessman. And ethnic groups exist along a spectrum of expectations, alternatively reinforcing and displacing each other. As Blacks flowed into the Northern ghettos Jews flowed outward. Explicitly Jewish writing creates a space for explicitly Black writing, which in turn displaces it as the predominant ethnic literature. In literature, politics, social status, and self-perception, Black and Jewish fates have been linked in America in a kind of codependency wherein each group watches the other for clues to its own status.

If Cummings is one Jewish figure against whom Douglass measures his fate, a far more sympathetic one is his wife, Allis. Her role is one traditional to women and occasional to Jews in literature: provider of sympathy. She sustains Douglass in his personal life and career, and nurtures his children. Having lost family in Nazi concentration camps (200), Allis is a prototypical figure of Jewish suffering and compassion. In a moment of solidarity with Douglass and his son by an earlier marriage, Allis declares: "*I* am not white; I'm a Jew" (154), a similar figure of dispossession. Together, these survivors of historical disaster strive to transcend history; at the scene of their marriage, a friend considers them "terribly in love, awfully courageous, and the parents of the new world the sixties were creating" (154). Williams glimpses themes of a cultural hybridity transcending past hatreds, a new generation creating a new world.

Allis's pure goodness is balanced by the racism of her father, who cannot abide a Black son-in-law; he avoids her wedding and shuns Douglass. Douglass wonders, "[W]ho *was* he, with the grime of Ellis Island embedded still in the creases of his being, to jar *my* life, to fuck up the head and heart of my wife, who had been his daughter?" (231). Literally, this refers to the Jewish status as recent immigrants, in contrast to Blacks, who have been in America for centuries; symbolically, it protests the absurdity of racism in a people who have long been victims of racial hatred. Though the father's racism is unexplored, its wellspring may be that same fear of difference, the need to fit into American society, which debilitates Cummings. In overcoming this fear to live out an American myth of harmonious difference, Allis represents an ideal purity, the best part of the Black-Jewish alliance, however frayed and contested it may otherwise be.

Williams's overall sympathy, then, is with Jews, whose history briefly converges with Blacks in the dream of a new America. If Allis's love is one symbol of this connection, another is their son. Only touched upon is his dilemma, that of the hybrid given the implicit gift—and burden—of making a new America (a theme further explored in Grace Paley's "Zagrowsky Tells"). The son complains about being reduced to a symbol: "I know I'm part black and part white, part Jewish and part Gentile, but I really don't want to be part, I just wanna be a whole *me*, okay?" (343). Cultural fragmentation—with all its attendant richness and possibility—is rejected in favor of the ideal of whole self, a member of universal humanity, yet the reader senses that the child will not escape his heritage. *!Click Song*, while gazing back at the frenzied changes of the 1960s, surveys the mixture of stagnation and hope still emanating from that decade. In its glimpse of a new dispensation, even in the midst of pervasive commercialism, the novel retains some optimism. Allis's final poetic dream-prayer to her husband expresses a blending of ancient peoples in an American setting: "He speaks in clicks. I know / his tongue. I !click back to him. / I know the language. It is ours" (430).

III

The bends and curves of hatred—internalized or projected upon a variety of others—lace themselves through Alice Walker's *Meridian*. Yet the novel is ultimately a celebration of the Civil Rights movement that, like *Click! Song*, intimates the possibility of a harmonious, interracial future. Like

Marshall's *The Chosen Place, the Timeless People*, the novel concentrates on individuals in the vanguard of change. Intertwined in all three
novels are the complexities of a Civil Rights movement rooted in a vision
of peace and harmony in juxtaposition with a Black Power movement.
The interaction between nationalism and multiculturalism has been complex and ever changing, sharing a foundational struggle to create an identity based upon a specific history and traditions, yet stressed by the demands
of universalist inclusion. Added to these, in Walker, is a third strand: the
adaptation of a feminist—or, in Walker's phrasing, womanist—perspective. As with Blacks in a society defined by Whites, women who wish to
stress their own identity in a setting defined by men may feel solidarity.
Gender is one element binding the Black Meridian Hill to the White Lynne
Rabinowitz. That is, if Black/White might be read as bipolar elements
driving Lynne and Meridian apart, woman/woman pulls them together.
Such terms would mean little, though, without a common purpose, not
just political but spiritual. Emily Miller Budick defines *Meridian* as a
religious allegory, with the protagonist as a female Christ (1998, 180),
and certainly a religious communion joins Lynne and Meridian. Categories of race and gender, together with a common political purpose, shape
the nature of their relationship, yet a deeper compatibility ultimately binds
their friendship.

A final complicating element is Lynne's Jewishness, which ties her to
Meridian's blackness as an outsider in American society. If Lynne
Rabinowitz, by the example of her life, is paradigmatic of a Jew who,
remembering her own past, struggles for the oppressed, in *Meridian* Jews
who identify primarily with Whites are abundantly present. Lynne's extreme and brutal split with her family is a microcosm of larger social
divisions. Her childhood room features "no black faces, of course. . . .
Not even any really Jewish faces" (Walker 1976, 155). The house is normalized, freed of any vestiges of difference. It is therefore not surprising
that when Lynne takes up with a Black man her mother "screamed without ceasing" (156), a scream less of hatred of Blacks than a denial of her
own difference, a culmination of the Rabinowitz family history. Her father seems the opposite—"always so gentle, so fair"—yet beneath his
calm surface he hides a similar torrent of rage. When Lynne's half-Black
child dies, she reports, "I told him my daughter was dead and he said,
'So's our daughter,' meaning me" (152). Such understated rage may be
more cruel than the mother's screaming. The stress that tears the Rabinowitz family apart is due to a denial of history, a festering wound beneath
a placid surface. For many Americans the coerced denial of ethnicity has

created a great loss. Most likely Lynne's identification with Blacks is a reaction to her zealously assimilationist family, an attempt to heal through introducing an intermediary agency.

Lynne's awkwardness and alienation regarding her ethnic heritage are captured when she enters a Jewish deli in the deep South. When the owners, conscious of her status as a Civil Rights worker living among African Americans, shun her, "they made her conscious, heavily, of her Jewishness, when, in fact, they wanted to make her feel her whiteness" (183). To a Jewish family striving to fit in as Americans Lynne, in her alliance with more blatant outsiders, is a reminder of their own provisional status, that "they were transplanted, as they had always been, to a place where they fit like extra toes on a foot" (184). The deli owners exemplify one Jewish reaction to issues of race: avoid them, as an embarrassment. Lynne chooses the opposite reaction—identification—yet transposes it onto an even more marginalized group. As so often, social and personal relations are channeled by rigid categories, which force Jewish Americans into difficult choices.

In embracing her alienation, rebelling from mainstream American society, Lynne enacts a phenomenon common to second-generation Americans, who wish to retain a heritage their parents have bitterly striven to escape. Lynne does so not through returning to her own family history, but through adopting, and romanticizing, that of African Americans:

> To Lynne, the black people of the South were Art. This she begged forgiveness for and tried to hide, but it was no use. To her eyes, used to Northern suburbs where every house looked sterile and identical even before it was completely built, where even the flowers were uniform . . . the shrubs incapable of strong odor or surprise of shape, and the people usually stamped with the seals of their professions, to her . . . the South, and the black people living there—was Art. The songs, the dances, the food, the speech. (128)

Counterposed to the stereotype of homogenized middle-class suburbs, with all individuality, and history, bleached out of them (satirized in the Pete Seeger song "Little Boxes on the Hillside") is the exotic Black South. While Lynne feels guilty about her sentimentality and reverse stereotyping, Walker has herself described Southern Blacks in a similar fashion: "black women whose spirituality was so intense, so deep, so *unconscious*, that they were themselves unaware of the richness they held" (1994, 39). Walker goes on to celebrate the many manifestations of this spirituality,

not just in oft-praised blues and jazz singers but in the quilting and gar-
dening of Black women. While one might accuse Walker herself of senti-
mentalizing Black women, it seems more truthful to say that every life is
a kind of poem, and that the specific cultural content, the heritage of that
life, provides the form. This poetry, absent in Lynne Rabinowitz's life, is
found by her in the African American cause, and in the people.

Yet if ethnic heritage can convey beauty and spirituality, in the form
of a reductive racial identity it also acts to separate people. In the Deep
South, even in the midst of the Civil Rights movement, Lynne finds a
hatred and divisiveness different in circumstances, but similar in character, to that she experienced in her own family and community. Given the
status of White women as icons of success forbidden to Black men, invasion and penetration becomes one substitute for possession. Tommy Odds,
who assaults Lynne, has been crippled in the freedom struggle and so
becomes a living symbol of both physical and psychological mutilation.
His rape, too, is made ambiguous by just a hint of acquiescence. He plays
upon the worst aspects of the White-Jewish-Black Civil Rights movement axis, the guilt inherent in an unbalanced coalition in which one party
acts from a position of sympathy. Odds plays blatantly upon this guilt:
"You think I'm a cripple? Or is it just that you really don't dig niggers?
Ones darker than your old man?" (Walker 1976, 160). Lynne's reaction to
this brutality reveals the complex emotional state of someone who has
given herself to a people, has come to identify and sympathize with them,
for, understanding his hurt, during the rape she hugs him and kisses his
stub of an arm. The entire passage plays out the most odious aspect of
Black-Jewish relations at the time, of pure anger deflected onto a substitute target who nevertheless feels guilty and puts up no fight. To Odds,
Lynne's lingering empathy is a kind of scorn, a symbol of his need to be
pitied. The abuse of a White woman is enacted as a social statement, a
playing out of the philosophy Eldridge Cleaver propounds in *Soul On
Ice:* "Rape was an insurrectionary act. It delighted me that I was defying
and trampling upon the white man's law, upon his system of values, and
that I was defiling his women" (33).

In inviting his friends to join in the rape Odds makes of Lynne a symbolic object, a representation of White society awaiting revenge. Yet—as
Walker illustrates throughout her work—this cycle of hatred and retribu-
tion is not inevitable; it can be opposed by personal action. Implicitly
criticizing Eldridge's version of Black nationalism, Walker deconstructs
the socially engendered abuse of White women. To Odds's invitation to
"have some of it," Odds's companions react: "It? *It*? . . . What *it* you

talking about? That ain't no *it*, that's Lynne" (162). Despite the power of racial hierarchy, the novel implies, personal agency is possible. Individual conscience and choice may, at times, overcome social brutality, a lesson of the Civil Rights movement. In combination individual choices can change society, an ideal which infuses Walker's work.

Like Meridian, Lynne is a liminal figure, one with no home identity, wandering and rejected by all; she is almost a paradigmatic Jew, like the displaced Jews in Bernard Malamud's short stories. Coming from two worlds, Meridian and Lynne are psychically connected, soul sisters. The boundaries of race and gender are not what create them as such; rather it is the choices they make, intensified by the dramatic presence of the Civil Rights movement. Lynne's romanticization of the Black South fades. "Black folks aren't so special," she says, and Meridian replies that "Maybe . . . the time for being special has passed" (185). Neither Blacks nor Jews are the chosen people; rather, people must choose for themselves, must make moral decisions, or not, as they construct their own lives. Arising out of the Civil Rights era, *Meridian* suggests an ultimate integration: not that the twists of history, the hard facts of race and gender, can ever be discounted, but that the human soul knows no color and may finally be stronger than race.

A New Dispensation

The range of African American portrayals of Jews in the brief period at the end of the 1960s indicates that, while historical conditions shape perceptions, these are arranged and interpreted in a variety of individual ways. Jewish portraits of Blacks, too, vary greatly, from lingering racial mythologizing and countermythologizing to humanist interior portraits. Fear and conflict were not the only Jewish reaction to the Black expressivism that ended the 1960s. After all, Jewish Americans maintain a tradition not just of liberalism but of radicalism. For activists steeped in radical thought, African American life moved beyond an object of study. The Black struggle, Black music and style, and Black thinkers from James Baldwin to C. L. R. James to Angela Davis to Frantz Fanon permeated the worldview of the counterculture. The rhetoric of Black nationalism was forgiven, ignored, or even embraced by Jewish radicals. An alternative set of beliefs was built upon criticism of mainstream society, a renewed version of earlier socialist and antiracist movements. By dialectic and bricolage such thought hints at an eventual synthesis of radicalism and integrationism. If bitterness and despair followed the shortcomings of the Civil Rights era, so too did a revived social vision.

I

Jay Neugeboren's identification with Blacks is evident in his attempts—tellingly unlike those of Bellow and Malamud—to penetrate the veil of

African American life. In his work the increasing accessibility of African American writing is evident. Active in the protests of the 1960s, Neugeboren felt external to American society, claiming that "my way of seeing things, I noticed, came more and more from the Black man's point of view" (1970, 98). If Neugeboren's perspective contrasts starkly with Bellow's, he differs also from Malamud in his outright rejection of American values, an attitude inherited partly from the tradition of Jewish radicalism and partly from the beatniks and their later relatives, the hippies. His social position is related to his attitude toward African Americans, directly in his willingness to critique American society through Black eyes, and indirectly in the implicit linkage between Black and Jewish marginalization.

The arena Neugeboren chooses to display relations between Blacks and Jews is sports, in America a culturally binding force in which the athlete is reified in a heroic fantasy. In Neugeboren's work, as in contemporary America, this usually means Blacks performing while Jews watch. As a spectacle for a surrounding, curious gaze, Black athletic success means a continuation of the minstrel role in which the audience may hoot and insult, releasing their aggressions freed from the constraints of "civilized" daily life. Yet athletic success is also a key point of recognition by American society, one in which African Americans fought long and hard to participate. Paradoxically such success may, in isolation, act to maintain stereotypes of Black physicality.

Into the contested sports realm Neugeboren brings versions of African Americans derived from the rich variety of Black writing available by the 1960s. *Big Man* (1966), which rather crudely portrays an African American consciousness, is actually a version of Richard Wright's *Native Son* transposed to a basketball setting, with Bigger Thomas's crime downsized to fixing college games. Mack Davis's punishment is not the death faced by Bigger Thomas, but banishment from professional sports, a kind of death-in-life. The novel's main events, occurring five years after Davis's fall from grace, correspond to the last section of *Native Son* in which Thomas is judged by a hostile society. Mack Davis, too, has his case articulated by a Jewish intermediary, in his case the sportswriter Ben Rosen, who explains his motivation for helping Davis: "You and the boys like yourself, all doors are closed to you. Like Jews, heh?" (Neugeboren 1966, 99). As with Boris Max, the memory of historical Jewish suffering connects Rosen to Davis while obscuring, in Rosen's mind, the great gap between Blacks and Jews in American society. Rosen translates for a White

audience the reason for Davis's behavior, the double standard of a hypocritical society. Yet like Bigger Thomas, Davis understands more realisti-
cally than his White, Jewish spokesman the entrenched nature of the power
structure: that society cares only for spectacle and will not respond to
revelations of corruption. In *Big Man* a Black center of consciousness is
the agent for exposure of social faults; Jewish marginalization is no longer
powerful enough to be a primary axis of subversion.

Neugeboren's "Elijah" (1969) pulls back from Black consciousness
to render a Jewish perspective; the result is both more sophisticated and
more convincing than *Big Man*. The exteriorized viewpoint may be partly
a reaction to the jolt of Black nationalist rhetoric, engendering a move to
a small fable about Black and Jewish relations. "Elijah" opens with a
group of Hebrew school students gazing upon a Black athlete with a mixture of awe, admiration, and envy, a characteristic scene of Black spectacle and Jewish spectatorship. As these students prepare for a track meet—
the only athletic event at which their school regularly succeeds—they are
outdistanced by the fleet Elijah, who races past them yelling "C'mon
Jewboys." Anti-Semitic slurs pepper the story, yet are presented merely
as boyish taunts. More serious are Elijah's misconception that Jews have
all the money, that they "run everything in this city" (Neugeboren 1969,
184). While this is presented as good-natured ignorance on Elijah's part,
the implications concerning the African American community are ominous. The oral tradition keeps alive what Earl Raab has called a
"generationally transmitted reservoir of cultural anti-semitism" (1969, 21)
and Fanon a collective unconscious, here of anti-Jewish myths. In 1969
Jewish awareness of Black anti-Semitism is newly awakened.

If Elijah is the visible surface, the sign of dangerous anti-Semitic currents, the Jewish community presented here is only affirmative. The coach
lectures that, "as Jewish boys we had a special responsibility to befriend
those others of the world who had suffered as the Jewish people had"
(Neugeboren 1969, 170). Jewish liberalism could not be more plainly
stated: Jews are part of a community of "others of the world" obliged to
help each other. This protophilosophy of multicultural brotherhood, however, assumes that in America Jews are among those privileged to help, a
circumstance that renders problematic Jewish "otherness." Elijah, by contrast, is portrayed as physically gifted but economically, and perhaps
morally, disadvantaged, coerced to traffic in stolen trinkets.

When the Jewish kids arrange for Elijah to run on their team he seems
to be doing them a favor; in reality, however, they are saving him from the

life of the streets, bringing him into the wellspring of (Jewish) civilization. Begging the coach to allow him onto the track team, Elijah exclaims:

> "I *want* to be a Jewboy—" He lifted a chain from under his T-shirt and
> showed it around. It had at least a dozen Jewish stars on it, all different
> styles. Mezuzahs too. "Izzie been working with me, teaching me." . . .
> He whipped a *yamulka* out of his pocket—a white silk one—put it on
> his head, and then—just like that—began talking in Hebrew. *"Baruch
> Atoh Adonai Shalom Shalom."* (190)

Just as Jews may usurp Black symbols to create themselves as Americans, Elijah hopes to write himself into dominant society through the
medium of Jewish language and symbols. His strange bricolage of
stereotypically "Black" characteristics—dialect together with an array of
(probably) stolen goods—and Jewish icons symbolically ushers a Black
American into "civilization." Even his name is Jewish, that of an Israelite
prophet. Jews are again the intermediary, with Jewish characteristics written not only onto the body but into speech, though in garbled, pidgin
form. This is the story of the making of a distinctly American culture in
which blackness is simultaneously a sign of a unique American bricolage
and an *absence* of culture, an emptiness waiting to be engraved with em-
blems of civilization. Ancient Jewish icons serve the role that Christianity
and a Western education perform in conventional colonial ideology.

Yet resistance intrudes onto the scene of "civilization." As in "Black
Is My Favorite Color" naive Jewish liberalism runs into something unex-
pected, inexplicable from its standpoint: the confrontational figure of
Elijah's father, a Black minister who appears as the rabbi's sinister double:

> He was a short man, about the same height as the rabbi and wearing a
> black suit just like him. The only difference was in their hats. The rabbi
> wore a black one, but the Negro man had on a crazy turban thing with
> capes and scarves flowing from it. . . . There were jewels in his turban,
> and rings on his fingers. . . . and there were two long scars that criss-
> crossed his right cheek. (194)

Both the patriarchal Black and the patriarchal Jew are short in stature,
reduced to comical characters in the scheme of a dominant culture that
diminishes traditional societies. Ethnic tradition is dwarfed by an invisible but omnipresent whiteness. The Black minister, moreover, is equipped
with an orientalist assemblage, a proto-African turban flowing with exotic

images decontextualized from any actual history. His scars represent the
brutalization of slavery and Jim Crow engraved upon his cheek. Overall,
his appearance is a prophetic postmodern decontextualization, a network
of disconcertingly juxtaposed images. In punching the rabbi he plays out
the mugging of Nat Lime in altered form, a scene that will recur, with
variations, in the 1970s work of Bellow and Malamud. Repeatedly, Jewish liberal assimilationism is confronted with anger it cannot understand,
emanating from outside its frame of reference.

   In this story, however, the last word is from the young Elijah, who
races with the Bar Kochba Trophy away from the scene of dispute. The
young, the implication is, will outrun the anger of the older generation;
history is fluid and will be overcome. In our strong, youthful country,
youth will finally absorb and transcend the network of meanings engraved
in language and on the text of body and clothing. Just as the prophet Elijah
symbolizes the coming of the Messiah, the character Elijah symbolizes a
new American covenant. In the late 1960s this message probably seemed
both plausible and inspiring; given thirty years of continuing economic
and racial barriers it now seems naive. Images planted deep within the
psyche are not so easily uprooted, nor are habits and privileges of class.
Rather the small, comic rabbi and minister gain stature with time, their
visages more threatening following a period of revived nationalism. Their
conflict presages that of Crown Heights, in which separate communities
clinging to traditional garb and lifestyles live atop each other as strange
and threatening entities.

   In the wake of turbulent Black nationalism and strained relations between Blacks and Jews, Neugeboren created his most effective portrayal
of Black consciousness in *Sam's Legacy* (1973), a novel that combines
the interiorization of *Big Man* with the greater (multi)cultural sophistication of "Elijah." The scope of African American literature implicit here is
far more varied than the single-minded portrait of *Native Son*. Drawing
upon a rich legacy of sources, Neugeboren portrays the complexities of a
psyche positioned between societies, forced to make a choice yet eternally unhappy with this choice, unsettled in both Black and White worlds.
The Black bourgeoisie, particularly light-skinned Blacks able to pass as
White, is the portion of the African American community whose experience is closest to the Jewish American predicament.

   Sam's Legacy, then, suggests the relevance of the African American
search for identity to the Jewish present. Representing this legacy is the
gift that Tidewater, a light-skinned Black, presents to Sam Berman: a

manuscript entitled "My Life and Death in the Negro American Baseball
League: A Slave Narrative." This gift reveals Tidewater's role as "The
Black Babe Ruth," while Ruth himself is depicted as a Black passing for
White, a subversion of the American myth of whiteness. As Eric Solomon
argues, while the major narrative is "a disorderly melange of fictional
indulgence, buried in this baggy fiction is a superb novella, a true inside
narrative" (1987, 57). The two novels are linked, albeit loosely, through
the Jewish protagonist, who "shift[s] the outsider's burden onto an even
more marginal man" (63). Marginalization is displaced onto a people not
only physically darker than the Jews, but further from the sources of European (and Mediterranean) culture. For Jews, then, one Black "legacy"
is displacement to insider status in American society. Yet ironically the
Black "marginal man" is represented as the authentic talent, as a buried
source of American achievement, while the Jewish character in *Sam's
Legacy* is a parasite existing on the social margins. The confusion and
multiplicity of identities created by Tidewater's ambiguous narrative is
confounded by its contrast with a Jewish milieu. The Jewish characters,
however, are not those professionals noted for increasing success, but
shady characters, outcasts, the "Blacks," so to speak, of the Jewish world.
As a loner and a gambler Berman has far less legitimacy than that available to Tidewater *if* he had chosen to pass for White. Like many Jewish
characters in Neugeboren's fiction, Sam is a spectator to Black performance; that Sam gains his livelihood by betting on Black athletes makes
his role blatantly parasitic.

   Sam's Legacy depends upon fertile historical and literary material to
enable Neugeboren's creation of an internal minor masterpiece dealing
with a cultural phenomenon removed from his own. The existence of separate Black baseball leagues is itself a hugely ironic commentary on American society. Yet Neugeboren could never have capitalized on these ironies
without borrowing from the insights and style of African American literature. One apparent source for Tidewater's narrative, as implied by the
title, is traditional slave narratives (whose themes continue in the twentieth century through the journeys and struggles of the dispossessed). Yet
Neugeboren seems to have relied most upon James Weldon Johnson's
Autobiography of an Ex-Colored Man, which shares with Tidewater's
narrative an overly formal prose that contrasts tellingly with Neugeboren's
usual loose, colloquial style. A Black writer adopts the pose of "White"
narrative in the hands of a Jewish writer. In both Johnson and Tidewater/
Neugeboren, the narrator is able to pass for White, to move surreptitiously
between worlds. In both the narrator excels at some talent for which Afri-

can Americans are noted—ragtime piano in Johnson's work, baseball in Neugeboren's—which draws notice and admiration through creating a dynamic spectacle (which the Eurocentric eye may mistake for primitivism). Finally, in both color exacts a cost, submerging a final legitimacy, though in Johnson's novel the protagonist eventually chooses to pass for White, while Neugeboren's narrator rejects this choice.

Although Tidewater grows up in a dark-skinned family and identifies with blackness, his mother, hoping he'll act as an envoy into mainstream society through his color and his strong educational performance, calls him "White Star." But these same qualities alienate him from his father and brothers: "[W]e construct our universe on the model of our immediate world; mine was black, and I, dependent on it, felt as if I were its white victim" (1974, 72). Blackness for him means warmth, family life, and athletic success. When his tremendous baseball skills become evident he refuses to play as a White, refuses the money and status, exclaiming "I'm a colored boy" (77). He further asks, "[H]ow could I, disguising myself as a white man, have retained the speed of my fast ball, and the superb control I had of that speed?" (78). Cultural blackness is enacted as integral to both athleticism and authenticity, part of a single self crucial to Tidewater's identity. Blackness is furthermore portrayed, here and throughout the novel, not as a stain on American life, but as a hidden source of cultural achievement.

In choosing blackness Tidewater chooses marginalization, alienation from a recognized American center. Despite his superior talent he will never attain the recognition of Babe Ruth or Lou Gehrig, but plays in a league relegated to minstrelsy. Black leagues at that time were, indeed, literal minstrel shows; participating in them meant

> Riding around in broken-down cars, playing games that were preceded and followed by minstrel shows, being teammates with men who were generally of little or no education—this was not . . . the life that had been envisioned for me . . . the life of a gentleman. (75)

Tidewater rejects two possible roles—race leader and White sports hero—for an unacknowledged heroism among his own people. Simultaneously, his light skin and education separate him from much of Black society, driving him to "a hatred for other black men" (80). Resenting his marginalization he internalizes social hatred of Blacks as an outlet for his own rage. Like Alexander Portnoy he is alienated both from mainstream society and from his own people; for him double consciousness means a brutal polarization that effaces the gifts of cultural hybridity.

Tidewater's role as "the Black Babe Ruth" is the crucial irony from which the narrative's theme unfolds. Meaning emanates via inversion and cynical paradox, through an "outrageous deconstruction of history" (Solomon 1987, 58). Black players, named after the Whites who captured America's imagination (Neugeboren 1974, 70), play out a secret history as shadow versions of the recognized greats. Tidewater's whole career is a hidden version of Ruth's; both began as pitchers and achieved great success as home-run hitters. The obscure margins hide the players who most deserve to be memorialized. In postseason exhibitions the best White players were often beaten by Blacks, just as at the narrative's climax Tidewater repeatedly strikes out Ruth. Yet Neugeboren's version of Ruth has made the choice that Tidewater refused, to pass for White, and basks in the greatest hero-worship that America can give. The novel ruptures myth, reinterpreting an American hero as a racial sellout. The irony is multiplied by Ruth's homosexual affair with Tidewater that consummates their parallel lives. A cross-racial, same-sex love affair breaks every taboo simultaneously; that it occurs at the instigation of Babe Ruth, with his Black double (who is in fact lighter than he), subverts all of our basic myths. Tidewater himself scoffs at "the great hero of America lying in bed, locked in that most absurd of positions with a fair-skinned nigger" (309). Despite his great athleticism, society has forced Tidewater into a feminized position, passive and invisible, a position secretly shared by Babe Ruth, here a doubly closeted figure. *Sam's Legacy* portrays a hypocritical society in which even a great American hero must hide his past, replaying in miniature a racial history long obscured in the public imagination.

Because he has forsaken the blackness imposed on him by American apartheid—for which even a drop of "Black" blood makes one Black—Ruth, in both Tidewater's estimation and in the novel's cosmology, cannot be the greatest baseball player. Tidewater, who magnifies his racial identity within the confines of American definitions, strikes out the hypocritical Ruth. His success may support a reading of the novel as accepting Black nationalist notions of an essential self, of blackness as inherent to Tidewater's athleticism. Just as easily, the ability to make that choice allows a reading in which Tidewater creates his own identity, albeit within a narrow framework of racial constraints. In this reading racial definitions are all "make-believe," artificial categories by which America classifies and separates its people. Mixed blood challenges these categories by its very existence and so must be denied. A light-skinned Black—in White ideology an oxymoronic noncategory—must choose between absolute categories, White or Black, in doing so choosing either a dishonorable success or an honorable failure. For Tidewater either choice means a denial of complete identity. As William Faulkner's Joe Christmas epitomizes through his tortured life, mixed blood is a curse in America, enforcing an ambiguous outsider status. Tidewater will never approach Ruth's public stature; his revenge is to prove himself superior: "I wanted . . . to defeat him so utterly that he would cease to exist" (317). His nihilistic rage is directed at a society that refuses to grant a public identity to an African American. Like Bigger Thomas he defines himself through destruction, through defeating an icon of dominant society.

Upon a lifetime's reflection Tidewater finally accepts the path he has chosen; he finds peace of mind in the fact that, though his choice precluded recognition, it also precluded hypocrisy. He writes, "I find at the end what I did not expect to find when I started to set these thoughts down: that, except for the fact that I have not been able . . . to sustain those friendships which might have been begun in my earliest years, I regret nothing" (336). Despite the constraints he has faced, Tidewater has been honest to his race and to the talents he has been endowed with. How different from James Weldon Johnson's protagonist—who, after giving up his blackness for security and family, confesses that "I have sold my birthright for a mess of pottage" (1989, 211). Neither statement reflects the ambiguity of the choice made; both are likely rhetorical exaggerations dramatizing the moral urge of selecting an identity commensurate with one's birth. Such concerns undoubtedly affected Neugeboren, struggling to find his Jewish roots in a society that encourages assimilation.

The question remains of Tidewater's legacy, the meaning of his narrative to Berman the marginalized gambler and, in a larger sense, the heritage of Black narratives to Jewish American identity. As a Jew Berman is positioned to balance various identities, while Tidewater faces an either/or choice between mainstream respectability and ethnic heritage. Yet as an outstanding athlete (albeit an invisible one), Tidewater is a living exemplar whom Berman greatly admires. Berman inhabits a neighborhood in transition, in an America in transition: "[W]indows were covered now with posters of ferocious-looking black men and signs saying that black was beautiful" (Neugeboren 1974, 40). To the remaining Jewish residents of this marginal neighborhood, Black pride and criminality are intertwined. As a small-time gambler Berman grafts easily into a racial liminal zone, a neighborhood marked by fear for most of its remaining Jewish residents.

In contrast to Berman many Jews, by conforming to mainstream society, relegate Blacks to the social margins. *Sam's Legacy* directly confronts Jewish racism, the extreme of this attitude, which views Blacks as dangerous and unfit. This legacy of White racism is a stark counterpoint to Tidewater's subversive narrative, the gift of which implicitly links Jews and Blacks. Berman's friend complains of the African American presence: "They think they own the city now. They're always bumping into you, daring you to say something. . . . You know how I'd take care of the problem? With one big bomb" (153). The Jewish voice here transforms into the judging voice of dominant culture, borrowing words that are so often used against Jews: "They think they own the city." The solution— one big bomb—echoes that of the Holocaust: exterminate the unwanted presence, cleanse the unclean manifestation in order to save civilization. Jewish racists exemplify a need to become part of the flock, to find safety in dominant society. Says Nate:

> My aunts and uncles—my mother's brothers and sisters—they didn't die in Hitler's gas chambers so that a bunch of dumb *shvartzehs* could knife my wife in the park. . . . did our mother's and fathers sweat their hearts out in Brooklyn so that some day a dumb boogie could knock up your daughter? (155–56)

When used as a means of fitting into dominant society ethnic history becomes a tool not of dialogue, but of increased fear and repression. Jewish suffering and horror are compacted into a miniature history justifying racist judgments similar to those used against Jews. Ethnic nationalism often replicates the hatred of the dominant society against which it defines itself. Fear of Black criminality may be an extreme version of fear and fascination with Black sexuality, of losing power and control. The mother may fear the rapist, but the daughter faces the seducer whom she may welcome. The "rapist" is a contained, demarcated version of Otherness, while the seducer implies a blurring of boundaries, a shifting of cultural and racial standards.

Tidewater's legacy, the larger legacy of African American writing, is to make impossible a replication of old racial fallacies, to impel a new American vision. Civil Rights–era integration promised an end to the impermeable concepts of Black and White, a remapping of psychic and genetic maps of America. Integration leads to new racial fears along with new possibilities, a situation dramatized in Grace Paley's "Zagrowsky Tells." The breakdown of old definitions of Otherness, increasing intermarriage and multiculturalism, leaves fewer and fewer social groups demarcated as legitimized objects of hatred. While often undertaken more in theory than in fact, this inclusive vision of America is Tidewater's ultimate legacy to Berman, one that defines Jewish and Black history not as a dissolving into American society, but as an interactive process. As Jews and Blacks occupy the dominant landscape they simultaneously alter it.

Yet the optimism of the 1960s was misplaced, or at least premature; bigotry, insecurity, and hatred would not vanish so easily, particularly given the failure of cumbersome bureaucratic attempts to end centuries of economic stratification. The history of multiracial intermingling exemplified by Tidewater is one of apparent false starts and dead ends, of often fruitless struggle for acceptance. Proponents of a linear progression regarding racial acceptance face the dismal meanderings of history, of at least one step backwards—and many sideways—for every two forward. Ancient national, ethnic, and racial hatreds are stubbornly persistent. The overlapping problems of class—of how to fairly share resources, create equal opportunity, and still provide incentive for a productive economy—are at least as difficult.

Both ethnic and economic divisions encompass questions of power, questions approached in utterly different ways by Bellow and Neugeboren. If Bellow's acceptance of Western values leads him to exteriorize Blacks, Neugeboren's radical questioning of American society prompts him to identify with them. In novels such as *The Stolen Jew*, Neugeboren would further explore his Jewish heritage; his adoption of Black perspectives may be an intermediate step toward claiming this heritage. Yet Neugeboren's work privileges ethnic heritage in a more multiple way than does Malamud, by implying an America of cultural essences existing side by side. This approach, born of 1960s radicalism, continues in today's multicultural ideals, which celebrate the maintenance of a strong ethnic heritage alongside an awareness of, and respect for, diverse traditions.

II

In the early 1970s the Jewish author who best retained the values of community, activism, and the struggle for transformation was Grace Paley. Rooted in the socialist tradition of East European Jewry, Paley remains a strong voice in radical and feminist movements. Political activism is so integral to her writing that Judith Arcana exclaims: "Grace Paley absolutely intends to effect social change—if not revolution—in her work" (1993, 6). Like the Black nationalists, Paley does not separate life and art. Like them she struggles to give voice to the marginalized. She differs,

however, in her portrayal of a multiethnic cross-section and in her exploration of internal psychological complexity. Her middle-class status allows
for a less urgent, more inclusive approach, one enamored of modernist
experimentation. Like her politics, the often noted power and charm of
her literary voice is not just a personal expression but derives from extensive roots. Her Yiddish heritage blends with urban dialect and African
American inflections to create a quirky expressive bricolage.

Grace Paley's locale is New York City, the scene of a barrage of cultural
intersections, a plethora of voices and dialects. She is the prototypical
urban writer, a status critical in the development of a Judaism branching
out, cross-pollinating with other peoples, creating a modern, humanistic
version of Jewishness, treating the city as generative of rich new beginnings: "What for Bellow is the conclusion of modern city writing, for
Grace Paley . . . is opportunity" (Baumgarten 1993, 397). Paley's community of voices transforms and transcends the hostile cityscape, generating a literature exploratory of difference. Simultaneously she tests and
refines Jewish American identity against the Black experience. Paley seeks
to define herself not just as a Jew within an American whole, but to recu-
perate and legitimize the lost history of Otherness, both Black and Jewish.
Americanization as simple assimilation into a preordained culture becomes
untenable. There is no center, no stable framework into which one fits
one's cultural patterns, but an ever changing aggregation never quite definable. .

Paley is most effective when using her trademark inflections and perspective, an unabashedly New York Jewish viewpoint.[1] She does so while
scrutinizing Black America; or rather scrutinizing, through the disrupting
lens of Black America, her own history as a minority. In two stories, "The
Long Distance Runner" and "Zagrowsky Tells," an easy assimilation
becomes untenable; America is redefined as a collection of unfinished,
interlocking histories. Yet even in the midst of stylistic and cultural
blendings, ethnic communities often remain segregated. This is particularly true for Black America, which continues to act, willingly or not, as a
test case against which other peoples define themselves. For Jewish Americans the Black presence becomes a jarring reminder of a past history of
ghettoization and marginalization. A comfortable version of assimilation
in which ethnic groups participate fully in American life while maintaining their traditions (at least in token form) is called into question. A more
extensive American vision is needed, one epitomized by multiethnic New
York. Yet this new vision is fraught with uncertainty.

Issues of racial and ethnic interpenetration remain controversial, making for a vexed literary treatment. "The Long Distance Runner" and "Zagrowsky Tells" employ vigorous yet highly divergent Jewish narrative viewpoints that powerfully compress and individuate a larger interaction. Triangulated between tradition, exclusion, and assimilation, Jewish Americans perceive Blacks from a complex, often conflicting, variety of perspectives: as a people alien to the traditions of Judaism; as a similarly oppressed minority group; as a nonassimilated version of the Other. Like many progressive Jews, especially during the social movements of the 1960s, Paley seems determined not to forget her people's past; she is resolved to help similarly oppressed groups join a larger social collectivity (and in doing so end the history of terror inflicted on subnational groups which has so devastated world Jewry).

Paley's recurring protagonist, Faith Darwin Asbury, is the narrator of "The Long Distance Runner" and a central character in "Zagrowsky Tells." Like Paley, Faith is a free-spirited Jewish radical; unlike her, Faith has survived a difficult divorce and raised two children singlehandedly. This removal from a traditional female role establishes a perspective sympathetic to the similarly—though not equivalently—displaced African American community. Despite her newfound independence, Faith begins "The Long Distance Runner" ill equipped for the kind of freedom romanticized in the masculine adventure novel. As a middle-aged woman she starts to run, explaining that "though I was stout and in many ways inadequate to this desire, I wanted to go far and fast" (Paley 1974, 179). Rather than vast sea journeys or cross-country excursions, she embarks upon the middle-class equivalent. The journey takes on a fantasy quality, an exploration of inner terrain as much as outer; indeed, it is impossible to tell how much of "The Long Distance Runner" is literally supposed to happen and how much occurs in Faith's imagination, as mounting implausibilities render much of the story fictive (from the viewpoint of the fictional Faith). Her journey out is also a journey in, or rather back to her original home in Brooklyn. In this physically close location she explores social and psychic distances that parallel—and parody—the male explorer of countless adventure novels. This is true not just psychologically but literally; like them she finds the alien, the dark Other, in large numbers: "Suddenly I was surrounded by about three hundred blacks" (181). As in Joseph Conrad's novels, in confronting these others she is confronting herself, her heart of, not darkness, but that strange realm which may be objectified as Other. Yet the terror often generated by the appearance of the Other, particularly on its own terrain, is not prominent; rather Faith, true to her heritage of striving for sisterhood and brotherhood, attempts to familiarize the strange, to bring it into harmony with her notions of identity and culture. America is to be remade in the image of the many.

The Blacks Faith sees are people like herself, living lives as best they can in a neighborhood alienated from mainstream norms, as she did when a child. In confronting the history of her neighborhood she reacts not only with fear but, more so, with a delighted curiosity. Unlike the formulaic White male explorer, Faith is anxious to make connections, to humanize. She exemplifies the well-meaning progressive White, telling the gazing Black crowd that "I like your speech. . . . Metaphor and all" (181). In praising the richness of the Black vernacular she does more to explain her own sympathetic position than to engage the crowd. She makes, also, a historical connection: "Yes my people also had a way of speech. And don't forget the Irish. The gift of gab" (181), a statement prefiguring current notions of American multiculturalism, of converging streams of languages, customs, approaches to life. The ideology of assimilation *into* a prefigured European-based culture is called into question; the philosophy of many peoples continually inventing and reinventing themselves is ascendant.

The gazing Black crowd is handled far differently in Paley than in Conrad. Given a voice, they are part of a progression in "dominant" cultural representations of Blacks, a shift in the perceiving gaze from rugged individual facing the wilderness to hybrid urban environment. Conrad's Africans are faceless and endowed with savage whoops as their only means of communication: "[A] very loud cry, as of infinite desolation, soared slowly in the opaque air. . . . as though the mist itself had screamed" (1989, 54). Lacking language, these Africans lack the ability to articulate themselves into being, at least in a European epistemology. Some sixty years later Saul Bellow invents an encounter with "a band of African kids, naked boys and girls, yelling at the sight of us. Even the tiniest of them, with the big bellies, wrinkled their faces and screeched with the rest" (1976a, 47). In Paley, too, the Black crowd represents a return to origins, a remaking of identity outside the overlapping social artifices of adulthood. This return is more literal than in Conrad and Bellow as Faith carries an awareness of her Jewish childhood to this neighborhood on the margins of America. Paley struggles also to give the "natives" a sophisticated language of their own, one through which they can appear as independent subjects. After all, Faith's family has been in the situation of outsider, of immigrants who may be perceived as incomplete humans unable to speak standard English. Faith's encounter is tempered with a newfound awareness, a struggle to embrace the viewpoint of the Other, to escape the role of judging, patriarchal eye. Simultaneously her work begins to incorporate another's speech as part of a common tongue.

From her position as sympathetic political activist, vastly separate from the realities of Black life yet committed to bridging the gap, Paley plays a delicate balancing game. Blacks can never entirely escape their role as a projection of White—in her case left-wing Jewish—needs. Although Paley struggles for an authentic portrayal of African American society, struggles to give her Black characters agency, a life of their own, the projections of the White Jewish narrator persist. In contrast to Faith's consciousness, the Black dialect is stark and blunt, demanding that the reader supply a larger context and meaning. Faith's viewpoint, though sympathetic, shades into a liberal version of the discerning White gaze, a judgmental stance that the story itself satirizes in Faith's interactions with the crowd, and in her later relationship with Mrs. Luddy. Adam Meyer argues convincingly that "the fact that Paley is aware of her own limited awareness only intensifies her self-consciousness and self-questioning" (1994, 80). Yet silence is a worse alternative; given her political motivation and the close relation of African American issues to Jewish progressivism, she cannot but speak.

Paley endows her Black characters with dialect as authentic as she can manage, as when one member of the crowd exhorts respectful treatment of Faith: "Poor thing. She ain't right. Leave her you boys, you bad boys" (Paley 1974, 181). A moral sense, a sympathetic reaching out, is evident. Rather than remaining a monolithic whole, the Black crowd begins to acquire individuality through dissension, dialogue, and brief, telling description: "You blubrous devil! said a dark young man. He wore horn-rimmed glasses and had that intelligent look that City College boys used to have when I was eighteen and first looked at them" (182). This description purposefully defies preconceptions of the "nonintellectual" Black, while linking its subject to intimate memories of adolescent anxiety and hope outside the barriers of color.

Simultaneously, however, a difference remains, a feeling that Faith is out of place: "She ain't right." Reversing American expectations, Faith hears herself perceived as alien, a White Other. Whatever her intentions, to the crowd Faith is an exemplar of whiteness, tied to an inescapable past: "the white old days. That time too bad to last" (181). The dialect meaning of "bad" as "good" ironically reverts to its original meaning. From the perspective of the ghetto residents the good old days were a nightmare of exclusion, with whiteness an omnipresent force surrounding the Black ghetto both physically and culturally. Whiteness in the Black psyche is at least as eternal and inescapable as is blackness in the White psyche. Paley's rendering of Black dialect subverts the European gaze, presenting Faith as the Other, her White self viewed startlingly through Black perspectives.

The dialogue in which Faith engages the Black crowd is limited; to them she retains an insurmountable difference. Trying to bridge the gap, to move from curious stranger to family, she offers one child, Cynthia, a place in her apartment. The child reacts: "Stay away from me, honky lady. They just gonna try and jostle my black womanhood. My mother told me about that, keep you white honky devil boys to your devil self, you just leave me be you old bitch you" (187). Black fear and suspicion is unleashed, specifically of White male sexual exploitation, an image that personifies a deeply entrenched economic and psychological barrier. If Faith feels secure enough to visit an African American neighborhood, the opposite is not true. If she believes herself to be returning home, viewing it with eyes both old and new, Cynthia views her as representative of an alien society, one powerfully mythologized in the collective Black consciousness.

Despite intimations of an African American perspective, "The Long-Distance Runner" remains centered in its Jewish protagonist. Faith revisits her past, updating and revising a crucial part of her psyche. She stops at the former apartment of the fat, tragic Mrs. Goreditsky, a Jewish resident from the old times left behind in the ghetto, whose death was discovered due only to the smell: "They couldn't get through the front door. It scraped off a piece of her" (185). Just as history, as the old neighborhood, remains with the Jews who have left, so a piece of them remains, part of the overlapping cultures, the palimpsest of American society. The old, the impoverished, are left literally behind to die, while symbolically the history of ghettoization remains in the Jewish people, its vestiges not yet expunged.

Mrs. Goreditsky exemplifies one fate for America's Jews; Faith tells of the extreme opposite in one deserter from the neighborhood who is now

> the president of a big corporation, JoMar Plastics. This corporation owns a steel company, a radio station, a new Xerox-type machine that lets you do twenty-five different pages at once. This corporation has a foundation, The JoMar Fund for Research in Conservation. Capitalism is like that, I added, in order to be politically useful. (185)

Capitalism with its plastic facade (like plastic both ever changing and superficial) is endlessly accumulating, multiply tentacled, and ideologically self-replicating (through its incessant funding of think tanks). Implicit here, derived from Faith's socialist background, is her critique of the evils of capitalism, her need to lecture, "to be politically useful." Between the extremes of impoverished ghetto resident and capitalist entrepreneurship lies Faith, who struggles to reclaim her people's history while developing a modern identity.

When Faith flees back into the apartment of her childhood, "my old own door" (187), the story has certainly entered the realm of the metaphorical. Faith imaginatively explores her homeplace transformed by a Black America that has taken over both the neighborhoods and the estranged status formerly occupied by Jews. Despite being "attacked by local fears" (188) Faith engages Mrs. Luddy in conversation. Yet she cannot resist the impulse to lecture, despite her awareness that she "is constantly intruding into the lives of these black people, offering advice as if she knows, and can teach them, what is right" (82). She discusses, analyzes, criticizes, and seeks to improve. Faith's good-natured liberalism often borders on the self-righteous, as when she suggests that "someone ought to clean up" the terrors of the slum, and Mrs. Luddy rebukes her with "Who you got in mind? Mrs. Kennedy?" (190). The dialogue is between the idealist, spewing her opinions in long streams, and the realist, blunt and brief, tempered by harsh reality. Faith's and Mrs. Luddy's differing attitudes derive at least partly from their histories: the African American of promises repeatedly denied, of the slow-paced life of a recently rural people; the Jewish American of purposeful immigrants who, in a generation, escaped the New York ghetto.

From her "three weeks" in the slum with its fatalistic psychology, Faith returns home with her questing spirit intact: "A woman inside the steamy energy of middle age runs and runs. She finds the houses and streets where her childhood happened. She lives in them. She learns as though she was still a child what in the world is coming next" (198). Her position as middle-aged explorer, driven to run but thriving on the forces that drive her, is interrogated but not greatly changed by her glimpse of an ethnic Otherness. She has seen what her preconceptions led her to. As an exemplar of the enlightened subject, but one interpellated by other positions—Jewish, feminist, socialist—she remains convinced through her encounters of the value of exploration, of breaching barriers. From her childhood poised on the edge of society, she imaginatively (re)constructs Black circumstances and glimpses an American future.

In "The Long Distance Runner" Blacks and Jews ultimately remain separate, paralleling the aftermath of the Civil Rights era, when relations

between the two fractured into mutual accusations. Yet Black-Jewish relations of the closest kind did arise out of the 1960s, leading to mixed-
race children (as well as more open acknowledgment of such children). If
in "The Long Distance Runner" a Jewish character crosses into terrain
ostensibly reserved for African Americans, in "Zagrowsky Tells" a Jewish milieu is infiltrated by a Black, the child Emanuel, a name that means
Messiah in Hebrew, the harbinger of new beginnings (reminiscent of Jay
Neugeboren's Elijah, a character who also crosses ethnic boundaries).
Surprisingly it's not the sympathetic Faith but Izzy Zagrowsky, a character tinged with racism, who appears with a (half-)black child, quickly revealed as his grandchild. The confrontation between Faith, an exemplar of
Jewish progressivism, and the more conservative Zagrowsky allows Paley
to explore a range of Jewish attitudes regarding African Americans. The
use of the slippery Zagrowsky as narrative consciousness exemplifies the
ambivalent, multiple nature of Jewish and Black responses to each other.
The child, oddly given a Jewish name, in America the label of an outsider,
is the object of these responses. He is the element upon which the story
hinges, the motivating force in Zagrowsky's changing attitude and the
internal contradictions provoked in him. Judith Arcana explains how he
serves "to heal the grief and misery in his family, embodying a bond that
holds the generations together" (1993, 163). The healing involves not just
Zagrowsky's immediate family, not just the split between conservative
and progressive Jews, but society's larger racial wound. The child is the
catalyst for confronting the pain of old enmities; yet ultimately such racially mixed children must become active agents in re(de)fining the meaning of ethnicity in America, a role only hinted at in "Zagrowsky Tells."

These enmities remained in the aftermath of 1960s protest, a period
of trauma that, in its search for a new beginning, brought ancient divisions to public scrutiny. The mistreatment of Blacks, a flaw in the American republic since before its inception, was confronted but not rectified. If
among Jews and Blacks accusations of betrayal persist, in "Zagrowsky
Tells" the division is local and specific. Years before Faith had confronted
Zagrowsky in a boycott of his pharmacy, accusing it of refusing to serve
minorities. Having previously delivered medicine to Faith's deathly ill
child Zagrowsky feels betrayed; the tension between the two becomes a
microcosm of difficulties between progressive and more conservative Jews.
To Zagrowsky, Faith is patronizing and self-satisfied as she suggests ways
he should raise his grandchild. The edge of satiric self-criticism that permeated "The Long-Distance Runner" is explicit in Zagrowsky's characterization of Faith as the "Queen of Right" (Paley 1974, 164). Yet when

Faith tells Zagrowsky that "we were right" to protest segregation (157), it's hard for him to disagree, given his subsequent acceptance of a mixed-race child. A distinction between right and wrong is implied, whether defined by evolving social attitudes or by a larger moral code.

Yet Zagrowsky cannot admit that he was wrong in his treatment of non-White customers; instead he serves up a litany of conscience-relieving excuses: "[N]aturally, you have to serve the old customers first. . . . and to tell the truth I didn't like the idea my pharmacy should get the reputation of being a cut-rate place for them. They move into a neighborhood . . . I did what everyone did" (158). Zagrowsky's morality is multiple and contingent, implicitly based upon shifting social standards. That Zagrowsky's people have been similarly isolated escapes him at this moment. Running through his head is a zigzagging and contradictory catalog of Jewish reactions to African Americans. He remembers his wife's comment that "We kept them down," and his reply: "We? We? My two sisters and my father were being fried up for Hitler's supper in 1944 and you say we?" (159). The Holocaust serves as the ultimate protection from guilt; my people, my immediate family, have been the victims, not the perpetrators, of racism, Zagrowsky indicates here. Just one page earlier, though, he had willingly if guiltily participated mentally in the racist discourse responsible for segregation. Mentally his role shifts from a member of the dominant culture to a marginalized outsider, depending on his immediate needs. Later in the story he shifts again, pondering about his blond-haired daughter: "Out of my Cissy, who looked like a piece of gold, would come a black child" (168). Zagrowsky understands the irony of blond and black miscegenation, an understanding approved of by dominant society in its attempt to keep the races separate. The irony he misses is that Cissy's blond hair might come from some long-ago rape by a Polish peasant (153)—that she herself is a product of miscegenation from a violent society practicing its own racial politics, that her people were once the "dark Other."

Yet elsewhere Zagrowsky shows himself aware that both Blacks and Jews have been victims of racism. Worried how outsiders will take the sight of him with a black child he rationalizes, "They think the Jews are a little bit colored anyways, so they don't look at him too long" (169). Here it is useful for him to identify with Emanuel, so he does. His awareness of racial ideologies is acute yet inconsistent, running a wide spectrum; at times he identifies with dominant society; at times he views himself as Jewish, an outsider, almost a Black. The ability to hold contradictory views yet remain unaware of the contradictions is psychologically realistic.

Zagrowsky repeatedly applies the assumption most convenient for his immediate needs to fend off threats to his ego at the most personal level of business and family.

Paley, master of compression that she is, has fit many themes of contemporary black and Jewish relations into her story; contradictory impulses, loyalties torn between dominant and marginalized expectations, drive Zagrowsky's oscillating consciousness. The Holocaust is an important bridge from Jews to Blacks in their role as the oppressed. Simultaneously it is (mis)used to posit Jews as the ultimate victims, to deny responsibility for other forms of racism. Miscegenation makes these themes and confusions vitally personal, driving Zagrowsky to contemplate his ethnic status. Emanuel's very existence calls into question racial ideology. As Zagrowsky puts it: "A person looks at my Emanuel and says, Hey! he's not altogether from the white race, what's going on? I'll tell you what: life is going on" (158). Life inserts interrogatory fragments into the facade of ideology. Zagrowsky has changed to the point of accepting the complex fluctuations of contemporary America.

Racial mixtures such as Emanuel are one means of undermining hatred, forcing a coming to terms with difference. Neil Isaacs explains that Zagrowky's "experienced love" speaks "louder than his learned hate" (1990, 91). Experience may be the best teacher, yet it converges imperfectly with historical and cultural ideology. Bicultural individuals are especially prone to confusion. From Zagrowsky's Jewish background he begins to unearth primeval kinships: "They tell me long ago we were mostly dark" (Paley 1974, 171). An immediate family link awakens prior historical parallels of marginalization. Zagrowsky, like Faith in "The Long Distance Runner," has confronted a past and in doing so redefined a present, redefined his status as both an American and a Jew, making of both a more flexible, inclusive identity. If Faith's identification as a progressive feminist is a motivating factor in exploring her Jewish past as mediated by the Black presence, Zagrowsky's ties of blood are even stronger.

Within the story Emanuel is a focal point for others' reflections, stimulating change through his very existence. He is a product of historical upheaval, of a time fraught with questions and changes. If the sixties produced crises—gaps between generations, genders and ethnicities—they were a time also of struggle for togetherness, of hope for an eventual end to the racial divisions that have tainted this nation's history. Emanuel is a long-term product of sixties ideology and "Zagrowsky Tells" is a parable of healing. Yet, outside the story's time frame, those like him will need to actively confront their uncertain status. Emanuel will be an outsider to

Black America through his Jewishness, an outsider to Jewish America through his blackness, an outsider to mainstream America through both. Paradoxically this alienated, indeterminate status will make him proto-typically American, a progenitor of new identity. Narratives such as Emanuel's are helping to define an America in transition, a world in flux where the meanings of color and transracial identity are perpetually reinvented.[2]

Fragmentation and Multiculturalism

In the past quarter century the flow of history has seemed less intense, less coherent, than in the 1960s and the shock waves of its aftermath, a time conscious of its own importance and destiny. In a static and conservative atmosphere relations between Blacks and Jews seem less momentous; contemporary cultural change is relatively incremental, consisting of a growing awareness and acceptance of a variety of minorities, but also of visible tension as submerged identities surface.[1] Furthermore, if the 1950s and '60s were a period of great visibility for Jewish writers, the African American writers currently prominent seem less interested in Black-Jewish relations; Jews are simply a smaller, and more assimilated, part of the American landscape than are Blacks. Nevertheless, writers both Black and Jewish continue to depict relations between the two peoples, albeit in a fragmented fashion.

This literature diverges from media depictions of increasingly hostile Black-Jewish relations during periods of faltering Jewish support for affirmative action, heated disagreement over the status of Palestinians, and anti-Jewish rhetoric from the Nation of Islam. In a time of media excess and strained rhetoric it is all too easy to reduce relations between Jewish and African Americans to a ruthless narrative of confrontation. The reality is far more complex; the two peoples envision and interpret each other in an intricate array of formats, through a variety of mediums—written,

spoken, visual, and musical—and, of course, through individual encoun-
ters. Much goodwill remains from the distant-seeming—yet ever present—
Civil Rights era. Recent literature shows the multidimensional nature of
Jewish-Black relations while fostering tendencies toward reconciliation.
While contemporary literature emanates from the Civil Rights era, at least
as important is the Holocaust, an unspoken backdrop to the 1960s that
linked Jews and Blacks as victims of racial violence. Toni Morrison's
Beloved, for instance, may be read as an attempt to commemorate Black
trauma in the way that Jewish thinkers and novelists commemorate the
Holocaust.

The Holocaust was often treated with embarrassed silence in its immediate aftermath; it was not yet recognized as an ultimate evil aimed at
eradicating a specific ethnic group. Kurt Ditmarr mentions "the necessary
restraint which forced American Jewish writers after World War II to approach the Holocaust in an oblique rather than in a direct manner" (1991,
64) Since then, of course, the Holocaust has been memorialized as an
event the horror of which must never be forgotten. In recent works about
Black-Jewish relations the Holocaust looms surprisingly large, a crucial
yet contested symbol.

Racial and ethnic movements, to avoid a breakdown into warring
entities defined by narrow boundaries, call for some common language
that acknowledges also particular cultural worth. The Holocaust is a primal symbol of the failure of liberal humanism to provide such a voice, to
transcend its Eurocentric origins. The ur-site of European "civilization"
bred the most intense, mechanized slaughter—the greatest number of victims in the shortest time span—in history. Incomprehensible as it is, the
Holocaust is endowed with meaning by various thinkers to suit their own
purposes. For Blacks and Jews it may be a touchstone of similarity, of
common suffering. As James Baldwin argued in 1962:

> If one is permitted to treat any group of people with special disfavor
> because of their race or the color of their skin, there is no limit to what
> one will force them to endure, and, since the entire race has been myste-
> riously indicted, no reason not to attempt to destroy it root and branch.
> This is precisely what the Nazis attempted. Their only originality lay in
> the means they used. (1993, 83)

Baldwin articulates the unity of racial ideology; to him the Holocaust is
simply the ultimate version of what Blacks, among other peoples, have
already undergone. This argument remains open to the charge of trivializing

the Holocaust, of simplifying hatred into a single phenomenon. The converse argument, that the Holocaust is beyond compare, essentializes it. What meaning has the phrase "Never Again" if the Holocaust is an unreplicable event? And what application has study and remembrance of the Holocaust to non-Jews if only Jews may suffer such a crime?

Crucial differences between slavery and the Holocaust are illuminated in Laurence Thomas's *Vessels of Evil* (1993). Attempting to negotiate arguments over the uniqueness of the Holocaust, Thomas argues that differences do not imply a moral scale; he acknowledges that neither atrocity can be judged as worse than the other: "I write with the conviction that the moral pain of neither [Blacks nor Jews] can be subsumed under nor assimilated into the moral pain of the other" (1993, x). Slavery attempted to reduce its victims to a childish obedience and erase their past; the Holocaust acted to physically destroy an entire people. As Thomas puts it, "The very telos of Slavery was to bring about the utter dependence of blacks upon slaveowners. The very telos of the Holocaust was the extermination of the Jewish people" (11). To overly equate the two may reduce one to the shadow of the other, minimizing the horrific nature of each.

Still, the overall pattern of a people dispossessed, in diaspora, and suffering persistent, inexplicable oppression holds for both Blacks and Jews. For both, significant racial features were defined by an outside society, which used these features as justification for unremitting acts of violence. Both could be verbally abused, physically attacked, even killed, seemingly at random based on the whim of an outsider. Given these circumstances, Baldwin's view is not so wrong. The physical destruction of the Holocaust was merely the next logical step in an ideology of racial outsiderness that permanently removed these groups from being considered a part of humanity. Thomas sarcastically defends himself from potential charges that his distinctions are overstated: "[W]ith a kind of rhetorical flourish, someone might want to say that death is the ultimate form of natal alienation" (152). Thomas has anticipated his argument's greatest weakness, yet fails to adequately defend it. This becomes clear if we reverse the terms: natal alienation is in fact a form of death. The death is not physical, but historical and cultural. European society has told Blacks, essentially: "You are not human; you have no culture or value; your languages and traditions have no meaning; you are therefore at our disposal to do with as we please." Jews, too, are placed outside the realm of culture, value, tradition, of anything defining enlightened humanity; lacking any use (as could be found for Blacks), threatening the moral and biological purity of society, they must be killed.

The equivocal nature of Thomas's argument is a response to heated comparisons of Black and Jewish suffering, often turned to immediate political purposes. The status of the Holocaust relative to other historical crimes, from the slave trade to the slaughter of aborigines in the Americas and Australia to the mass killings of Armenians, is the subject of bitter debate. The anthology *Is the Holocaust Unique?* presents extreme positions from a variety of perspectives. To Steven Katz's contention that "The Holocaust, that is, the intentional murder of European Jewry during World War II, is historically and phenomenologically unique" (Rosenbaum 1996, 19), David Stannard replies that "not only is the essence of [this] argument demonstrably erroneous, the larger thesis that it fraudulently advances is fundamentally racist and violence-provoking" (Rosenbaum 1996, 167). Such excessive claims have the feel of a game of comparative suffering, a contest for the status of history's ultimate victim. At times Jews and Blacks may be bound so much by their own belief systems, derived from their specific histories, as to be unable to fathom each other. It is here that the literature of Black-Jewish mutual representations offers at least the hint of the possibility of an escape.

I

The employment of the Holocaust as the final criterion of victimhood is illustrated in elegant microcosm in a scene from Lore Segal's *Her First American* (1985), in which the Jewish Fishgoppel engages in a verbal dual with the African American Ebony:

> Fishgoppel said, "Jews care enough about their children to give them an education."
> Ebony said, "Negroes were lynched if they learned the alphabet."
> "We had pogroms," said Fishgoppel.
> "Slavery," said Ebony.
> "Holocaust!" cried Fishgoppel. (1985, 273)

Each character is immersed in her own history. A few key words—"Slavery," "Holocaust"—are signifiers for an immense horror, uncountable individual struggles and defeats, humiliation and despair. From outside these histories, however, the words may appear as large abstractions, excuses for ethnic isolationism. Here each participant is guilty of such evasion, steeped in her own misery. Each privileges absolutely her own position, remain-

ing willfully blind to the other's. Finally Ilka Weissnix, the novel's protagonist, intervenes: "Are there no griefs that aren't racist or anti-Semitic!"
(273). This outburst attempts to establish a common humanity, to shock
the adversaries away from exclusive preoccupation with their own
victimhood. Such avoidance of historical confrontation allows for universality, but drains the reality of difference. In microcosm it replays early
Civil Rights movement assumptions of a universal humanism that elides
awareness of difference, of ethnic particularity. Even Ilka's attempted
compromise is futile as Fishgoppel and Ebony end up stalking from the
room, a graphic illustration of Black-Jewish compartmentalization, an
almost willful misunderstanding.

Despite this scene *Her First American* is not predominantly about
irresolvable difference but about mutuality. Ilka Weissnix's cry of horror
might be an epigraph for a novel in which the suffering of both Jews and
Blacks develops into a search for mutual transcendence. The central agent
of a common humanity is Ilka's romantic relationship with the African
American Carter Bayoux. His ironic humor and penchant for storytelling
entice Fishgoppel into what for her is the highest compliment: "Carter
has a Jewish mind" (125). In their psychological combat with dominant
culture both peoples employ sardonic humor; this seems to be what cap-
tures Fishgoppel's imagination. The sophisticated, urbane Carter, an envoy to the United Nations and friend of celebrities and musicians, might
superficially seem protected from racial victimization. His alcoholism
implies otherwise, for his dignity has been incessantly undermined by a
society that refuses to recognize him. He misses appointments, is repeatedly hospitalized, and mishandles personal relations. This is not merely
an individual condition, but is a response to socially generated stress.
Having internalized group degradation, Carter flounders almost willfully
in the squalid state that American society expects of Negroes. Certainly
Carter's pervasive concern with race relations motivates his essays upon
the African American "hate-fear-hate" complex, inflamed by "daily, small,
casual hurts and slights" (104). Guilt and helplessness culminate in alcoholism.

Ilka's mother offers a Jewish parallel to Carter Bayoux. Like him the
mother is unable to escape the tragedy of her personal history, which stems
from her people's history. Her most terrible memory is of leaving her
husband alone on a road to be shot by the Germans. If Carter uses alcohol
as a means of escape, the mother suffers from nightmares. She cannot
submerge the Nazi past; he cannot abide the American present. Following
the pattern outlined in both Fanon's *Black Skin, White Masks* and Cobbs

and Grier's *Black Rage*, a traumatic history replays itself in individual psyches. Ilka's attempt at reconciliation again includes a measure of evasion when she tells her mother that Blacks "have their own stories, Mutti. They don't need our nightmares" (Segal 1985, 151). Carter, however, listens patiently to Mutti's stories. Here it is the African American who articulates Black-Jewish similarities. Drawing from the Talmudic injunction that shaming another is the greatest sin, Carter asserts that "When a people—a whole race—is systematically humiliated, it is tantamount to genocide" (263). Carter's interest in Jewish thought and experience arises from his own situation, his immersion in historic humiliation, his need to comprehend racial oppression. The term "genocide" might seem misused, even trivialized, in the above quotation, yet it stems from a common sympathy, an understanding of the wrongs inflicted upon both Jews and Blacks. The "genocide" here is social and cultural, harking to the concept of natal alienation in which a people's historical identity is effaced.

Carter's sympathy with Jewish history, though, does not lead to harmony, for Blacks and Jews face radically different conditions in the United States. To the contention that the two share a parallel experience, Carter replies, "Yes, indeedy: parallels are two lines that run side by side and never meet except in infinity" (263). Ilka and Carter's affair might seem to contradict this statement: from oppressed peoples with differing histories in vastly different parts of the world the two have converged. Romance, the possibility of marriage and family, which seems very real through much of the novel, is the binding agent. Individualism, that part of American ideology which gives the human control over his or her fate, which discounts racial and class barriers, is briefly ascendant. Ultimately, though, personal communion does not overcome social destiny. Carter is unable to deal with his history, unable to control his alcoholism, and hence Ilka, unable to deal with his behavior, finally abandons him.

Just as the individual Black/Jewish relationship is not sustained in *Her First American,* so the political destinies of the two groups are fractured—the parallels do not meet—as the novel's African Americans struggle to claim an identity of their own. A negative version of this identity has already been partially determined by the fierceness of segregation. When a liberal Jewish couple seeks to adopt a Black baby, self-consciously to break the color line, Ebony among other Black characters sneers at their naïveté, their belief that social custom will simply melt away. When Ilka complains that the couple has been unfairly harassed, Carter replies with his customary irony that "Friends are the only ones close enough to get your teeth *into*" (220). Jews, as benefactors from a superior position in the American racial and social hierarchy, are vulnerable to resentment, to charges of being patronizing or hopelessly naive. The Jewish and Black experiences in America are different; parallel lines have not converged but remain as a ghostly presence of mutual awareness, two histories uneasily mythologizing each other.

African American isolation, initially imposed from the outside, may be continued internally through the development of a racial countermythology. After Carter's death his students, caught up in Black nationalism, wish to deny his involvement with the White Ilka, to claim his story solely as their own. Ebony explains their fear that Ilka will exploit Carter, that her book will appropriate his image for her own purposes. Rather, the students "want the book about Carter to be a black book," portraying him as "a black man among blacks, a man among men" (286). For them Carter's manhood is synonymous with his blackness; his true identity, his comfortable social self, exists only among his own people. The students, however, neglect the problematic, multiple nature of identity—that it can have many guises, changing to suit the context; that each such identity has its validity; that Carter had a genuine, if shaky, relationship with Ilka. Indeed, Carter's identity was created as much by context within White society—by his partial, problematic integration—as by Black segregation; the drunken, confused Carter, disgusted by his own status, is a vital ingredient of Carter the African American theoretician. Hybridization should not be romanticized; it is often a painful, haphazard process replete with false starts and dead ends. Carter himself considers Ilka a prime support of his identity when he jokingly proclaims that her last name, "Weissnix," means "Notwhite" (287). The signifier "White" here takes on the mythological characteristics of the oppressor; Carter's joke recognizes Ilka as outside of this category in her status as a Jew, a Holocaust survivor, and a human being.

Despite this recognition, the overall movement of *Her First American* is from togetherness to separation. John Edgar Wideman's "Valaida" (1989) reverses this direction, employing a Jewish narrator, a Holocaust survivor given the generic American Jewish name Mr. Cohen. Alienated from his Black maid throughout most of the story, Cohen experiences a final, spiritual epiphany that, however, may exist only in his mind. The narrative consciousness, distant from its African American author's perspective, forces an imaginative leap across social borders. Mr. Cohen evolves from evading and hence dehumanizing his Black maid, Clara Jackson, to an extraordinary empathy, a reversal of the author's own psychic border-crossing. As often happens the Holocaust becomes a crucial tool of identification, for as a child in a concentration camp Mr. Cohen's life was saved by the African American singer Valaida Snow, one of the few Blacks unfortunate enough to fall into Nazi hands. Driving an orchid-colored Mercedes and having been awarded a golden trumpet by the queen of Denmark, Valaida is an African American glamour symbol. Yet she too is degraded by the Holocaust, a larger-than-life figure dehumanized, made less-than-life, thrown together with the Jews. In "Valaida" it is her lonely act of saving a Jewish child, rather than her glitz as a performer, that ultimately raises her from sub- to suprahuman status, reversing her significance as a mythologized sign of blackness.

Neither idealized sign—superhuman or brute—allows Blacks a fully complex human status; in perceiving Valaida Snow, the lonely Mr. Cohen cannot bridge the barrier of myth. Unable to humanize Clara Jackson, and embarrassed by this incapacity, he has spent years avoiding her "systematically. Seldom were they both in the same room at the same time . . . because clearly none was large enough to contain them and the distance they needed" (Wideman 1989, 30). Jew and Black are here utterly separate; Mr. Cohen reifies his maid, making of her a necessary cleaning tool while evading her humanity. This behavior may be attributed simply to racism, but it is more likely caused by a guilt complex due to Mr. Cohen's status in American society relative to Jackson. Having been dehumanized himself, Mr. Cohen is embarrassed by his own dehumanization of another, even if on a relatively puny scale and in a manner bereft of violence or overt force. In the concentration camp, Jew and Black had been mutually devalued; Mr. Cohen now operates within an ideological and economic system that devalues only the Black. The way economic status defines relations between the two peoples contrasts with the Holocaust as the ultimate sign of difference. Mr. Cohen is unable to articulate his own dehumanization, his suffering unspeakable acts to which Clara Jackson's status doesn't compare. Paradoxically, both as master and as victim, his status is separate from hers, perhaps inexplicable. He may further fear her implicit hostility toward White people, her lack of understanding. His final reaching out to her, then, is a desperate cry for sympathy. Her uncertain reaction leaves Black and Jewish relations unresolved; any resolution occurs only in Mr. Cohen's head.

In "Valaida" the primary physical symbol of blackness, and to a lesser extent Jewishness, is hair. Initially a symbol of division, through a humanizing irony it metamorphoses into one of conjunction. Mr. Cohen's "thick, straight, black hair" (30) differentiates him from the gentiles, yet the more extreme difference of Jackson's hair from the dominant cultural standard becomes a means of separating her from Mr. Cohen:

> Hair he'd never imagined. Like balled yarn in his grandmother's lap. Like a nursery rhyme. *Black sheep. Black sheep, have you any wool?* So different from what he grew on his head . . . that he could not truly consider it hair, but some ersatz substitute. . . . (31)

This alien substance marks her as the dark Other, reinforced by her status as a maid, her entry into his home not through ties of family or friendship but merely to provide a service.

Simultaneously, however, Clara Jackson provides a link to humanity for the isolated Mr. Cohen through her motion and singing, which interrupt his static life, and through his increasing dependence on her to straighten his apartment, clean and repair his suits, bring order. Her hair proves symbolic here too, for "He'd been tempted countless times to touch it" (31), to explore difference while creating human contact. Finally one night near Christmas he breaks down, serves her coffee—reversing their previous server/served relationship—and tells of how "a colored woman once saved my life" (32). If the Holocaust has been an inexplicability, telling of it is an ultimate unburdening, an attempt to bridge barriers. The psychological effect of this release, of Cohen's sharing his terrible story, is not made explicit, at least not until the final epiphany. Jackson's reaction is even more opaque; the contact may be one-directional, with Mr. Cohen employing his maid as a device of unburdening. Indeed, her reaction implies a continued separation, a lumping of Mr. Cohen with the rest of the White world: "Always thought it was just you people over there doing those terrible things to each other" (39). Having reified European history as irrelevant, she has perceived no connection between Black and Jewish history. Whether the story of Valaida will alter Jackson's historical vision is left to speculation.

When Jackson leaves, Mr. Cohen again consigns her to an Otherness, but a changed one emanating not from a dominant cultural perspective but a Jewish one; he is estranged from not a dark, but a goyish, Other: "In every corner of the city they'd be welcoming their Christ, their New Year with extravagant displays of joy" (40). Jackson now melts into the Christian dominant society from which Mr. Cohen is isolated, that same society responsible for traditional anti-Semitism. The categories by which people separate themselves are numerous; Jews may be isolated from other minorities *and* from dominant culture, a multiplicity of alienations that vexes our multiethnic society. Yet, naked under the dominant cultural eye, minority self-awareness may lead to identification; the hair from which Mr. Cohen had been alienated now becomes a device of symbolic conjunction, at least for an instant, in his imagination: "The faces of her relatives become his. Everyone's hair is thick and straight and black" (40). If Valaida's physical characteristics threw her, due to Nazi ideology, together with Mr. Cohen's doomed relatives, these characteristics now serve, through story and imagination, to conjoin Jew and Black. For an instant the human family becomes one. In the hands of an African American writer portraying a Jewish consciousness art briefly overcomes the constrictions of subject position.

The focus of consciousness seems strictly African American in Gloria Naylor's *Bailey's Cafe* (1992), a work far broader in its narrative scope than "Valaida." The novel concentrates not on an individual consciousness, but assembles a larger cast, a cross-section of Black history, a plethora of voices creating complex thematic juxtapositions. *Bailey's Cafe* thus relies not on internal consciousness but on external dialogue, in conjunction with powerful symbols, to probe Black and Jewish relations. The physical setting of the novel is as much symbol as real, a café on the margins to which the dispossessed—outcasts and prostitutes—find their way, an ambiguous haven for those "hanging on to . . . the edge of the world" (Naylor 1993, 28). The setting is precarious in time as well as place; the action occurs in the late 1940s in a world recently decimated by war—by Holocaust and Hiroshima. Bailey is the only name given the narrator, the novel's guiding voice through a cacophony of stories. In this setting no Jews appear until the novel is some two-thirds of the way through, and then only sporadically. Nevertheless the symbolic Jewish role is vital, as Europe's outcasts whose remnants Black soldiers have just helped rescue. For once, Blacks are members of a triumphant army encountering a helpless people. Although Bailey himself fought on the Japanese front, Jews appear prominently in the figures of Gabe, a survivor of Hitler's Europe; and Mariam, a mystical Ethiopian Jewess.

Bailey and Gabe's discussions are misleading. *Bailey's Cafe* doesn't practice what it preaches, at least regarding Black-Jewish relations. Or rather the preachments of Bailey, the narrative tissue that holds the text together, contradict the novel's symbolic action. Bailey says of his friendship with Gabe, the Jewish pawnbroker,

He's a Russian Jew. I'm an American Negro. Neither of us is considered
a national treasure in our countries, and that's where the similarity ends.
We don't get into comparing notes on who did what to whom the most.
Who's got the highest pile of bodies. The way I see it, there is no comparison. When most folks come out with that phrase, what they're really saying is that their pain is worse than your pain. But Gabe knows
exactly what I mean: they're two different ball games. (220)[2]

Bailey's statement may seem a conversation stopper, effectively ending
Black-Jewish dialogue for want of a common history: the two peoples are
different—an extended comparison can only mislead. However, given the
current nature of Black-Jewish exchange, it really acts as a buffer designed to avoid the trap of endless competition for victim status, a disclaimer that reenacts, in a mutually sensitive way, Fishgoppel and Ebony's
stomping apart with no room for further dialogue.

Bailey's tactic of preferring disengagement to competitive victimization reprises Laurence Thomas's strategy of circumventing a controversy
that seems only to divide Blacks and Jews. The implicit thrust in *Bailey's
Cafe*, though, is to disagree with Thomas, to make the Holocaust part of
the continuum of a common history. So Gabe objects to Bailey's characterization of Hitler as an inexplicable anomaly:

We're talking about a real monster. But Gabe won't budge on this one.
He says, No, we are talking about a human being. I would like to believe you are right, he says; it would allow me to sleep at night. . . . No,
my friend, he was no more than a man. And Hitler had help. (219–20)

Slavery and the Holocaust are both horrors dictated by recurring (if often
submerged) features of human nature; the pain and suffering of Blacks
and Jews are comparable, examples of the same cruel historical phenomenon, even if the unique features of this suffering should not be blurred.
If, in *Her First American*, a Jewish author places remarks equating Black
and Jewish suffering in an African American mouth—"When a whole
race . . . is systematically humiliated, it is tantamount to genocide" (Segal
1985, 263)—here an African American author voices the argument that
both peoples suffered an evil explicable through the stream of human
history. Naylor has heavily stacked the argument against Holocaust essentialism by placing it in the mouth of the most unassailable character, a
Jewish Holocaust survivor. To Gabe, Hitler's place within a larger context makes the danger very real and underscores the necessity of remembrance. Hitler lives in the recesses of the human psyche that demonize,

that create the need for an enemy. To make of him a unique historical figure is to reduce the danger to an impossibility. Given the appropriate combination of circumstances other Hitlers may arise, have indeed arisen, and we may participate in their evil. Only through historical connection is the Holocaust relevant. The approach is tricky, fraught with dangers and reductions on either side: how to make of the Holocaust, and of slavery, full and unique historical events while retaining their universal character as warnings of the evil of which humanity is capable? *Bailey's Cafe* doesn't reconcile this contradiction, but instead juxtaposes versions of the two perspectives.

Symbolically, however, the novel does provide for a spiritual reconciliation between Blacks and Jews through the figure of Mariam, an Ethiopian Jewish girl about to give virgin birth. The world of the Falashan Jews from which she has come is archetypal for both the Jewish and African American diaspora:

> They're outcasts in their own nation and only allowed to be tenants on the land. . . . Keepers of the Commandments. Commandments given to ex-slaves. To the dispossessed. It is a poor man's faith so it has thrived among them well. A faith built on what is always attainable for the poor: prayer, children, and memories. (Naylor 1993, 146)

In a similar way, America's Blacks, ex-slaves long denied property, basic rights, and full American citizenship gave religion a central role in their communities. Even more than the wandering Jew or the bewildered African lost in America, Mariam is an overdetermined symbol of dispossession: female in a patriarchy; Jewish in a gentile nation; Black in a Eurocentric world; and migrating from a country ravished by Italian fascists preaching a neoclassical racism. Terror is at the root of our neocolonial, postmodern world; violence, the origin-point of cultural hybridity.

In an even starker contradiction, Mariam is a Christian symbol embodied in a Jew, new hope about to be born among the dispossessed, a new version of the Virgin Mary. She's also a symbol of America giving birth to a new beginning for the wretched from the far corners of the earth under the auspices of a culture known for conventionally snowy-white representations of Mary and Jesus. Mariam, then, is a version of what James Baldwin calls "the disreputable, sun-baked Hebrew" at the root of Christianity, rather than "the mercilessly fanatic and self-righteous Saint Paul" (1993, 44) who, to Baldwin at least, has undermined the original Christian ideals. Mariam's existence similarly threatens the reductive version of Christianity that European colonialism bore around the world; in her, Christianity is returned to both Jewish and African roots. She combines two outcast peoples in herself while embodying the holiest figure of the religion that, in its official version, cast them out. As a Christian figure, however, she never loses her Jewishness; her child undergoes a wondrous circumcision rite with Blacks playing the roles of honorary Jews, a kind of ceremony of outcasts on the margins of America. Like Emanuel in "Zagrowsky Tells," the child is a symbol of an America marked by crossbreeding, by fertile new possibility.

The hope is fleeting. The child disappears, taken to a homeless shelter, confounding the symbolic new beginning. The novel ends unable to satisfy the closure that traditional myth demands; it tells, rather, the tale of a late modernist, postcolonial world in which a grand climax is endlessly deferred. Similarly, Black America has had much of its hopefulness eroded. America is not a religious or mythic utopia, but merely a country failing to live up to its ideals. Bailey makes this same point about an Israel held up as the mythic Jewish haven: "[I]nside those borders it's the same old story: You got your haves and your have-nots. You got those who are gonna be considered inferior to others because of the type of Jew they are, the color of Jew they are, or whatever" (Naylor 1993, 222). History is always corrupt and fragmented; only symbol is pure. Even at the point of its creation Israel was compromised: secular Jew bickers with Orthodox; Ashkenazi with Oriental; the status of Black Jews is undetermined. So Mariam's baby tumbles off the map, out of the novel, while Bailey's customers gripe, "—There's no such thing as a black Jew. Ain't being one or the other bad enough? / —I'm not messing with those people . . . I don't trust those people . . ." (223). Naylor certainly wrote these words intensely aware of current Black-Jewish feuding. Even as the mystical event, the virgin birth, occurs, those on the sidelines snicker and slander. The haven of the dispossessed that is Bailey's café will not last. Only in the symbolic world of the novel may Blacks and Jews be reconciled, yet the novel calls brutal attention to the flimsy nature of this symbolism. In the real Israel Jew fights Arab; a continent away, at the ur-scene of a marginalized America intimating hope for a multicultural dream, the infighting has already begun.

Naylor's conciliatory approach to Black-Jewish relations, evident in speeches by both Bailey and Gabriel, is not developed through a probing exploration of an Other consciousness, as occurs in Wideman and, from an external perspective, Segal. Rather, Naylor uses the condition of post–World War II America as a platform from which to illuminate current issues. Like Farrakhan, she usurps the Jewish Holocaust in creating a myth of a chosen people; in striking contrast to Farrakhan, however, Naylor uses this myth to make terror and oppression a common human problem.

Segal and Wideman, too, appropriate the voice of the Other, of each other's people, to interrogate the concept of Othering. The Holocaust thus becomes a great connective event, an ultimate symbol of common suffering. In all three authors, however, the problems raised by vast historical comparisons can be resolved only briefly, only at the human level. Of course, this is the level at which we all live (although as individuals we are largely created by our history and circumstances). That these personal contacts remain ephemeral illustrates the current impasse in Black-Jewish relations. In a time dominated by mass media the complexity of multiple community interactions may be obliterated, fashioned into instant mythmaking. In restoring both personal and historical complexity, in the humanity of their portrayals, these stories reveal multiple perspectives, creating, through clashing discourses, a common dialogue.

II

Bailey's Cafe combines a complex exploration of consciousness—the "modern novel"—with an older form of didactic storytelling. This term should not be read in a pejorative way, for a hierarchical reading of narrative forms culminating in the modern novel is consistent neither with a postmodern sensibility nor with the kind of social/historical approach this book favors. Didactic and satiric literature, while different from an intimate exploration of consciousness, reveal not just social and political concerns but accompanying psychological conditions. Ishmael Reed's *Reckless Eyeballing* (1986) uses satire to decode as social constructs the multiple masks of race, ethnicity, and gender our society encourages. Perhaps it is the satiric mode that allows Reed the distance to confront current difficulties between Blacks and Jews more directly than other authors.

Much as Grace Paley exposes contradictions in Jewish attitudes through Izzy Zagrowsky's interior dialogue, Reed's novel uses exterior dialogues to mischievously depict contortions in Black perceptions. The contradictory ways the various characters perceive Jews says more about their social and psychological needs than about any actual Jewish characteristics. *Reckless Eyeballing* derives its force from the clash of various characters, each of whom is presented as an ideogram mouthing overblown clichés about Black-Jewish relations. As with *Invisible Man* the hapless protagonist, Ian Ball, is propelled by conflicting ideologies. A network of reductive characters who act as mouthpieces for particular ideologies form the matrix of his search for self-definition. However, these characters are so extreme—mirroring the absurd extremities of larger social configurations—as to forestall this search. Ball is characterized as two-faced, as "nothin' but a trickologist with . . . fuzzy quick lines" (Reed 1986, 106), a description well suited to Reed's own narrative strategy (and likely an autobiographical comment). If Ellison's invisible man naively accepts a variety of ideologies to end by rejecting all ideology, Ian Ball is more cynical, a postmodern figure for whom ideology is manipulable to suit individual ends. So he is capable of simultaneously paying tribute to (White) feminist values in order to achieve success as a playwright and engaging in a campaign of subversion against "feminist-sympathizers" who in his mind betray the Black male. He is the invisible man finally emerged from his hiding place in the form of another Ellison character, Rinehart, who metamorphoses through "Rine the runner and Rine the gambler and Rine the briber and Rine the lover and Rinehart the Reverend." Ball, too, through his multiple roles poses the question "Could he himself be both rind and heart? What is real anyway?" (Ellison 1972, 487). Identity, what one believes to be one's true or inner self, is defined largely by the masks one wears, which in turn are difficult to separate from one's actions. Ian Ball is an intellectualized, politically aware version of Rinehart fighting the good fight not just for himself but, in the guise of the Phantom Flower, for Black males. As long as Black men are stereotyped as criminals, the mask of blackness is one he can never shed.

The multiple identities and vulnerabilities of Black males are apparent in a spectrum of attitudes toward Jewish Americans. *Reckless Eyeballing*'s form as satiric fable alleviates the pain of a naturalistic presentation of social problems. In its simplest form the fable presents a coherent ideology, a single perspective on human personality and morality. In doing so it resembles in miniature such ideological systems as religion, communism, and nationalism, which organize the world through overarching principles or, less charitably, myths. Myths of Jewishness are multiple and variegated in *Reckless Eyeballing;* their clash is the creative tension that drives the novel. The fable form also prevents an overly blunt exploration of Black angst; layers of irony obfuscate the novel's "message" and protect against the kind of critical reception that greeted Chester Himes's *Lonely Crusade*.[3] Explorations of Jewish characters and, even more, of Black attitudes toward Jews have always been a risky business for Black authors; indeed, Reed claims that African American "attempts to write about other major cultures is considered a case of 'Reckless Eyeballing.' What you lookin' at" (Reed 1988, 60–61).

Reckless Eyeballing appropriates, from an African American position, some of the power of dominant discourse to control racial, social, and legal definitions. The title reverses the charge of "reckless eyeballing" used in the Jim Crow South to prosecute Blacks for looking directly upon White women. Reed has decried the ability of outsiders to "define me and even profit from interpreting what they call 'the black experience'" (59–60), a condition satirically inverted in *Reckless Eyeballing*. The position of surveying eye long forbidden to Blacks makes the novel an enactment of its title. Mechanisms of surveying and representation are co-opted by a Black male sensibility and turned brashly upon Jews, Irish Americans, and White feminists.

Dominant culture is the originary location of such surveillance, which resembles Foucault's panopticon, a prison system whereby inmates are constantly exposed to the view of a central authority (Foucault 1977, 200). While the panopticon is a powerful metaphor for the pervasive nature of ideology, it is a totalizing and reductive formulation, for ideology, in its actual workings, tends to be decentered, scattered among numerous social levels and locations, and contested by local resistance. The human psyche in Reed's novel acts as a playing field for a variety of ideologies—largely methods of dealing with dominant ideology. If each ideology is itself relatively coherent, their intersection reveals their absurdity in describing actual conditions. By juxtaposing ideological narratives in the mouths of a variety of informants, Reed accentuates their extremist, mythic character. Together these worldviews present a clashing, dissonant mess; the human mind, in its search for stability, organizes them, perhaps simultaneously accepting several, perhaps dwelling obsessively on a single ideology. This last, simplest solution is tempting to individuals burdened by extreme psychological stress, desperate for a unified explanation of their woes.

In *Reckless Eyeballing* contradictory ideologies clash through the encounters of a variety of dogmatic characters. Reed's obsession with history and with sociological investigation of racial and sexual relations makes the work as much a treatise as a novel, exposing the fallacies of the closed systems we humans reduce history to. Such self-defeating divisions—the kind that destroyed the Black-Jewish alliance—are an ultimate target of Reed's satire. In addition to dealing with Black anti-Semitism, the novel portrays divisions between Black men and women. To the extent that the White feminists Reed satirizes are tools of the upper

class—certainly a debatable proposition, but one that Reed seems to believe—they are part of the conspiracy against Black males. Rather than
tools it seems more accurate to say that they are members of the upper
and middle classes and hence bounded by a set of assumptions and interests that they can at best partially escape.

For two characters, Jake Brashford and Randy Shank, history is the
plaything of conspiratorial Jews. Both are playwrights from the Black
nationalist period who have since failed to please the opinion makers—
perceived as Jewish—who serve as a gateway to dominant cultural acceptance. Both conceive of Jews as neither Black nor White, but as sui
generis agents of dominant culture who appropriate Black achievements
as their own. To them Jews occupy the ultimate Rinehart position; they
are infinitely malleable, adjusting to all conditions (an ability Ian Ball
envies). Shank considers White Jews as wolves in the clothing of another
kind of wolf: "They [dominant society] let them be white now because
they serve the white man by keeping an eye on us, monitoring us, providing him with statistics about us, and interpreting us" (Reed 1986, 67). A
panoptical mechanism of constant surveillance is here policed by Jews.
There is a hint of identification in Shank's classification of Jews, like
African Americans, as outsiders; overall, however, Shank perceives Jews
as powerful servants of the dominant culture.

Besides their direct involvement in economic exploitation, Jews are,
in this ideology, usurpers of Black culture. Brashford blames his lack of
recent artistic accomplishment on the Jews having "stolen all of the black
material, so there's nothing for me to write about" (30). Paranoia about
Jewish usurpation of Black achievements extends to the idea that American Jews aren't the real Jews, the biblical Jews; as Shank puts it, "Black
people invented Judaism," and "Abraham was a black man who fucked
black women and had babies by them" (56). Traditional African American identification with the biblical Israelites mutates into jealousy; the
Black slaves in America converge with the Jewish slaves in Egypt as Shank
wills himself into a pseudo-Jewish identity. White Jewish usurpation of
African American culture becomes the extension of Jewish usurpation of
cultures and traditions originating in Africa.

Brashford and Shank's actions, however, reveal anti-Semitism as
cloaking a deep affiliation between Blacks and Jews, particularly among
intellectuals and artists. Complaining about Brashford's anti-Semitic ti-
rades on the phone, Brashford's wife reveals that "I'm Jewish and he has
a Jewish son" (117). The intensity of Brashford's emotions is that of an
alienated family member, a kind of bastard son, a literally Black sheep.

After his one successful play Brashford feels isolated from the literary establishment represented by Jews. The same is true of Randy Shank who, immediately following his brutal invective against the Jews, demonstrates a startling turn of behavior toward a distinguished, artistic, presumably Jewish couple: "'Oh, Mr. and Mrs. Epstein,' he said gushingly, almost falling over himself, 'shall I fetch you a taxi?'" (57). When the Epsteins ignore Shank and acknowledge Ian Ball's talent, Shank "couldn't stand it. Rage bristled at his insides" (57). The patrons whose recognition fueled his previous success have turned their attention elsewhere. Desperate for acceptance by these paragons of culture, Shank displays the complex hatred fueled by rejection, hatred characteristic of a failed love relationship. As *Lonely Crusade* exhibited fifty years ago, the attitude of the Black intelligentsia toward Jews may be marked by extreme contradictions, by love, rage, and envy.

If, to Randy Shank, Jews take on a kind of pseudoblackness—or perhaps Blacks a more authentic Jewishness—a similar identification is voiced by *Reckless Eyeballing*'s pro-Jewish characters. Paul Shoboater exclaims, "Black people are strongest when they emulate the Jews. How do you think they got through slavery?" (85). Shoboater further discerns the two groups as united through their victimization by such groups as the Ku Klux Klan and the Nazis. He explains that Jews benefit Blacks through acting as a defense against discrimination and violence: "The Jews are the only ones standing between black people and these barbarians from Europe that are over here" (83). The long European history of anti-Jewish pogroms is conflated with the enslavement, lynching, and ghettoization of Blacks. Jewish liberalism, according to Shoboater, is all that prevents continued discrimination, a theory that implicitly acknowledges the Jewish role in fighting for civil rights legislation. Tremonisha Smarts further articulates the connection between Blacks and Jews, though in a more contradictory, defensive way, with the two linked through the negative of victimization. Smarts describes "Nazi magazines and newspapers that showed Jewish men mugging and raping German women. The Jewish men were always drawn dark" (60). The classic Southern stereotype of Blacks as the dark Other, criminal and bestial, lusting after White women, is applied to Jews. Both Nazis and Ku Klux Klan members suffer from sexual fear and jealousy; a paranoid need to protect the purity of White women—actually a displaced anxiety, sexual and otherwise—incites racist violence. This sort of psychological-historical analysis is prompted by Smarts's feminist investigations of gender roles in conjunction with her racial position. As we shall see, her rebellion against White feminism is critical in her evolving exploration of Jewish history, since female Black artists are positioned relative to White feminists similarly to the earlier relationship of Blacks to Jews.

Although *Reckless Eyeballing* seems to play off all sides, to deconstruct history through offering contradictory worldviews, its overall movement, particularly filtered through the perceptions of Smarts, is toward an identification with Jewish history. The novel's action develops a mutual Black-Jewish interest in opposing bigotry. Jim Minsk, the Jewish director who supports Black playwright Ian Ball, speaks for Jews in their modern alliance with Blacks as well as their common historical experience: "The Europeans were massacring Jews before they went into Africa after the blacks" (15). When Minsk visits a Southern university he hears a radio preacher voice this same opposition between Europe and its Others, although in a horribly inverted fashion: "The Jews and the blacks are the children of Satan, ladies and gentlemen, descendants of Cain" (35). The university is located near the site of Leo Frank's lynching. At this place, emblematic of the racist threat to both Blacks and Jews, a ritualistic performance reenacts the death of Leo Frank, who appears as Dracula. Daniel Boyarin describes the terrain of the vampire as "a doubly Orientalist fantasy: the Jew as Oriental and eastern Europe itself as the Orient, the site of Dracula and his brethren" (1997, 41). Sucking the life from a pure Christian woman (Reed 1986, 42), Dracula epitomizes a metahistorical racism, the dark, cunning rapist, a figure conjoining stereotypes of Orientals, Blacks, and medieval Jews. Minsk's death at the hands of an angry lynch mob shouting racial epithets symbolically links Southern lynchings and European pogroms. Through racial murder Black and Jewish history conjoin.

If *Reckless Eyeballing*'s plot exonerates Jews, it features a substitute figure of conspiracy against African American males in the form of White feminists. The villain here is Becky French, the producer who embodies White feminist power over Black artists. Her preferred African American play makes Black men into vicious, oversexed killers. White feminists are represented by Reed as fanatics who level off race and class differences, creating a Manichaean view of history as, according to Becky French, a turf war between men in which women act as innocent pawns (59). History's multiply determined, irreducible complexity has been, as so often happens, reduced to a single explanation.

The immediate purpose of Reed's attack upon White feminists is to protect Black men from being portrayed as beasts, a motivation made clear in Reed's other writing, as in his complaint regarding *The Color*

Purple: "[C]ritics in the media have used both the book and the movie as excuses to indict all black men" (1988, 146). Reed's exploration of the twin themes of Jewish and female conspiracy stems from Black male vulnerability. Indeed, *Reckless Eyeballing* begins by depicting omnipresent vulnerability in describing Ian Ball's mother as "A woman who could look around corners and underneath the ground. He used to have nightmares of eyes with wings swooping down upon him" (1986, 4). This is ur-surveillance by a controlling eye at the very root of the psyche. Reed's matriarchal eye is connected to its ostensible antithesis, the patriarchal eye; supposedly nurturing, the motherly role is often to punish, to reinforce the norms of dominant society, to prepare the child for life within that society. For this ur-eye may be substituted two other figures: Jews and White feminists. The novel's opening paragraph parodies feminist patronage in explicitly exchanging matriarchy for patriarchy, describing a painting of the Puritan fathers whose faces are those of feminists. Escorted by his mother to the gallows (1) Ball replays the primal scene of sacrifice to dominant society. Ian Ball is predetermined guilty of an unknown crime. So society judges the baby who wears a Black skin always already guilty of Otherness, and Black mothers are charged with inducting their children into this society.

African American insecurities regarding women and Jews are evident in comparing *Reckless Eyeballing* to Chester Himes's *Lonely Crusade*. In both novels Black males find independent accomplishment stifled by the mechanism of dominant judgment. Just as Tremonisha Smarts eclipses Ball, Brashford, and Shanks, so Ruth Gordon's success undermines Lee Gordon's masculinity. If exaggerated Black masculinity is a pretense, a defense against acute vulnerability, it often appears quite threatening to outsiders. Perceptions of Black male sexuality have historically motivated lynching, a fear that persists in both Reed and Himes. The historical roots are deep; Katrin Schwenk explains that "Reed sees black men jeopardized by the feminist outrage against rape and black machismo, which fits all too well the myth of the black rapist" (1994, 317). These perceptions are one cause of the high rate of Black incarceration and of police brutality. Reed's concern with portrayals of Black males is legitimate, given that audiences tend to focus on that which reinforces their preconceptions.

Fear of emasculation is a root cause of Black anti-Semitism in both *Reckless Eyeballing* and *Lonely Crusade*, novels in which Black masculinity is threatened by both Jewish "femininity" and female "masculinity." African Americans may internalize the mores of a society that dehumanizes them, transferring their hatred of that society to some other object, a psychological drama that *Reckless Eyeballing* satirizes in its Black male characters' susceptibility to conspiratorial theories. The Jew takes on the contradictory—yet mutually intensifying—traits of enemy and benefactor. For Black men the Jew may be lawyer, advocate, political ally, and artistic patron, the same plethora of roles that White feminists have occupied relative to Black female artists and intelligentsia. The combination of gratitude and resentment that Blacks may feel toward Jews is also felt by Black women regarding White feminists. Like Jewish patronage, mainstream feminism laid the groundwork for a wide critical acceptance of Black women authors while remaining ignorant of vast areas of Black experience.[4] So Tremonisha Smarts's rebellion against Becky French resembles in miniature the Black nationalist rebellion against Jewish patronage. As she begins to disavow White feminism, as personified by Becky French, Smarts joins Shoboater in comparing Jewish and Black historical roles. To Ball's question, "'Are you saying that World War Two happened because Hitler was trying to pass for white?'" Smarts's curt reply, "'Overzealous assimilation, it happens all the time'" (Reed 1986, 65), dramatizes the hidden yet omnipresent nature of both Black and Jewish self-hatred. Extreme reaction to the assimilationist drive, the compulsion to fit into dominant society and to suppress Other identities, is a common trope for the marginalized. Smarts's remark posits self-hatred as extending from a denial of Hitler's own Jewish blood to a destruction of all Jews, a stunningly disproportionate cause-effect relationship. Extermination is the only means of expunging the Jew—or Black—within. In expressing the ultimate self-hatred as "overzealous assimilation," Smarts sardonically links Black and Jew, revealing a keen perception of the nature of racial ideology. As she rebels against her White feminist patrons, she grows sympathetic to another intermittent Black ally, Jews.

Reed may have personal reasons for satirizing White feminism. The success of such authors as Alice Walker and Toni Morrison, bolstered by the feminist movement, may be perceived as coming at the expense of Black men. In the short term it may be true that as Black literary women have prospered, the careers of Black male authors—including Reed—have stagnated. Still, the long-term effects of encouraging a larger reading public and advancing new themes probably help all African American authors. Among the Black males in *Reckless Eyeballing* only Shoboater, who accepts Jewish patronage, remains successful within his niche. Meanwhile the glamorous Smarts has chosen—or been chosen by—the currently dominant patrons: White feminists. Literary success in this cosmology is a result of pleasing the correct social and political group. Ian Ball's active pursuit of female patronage is a blatant attempt to receive a share of this success. In his double role of feminist sympathizer and Phantom Flower he personifies a splintering of old liberal coalitions into the conflicting demands of identity politics. The originary psychic split between White and Black, long ago punctured by Jews (among other groups), is pulled in yet another direction by feminism. Waiting expectantly are a host of othernesses—Hispanic, Asian, homosexual—to further fracture the psyche, confound loyalties, and call for new configurations and new judgments. Meanwhile the figure of Jim Minsk—the figure of Jewish patronage— lies dead. The Black male artist must find a path outside the constrained view of literary success in *Reckless Eyeballing*. Precarious and lonely as this terra incognita might seem, rich new possibilities abound. Ralph Ellison long ago recognized the array of sources that will guide the future evolution of American literature. African American authors, from Toni Morrison to Charles Johnson to Gloria Naylor, are even now exploring new facets of our hybrid culture.

Parallels and Paralysis

*You cannot have a friendship unless everybody is tall and
everybody is looking one another in the eye.*
—Roger Wilkins

Even as literature explores entrances into multiple subject positions, probing a common if tangled understanding, the economic divergence in Black
and Jewish status leads to discord. The dialogic dynamic, with its escalating hybridity and sympathy, has run counter to worldwide economic trends
that leave the poorest people ever more hopeless, more cut off from participation in the mainstream economy. The existence of a large, seemingly permanent Black underclass contrasts vividly with overall Jewish
affluence. Hence the undercurrents of rage that surfaced in the late 1960s
have been repeatedly aggravated. And hence relations between Blacks
and Jews have been marked by increasing stagnation and resentment

The 1991 clashes in the Crown Heights section of Brooklyn starkly
illustrate this divergence. As Anna Deavere Smith's performative documentary *Fires in the Mirror* dramatizes, Black and Jewish perceptions are
distinctly separate. Through exploring how Black and Jewish worldviews
are constructed by a specific cultural history, Smith shows a vivid humanity and an ideological extremism coexisting. Her perplexed human portraits extend Grace Paley's illumination of psychological contradiction
and Ishmael Reed's satire on self-deception. Perhaps the only answer to
these extremes of misunderstanding is *Fires in the Mirror* itself; its remarkable human spectrum creates a kind of dialogue composed of overlapping

207

monologues in which the participants refuse to listen to each other. In Anna Deveare Smith the clash of ethnic heritages that make up America is at once ugly, vivid, beautiful, and terrifying.

The Crown Heights situation was unique in bringing an impoverished Black population, largely Caribbean, together with a Hasidic population clinging to ancient traditions far removed from most of American Jewry. Yet Crown Heights was symbolically central; it isolated and displayed the clash of particularism at the margins of America, the search for identity as a shield against a bewildering world. In the 1980s and '90s the visible part of Black/Jewish relations has been the extremes. Most blatant, and most publicized, is the rhetoric of Conrad Mohammed and Louis Farrakhan, emanating from a desperate condition in which the American dream seems simply untenable. Cut off from both historical African culture and social and economic inclusion, poor urban African Americans are ripe for a charismatic leader presenting a heroic counternarrative to that of dominant society.

If Farrakhan's sound and fury (signifying almost nothing in terms of real power, at least within dominant society) have been amplified by a media hungry for newsbites, the change in Jewish attitudes is less dramatic, but perhaps more important in terms of actual consequence. A comfortable Jewish America has no need for a charismatic leader. Far more politically influential than the Black Muslims is the neoconservative movement, largely Jewish in origin, with its critique of liberalism and radicalism as utopian ideals that rarely achieve what they promise. Although the majority of Jews continue to follow a traditional, if moderated, liberalism, neoconservativism is influential beyond its numbers, initiating and legitimizing attacks on government, particularly on welfare and affirmative action. If neoconservativism signals the end of the Jewish American role as primary agents of critique and transformation, such leaders as Louis Farrakhan voice the intractable marginalization of a large segment of Black America. Viewed in proximity, the two movements graphically illustrate the current crisis in Black and Jewish relations. In literature, however, aside from Ishmael Reed, recent developments in Black/Jewish relations have been dealt with only indirectly. Representations seem increasingly removed from immediate political events; reflective of the 1960s as much as the 1990s, they are almost nostalgic. Aside from *Reckless Eyeballing,* only *Fires in the Mirror*, radically different from conventional literature in its use of performance, segmentation, and video—the techniques of postmodern pastiche—speaks to the 1990s.

I

The closest American Jews have come to a nationalist movement similar
to the Black Muslims is the Jewish Defense League (JDL), a highly publicized but relatively unimportant organization. Simultaneously modeled
on and reacting against the Black Panthers—an irony paradigmatic of
Jewish and Black relations—the JDL speaks for those Jews who feel most
detached from the promise of American affluence (Dolgin 1977, 17). Even
the JDL's symbol, a clenched fist emerging from the star of David, pays
homage to the Black Panthers. Paralleling Farrakhan's beliefs about Blacks,
JDL cofounder Meir Kahane decries a Judaism torn from its roots. Kahane
blames American materialism and complains about Jews "steeped in foreign, un-Jewish culture and ideas that stand in stark contradiction to Judaism" (1987, 319). Just as Amiri Baraka revolts from the Black bourgeoisie, Kahane scorns assimilationist Jews who substitute affluence for
historical and cultural memory.[1] In stark contrast to the Black Muslims,
JDL ideology has proved fragile in America, unable to survive the tide of
affluence. American Jewry lacks the broad base of disenfranchised people
necessary for a separatist movement.

Any political movement depends upon the makeup of its constitu-
ency; increasingly safe from anti-Semitism, Jewish America has veered
away from radicalism. Epitomizing this trend, the neoconservative movement accepts and defends American affluence and is cynical about the
possibility of social transformation.[2] Ideologically the neoconservatives,
balanced between assimilationism and a pro-Israel Jewish nationalism,
are less consistent than was the JDL, yet economically and socially they
are far more secure. Jewish neoconservatives struggle to reconcile Jewish
and American identity, with Israel regarded as a counterweight to assimilation. Overall, neoconservatives believe that America is the best country
possible, given the global reality of harsh religious and national feelings.
The earliest neoconservatives viewed themselves as former liberals or
radicals grown realistic, cognizant of the world as it is rather than fighting
for unworkable utopias. Whatever skepticism it may have had about
America, the neoconservative movement has provided intellectual respectability for those who believe in a capitalism uncurbed by government and
see no contradiction between materialism and traditional values. In this
way neoconservatism laid the intellectual groundwork first for Reaganism
and now for the global dominance of free-market ideology.

Neoconservatism arose as a response to 1960s radicalism. It saw

American liberty threatened by the rhetoric of the New Left, by extremist fantasies rather than the realities of human nature. So Nathan Glazer complains of "an untempered and irrational attack on American society, government, and university" (1996, 62). Glazer articulates feelings widespread in the Jewish community: fears of betrayal by Blacks and other minorities, and a disquiet regarding the proper Jewish stance regarding both political interests and larger moral issues. Since America has been good to the Jews, Jewish neoconservatives are supportive of America, accepting its premise as a multiethnic society dedicated to free speech and free enterprise, loosely tied together by a Europeanized elite. Government programs, they believe, threaten the order of this society through unintended effects: "[A] liberal and compassionate social policy has bred all sorts of unanticipated and perverse consequences" (Kristol 1995, 48). Welfare, for instance, discourages individual initiative, leading to cycles of poverty and to single-parent households. Yet, however pertinent some neoconservative critiques may be in specific details, they neglect powerful historical and economic causes of poverty. Government programs, rather than just failing to eliminate poverty, come to be considered the root cause of problems that existed long before such intervention. At one extreme, neoconservative critiques are used to blame the poorest and most oppressed for society's failings, and to discount a larger history of oppression, creating a fictional America whose downfall began in the 1960s with radical attacks upon humanist democracy.

II

Although not explicitly neoconservative, Saul Bellow echoes many of the movement's complaints regarding the shallowness of liberalism, while upholding the efficacy of American individualism. If *Mr. Sammler's Planet* remains silent on questions of economic stratification, Bellow's corrective is *The Dean's December* (1982). Fiction, he decided, was the best medium with which to approach the problems of the Black underclass. Justifying this decision, Bellow describes the novelist as "an imaginative historian, who is able to get closer to contemporary facts than social scientists possibly can." Bellow criticizes bureaucratic "solutions" to poverty that dehumanize the recipients, that leave them trapped in unending cycles of hopelessness: "[I]t became clear to me that no imagination whatsoever had been applied to the problems of demoralized cities. All the approaches have been technical, financial and bureaucratic, and no one has been able to take into account the sense of these lives" (Bellow 1994b, 182). Similar criticism of bureaucratic solutions has intensified throughout the 1980s and '90s as the underclass has come to seem a permanent feature of American life. The American dream has become a tantalizingly cruel fantasy for a significant population trapped economically and, perhaps more importantly, psychologically. Writing in 1994, Cornel West describes the despair created by an apparently irrevocable exclusion from American affluence among the Black underclass, which now faces a

> *nihilistic threat to its very existence.* This threat is not simply a matter of relative economic deprivation and political powerlessness—though economic well-being and political clout are requisites for meaningful black progress. It is primarily a question of speaking to the profound scenes of psychological depression, personal worthlessness, and social despair so widespread in black America. (1993b, 12–13)

Particularly in a society that values personal achievement and consumerism, the withholding of opportunity leads to a politics of victimization and blame. Bellow has proved accurate in his stress on the problem's intractable nature.

Yet, due to its emphasis on individualism, *The Dean's December* proves a limited vehicle for critiquing problems of the underclass. Through the mouthpiece of its protagonist, Dean Corde, and through a series of events that beset him, the novel attacks liberal solutions to poverty and racism. The left-wing attitude toward African Americans is satirized in Corde's self-indulgent nephew, Mason, who takes a voyeuristic journey into the Black ghetto and mouths facile solutions to entrenched problems. By contrast Corde's solutions require tough-minded individuals ready to take responsibility for their own actions, which the novel provides in the form of three Black characters. These positive role models constitute a kind of affirmative action in atonement for Bellow's earlier neglect of worthy Black figures. Relying upon the autonomous individual for a solution, Bellow, through the perspective of Dean Corde, replicates neoconservative simplification of complex historical and social phenomena. African American social and cultural achievements remain invisible in *The Dean's December;* Black society is portrayed through a dichotomy between a thieving, pimping underclass and a few strong individuals who have implicitly accepted the tenets of individualism. Bellow's vantage point, which allows him to create complex interior portraits of characters from his own background, limits him in portraying Black society.

Of course, limited subject position affects all writers, as the case of Grace Paley illustrates. The question is how authors deal with these limitations: how they portray characters removed from their immediate social environment and use intermediaries to portray various distanced and disenfranchised groups. Centered in Corde's consciousness, *The Dean's December* is twice-removed from the Black underclass. Reflecting upon this distance, Corde employs the perspective of Mason as a more leftwing intermediary: "Corde understood very well what his nephew was saying to him. He said it to himself, and this was how it went: You meddle in things you have no sympathy with. These people do what they can in the space they've been confined to" (Bellow 1981, 47). The same liberal guilt and embarrassed distance afflicts both Paley's Faith and Bellow's Corde. Indeed Bellow's decision to grapple with the problems of marginalized Blacks may be due to his awareness of Jewish history; certainly guilt and identification with marginalization flicker through *Henderson the Rain King*, and predominate by the conclusion of *Mr. Sammler's Planet*.

Yet in his journey to the Black ghetto, Corde clearly differs from Faith in "The Long Distance Runner," who revisits her old neighborhood to reestablish her past, to reconnect herself to an America of ethnic marginalization. Corde, by contrast, is a judging presence, one searching for solutions to problems rather than mutual understanding. In *The Dean's December* the narrative voice is that of an American ensconced in six generations of privilege (132). In Bellow the distance from Black society seems purposeful; the vehicles of Henderson and Dean Corde are more removed from any historical identification than a Jewish protagonist would be. Jews, after all, have historically been exoticized and have previously occupied many of today's Black ghettos (both figuratively and literally). By contrast Corde's role as keeper of Western civilization—partly self-appointed, partly inherent in his position as university spokesman—contributes to his distance from African American society. He repeatedly invokes Western virtues, largely through contrast with the horrors of Eastern Europe: "Capitalistic democracies could never be at home with the catastrophe outlook. We are used to peace and plenty, we are for everything nice and against cruelty, wickedness, craftiness, monstrousness" (199). Yet, from an African American perspective, Corde's description belies that core part of American history which engaged in slavery, lynching, and systematic denial of rights, creating wholesale institutions defined by monstrous cruelty and racism.

Still, Bellow does include a sympathetic portrayal of African American suffering, together with an analysis of entrenched economic factors. With mechanization, computerization, and cheap foreign labor, the underclass becomes superfluous, useless even as a reserve labor pool. These conditions lead Corde to ask, "Are they part of American society, or are they going to be eliminated from it?" (165), and to "speak in his articles of 'superfluous populations,' 'written off,' 'doomed peoples'" (192). In contrast to *Mr. Sammler's Planet*, *The Dean's December* acknowledges the dilemma of the African American underclass and their reduction to the margins of the margins, where they risk toppling out of the American narrative. Watching the endless parade of Black criminals in a Chicago court, Corde reflects upon people without a place or past, likely without a future: "No one seemed able to explain what he had done, who he was. It was all: 'You brought us here, you tell us who we are, and what you want with us'" (159). Indirectly, this quote is addressed to the heirs of those who brought slaves to America. The social and cultural amputation of those like the Black thief in *Mr. Sammler's Planet* and the criminals in *The Dean's December* is a long-term responsibility of American society.

Bellow dramatizes the perspective of poor African Americans only indirectly, articulating it through characters who epitomize individual responsibility, such as the American ambassador to Romani: "This man, quite black, very slender, had style, class, cultivation" (64). The admiration bears the intonation of the need to portray a Black man bearing the highest qualities of civilization. In Corde's cosmology, only such individuals can save the beleaguered underclass. Through one such intermediary, Toby Winthrop, who runs a drug detoxification center, the novel powerfully discourses on problems of the Black underclass, of human beings at the nadir of existence. Winthrop exclaims of his patients:

> Those people are down in the cesspool. We reach for them and try to get a hold. Hang on—hang on! They'll drown in the shit if we can't pull 'em out. . . . I'm telling you, Professor, that the few who find us and many hundred of thousand more who never do and never will—they're marked out to be destroyed. Those are people meant to die, sir. (192)

This is the novel's most eloquent plea, a central statement of Bellow's reason for depicting the Black underclass. A similar character, the prison warden Rufus Ridpath, struggles to clean up the corruption and squalor of the Cook County Jail. Ridpath is sabotaged by a liberal establishment unwilling to hold Blacks accountable for their actions, paternalistically reducing them to the status of children. Possibly this is an accurate depiction of the liberal mentality, which may transform the dominant gaze, with its (pseudo)analysis and systematic action, into a paternalistic caricature, a well-meaning yet naive, and in some ways self-serving, version of colonization. However, such a critique of liberalism contains no viable solutions. To depend upon a few isolated individuals to solve entrenched social problems is quite as much a "failure of the imagination" as the bureaucratized policies Bellow criticizes.

Given Bellow's social and economic distance, his appeal for the Black underclass is articulated from the perspective of paternalistic protectors, albeit Black ones. Still, *The Dean's December* develops a powerful sympathy with the condition of the Black underclass, at least as it pertains to the belief—recurrent in Bellow—in a decadent society. Corde confesses, "The worst of it I haven't gotten around to at all—the slums we carry around inside us. Every man's *inner* inner city" (207). The bleak recesses of the human soul, that perennial modernist theme, are symbolized by the Black underclass. Yet blackness also represents an antidote to the alienation, the detachment from emotions and physical enjoyment, of the prototypical modernist figure. In journeying to its dwellings, its slums and jails, for purported altruistic reasons, Corde undertakes the same journey as his nephew Mason, one filled with voyeuristic titillation. The depths of ghetto despair are construed as the depths of their own souls. This, at least, is a conventional modernist reading, one given weight by Corde's words. Corde's exploration of the ghetto is a search for self through contrast—rather than contact—with the Other. Black society remains the object of White psychological needs. In *The Dean's December* the narrative viewpoint is that of Western tradition, celebrating the freedom—but also the responsibility—of the individual. The rhetoric is that of an affluent professional class who gaze down upon the Black underclass in wonder, pity, and disgust as the embodiment of the antirational. Despite the invisibility of Jewish characters, part of the disgust is likely fear of what Bellow has left behind: the Jewish history of ghettoization and marginalization.

III

Literature loosens the boundaries of selfhood; the slippery nature of meaning and symbol is heightened by representations of other consciousnesses. Still, the process must be refracted through an individual author's sensibility, which is necessarily limited by time and place. *Fires in the Mirror* corrodes such limitations by portraying the Crown Heights disturbances between Blacks and Hasidic Jews through a variety of viewpoints taken from verbatim interviews, a "polyphony of perspectives . . . rarely aired and heard in the Black-Jewish dialogue" (West 1993a, xix). Smith articulates her purpose through her critique of acting techniques designed to project one's own emotions and experiences onto others:

> I wanted to develop an alternative to the self-based technique, a technique that would begin with the other and come to the self, a technique that would empower the other to find the actor rather than the other way around. . . . I became increasingly convinced that the activity of reenactment could tell us as much, if not more, about another individual than the process of learning about the other by using the self as a frame of reference. (West 1993a, xxvii)

Smith's performance continues the tradition of documentary filmmaking, of approaching a complex situation through a polyphony of voices. Yet she transcends this through her acting, through taking on the physical characteristics of the various agents in the drama, using this as a gateway to Otherness. Through a collage technique that intimately explores other identities, dialectic acquires new impact.

The video version of *Fires in the Mirror* relies partly on standard documentary techniques. Images of Blacks and Jews in the streets of Crown Heights offer historical contextualization, while depictions of rioting graphically illustrate the immediate conflict. Over this is heard music with African and Jewish roots, a quintessentially American blend of funk rhythms and klezmer horns. The rich sound of multiculturalism glides over the ugliness of ethnic conflict; the heart of Smith's work lies in her dramatic juxtapositions, revealing dreadful ironies and absurdities. To contextualize the Crown Heights conflict she quotes academics, among them Robert Sherman, who describes the contemporary state of American race relations as "a soup of bias—prejudice, racism, and discrimination" (Smith 1993, 64).[3] On this subject Sherman considers our discourse remarkably imprecise; "we have sort of lousy language on the subject and that is a reflection of our unwillingness to deal with it honestly" (66). Denial is ingrained in our language, as a society tied to myths of individuality and equality evades its shortcomings. Smith's Angela Davis describes how, for African Americans, race has been "synonymous with community," how, of necessity, Blacks have been forced to bond together so "that if anybody in the race came under attack then I had to be there" (27). This group defense, mandated by a hostile environment, has taken on a life of

its own. Davis believes that such racially based ideologies are "an increasingly obsolete way of constructing community" (30), that we need
mutual outreach.

But the dilemma remains: how to uphold difference, to welcome and
encourage other identities within an American context, without having
them simply melt into an assimilationist blankness? Theories of blending
and hybridity acknowledge that the old assimilationist model does not
work, that the margins contribute to and change the center (itself an increasingly problematic concept). If this is true culturally, economically
the margins are still very much intact. The Black community portrayed in
Fires in the Mirror is a prototypical example. In their inability to assimilate, the ethnic margins simultaneously announce the need for multicultural
tolerance and undermine schemes for a cohesive America. Through its
very existence, the Orthodox Jewish community of Crown Heights contests the idea of a cultural center, despite economic assimilationism. By
contrast, the Black lower class remains isolated through material and social constraints rather than through choice.

Of course, cultural mixture occurs constantly, regardless of the existence of "pure" ethnic communities, yet such blending does not necessarily create cohesion or a feeling of belonging. As the cultural and commercial apparatus appropriates various "marginal" cultures, the result may be
a token style, a depthless postmodern collage. Such considerations, however, have little direct relevance on the streets of Crown Heights, where
people cling tenaciously to their historical past, allowing culture to shape
them more than they shape it. Old ethnic identities and divisions remain
as immediate as ever. *Fires in the Mirror*'s juxtaposition of Crown Heights
violence with the idealistic search for new communitarian ideals dramatizes the utopian nature of Davis's vision.

The dilemma of Crown Heights is that Blacks and Jews continue to
define themselves through ethnic identity while living virtually on top of
one another. Hasidic Jews define community through ancient religious
and cultural tradition; Blacks, through shared cultural traits and a continued marginalization. Since oppression is a key element in both Black and
Jewish identity, comparative oppression takes on a macabre intensity as
the two groups diverge. The Holocaust, rather than fading with chronological distance, increases in importance as a symbol of exploitation; or
perhaps what was hidden has surfaced, actively contested in rhetoric.

Speaking for a people in the United States drastically more exploited
than Jews, the Black Muslims seek to undermine any continuing Jewish
claim to moral high ground by declaring the true Holocaust as their own.

So Minister Conrad Mohammed declares of the Middle Passage, and of slavery, that "no crime in the history of humanity has before or since equaled that crime. The Holocaust did not equal it[.] Oh, absolutely not" (Smith 1993, 54). Mohammed seeks to dwarf the Jewish Holocaust through sheer numbers: 100 to 250 million dead in the Middle Passage (a probably inflated estimate), versus 6 million Jews; over three hundred years of suffering, versus six years for the Jewish Holocaust (54–55). Yet Mohammed decrees the true horror of this crime to derive not from sheer numbers but from the loss of historical identity, for the African American is an "amnesia victim" who "has lost knowledge of himself . . . and he's living a beast life" (56). This reiterates Lawrence Thomas's argument from *Vessels of Evil*, while arriving at an opposite conclusion: that historical amnesia is the true Holocaust, while the Jews retain a historical identity.

Besides documenting Mohammed's words, *Fires in the Mirror* comments on them by slyly positioning them beside a tale of the Jewish Holocaust. Although Letty Cottin Pogrebin warns about the "tendency to make hay with the Holocaust, to push all the buttons" (59), Smith convinces Pogrebin to tell of her Uncle Isaac, who came to her family as a refugee from Germany shortly after World War II. The blond, blue-eyed Isaac, posing as an Aryan, had been instructed to survive by any means necessary to tell the story of the concentration camps. To prove his Aryan status, the Nazis forced him to pack his own wife and children into the gas chamber. After the war, Pogrebin remembers him wandering around the United States "with prematurely white hair and a dead gaze" (62) spreading the story to whoever would hear until his death after a few months. Like Mohammed, the Jewish councils who instructed Isaac were aware of the critical role of historical memory. The injunction "Never Forget," perhaps the central motto for the Holocaust, is most graphically illustrated in Isaac's tale. Mohammed, too, illustrates his account with graphic horror, describing how slave masters would slice a pregnant woman's "stomach open[,] push the baby out on the ground and crush the head of the baby" (56). Juxtaposed with Pogrebin's account, these stories illustrate not that either Blacks or Jews have suffered most, but the futility of playing a numbers game in vying for the status of history's greatest victim.

If the Holocaust is subject to extreme differences of interpretation depending upon social context and political agenda, in the case of Crown Heights facts themselves are debated. The Lubavitchers maintain a strong sense of separate identity based on a strict interpretation of the Talmud, which constructs both their daily lives and their ideology. So Rabbi Shea Hecht explains that kosher food prevents him from having Blacks over for dinner, because they cannot reciprocate (110). Religious and cultural traditions make basic social exchange difficult; still, it is questionable how much of Hecht's reaction comes from a genuine need to follow Jewish tradition and how much is an excuse for insular behavior, a justification for fear of outsiders. Lubavitcher tradition not only constructs day-to-day lives but, in conjunction with a larger sense of Jewish history, determines interpretation of events in the Crown Heights rioting. A Jewish version perceives Gavin Cato's death as a freak accident, at the scene of which an irrational Black mob brutally beat the Jewish driver. The killing of Yankel Rosenbaum is judged an act of opportunistic bloodlust, with the subsequent riots the work of outside agitators. Such depictions flirt with conventional racial images of Black savagery.

Perhaps more important to this Jewish reaction than racism is the ingrained fear of anti-Semitism, of words leading to mob action. The rioting is transferred in the Jewish mind to such an episode, confirmed by taunts from the Black mob: "Kill the Jews" and "Hitler didn't finish the job" (86). Jews cannot perceive such pronouncements outside of a brutal historical awareness, for it is this history which spurs the taunts, words calculated for maximum effect. Black hatred of Jews, the rioting that erupted in Crown Heights, and the death of Yankel Rosenbaum—in this version of events, all are merely continuations of a great historical pattern of Jew hatred, tacitly backed by authority, that transcends time and place. Rosenbaum's parents were Holocaust survivors; in a context quite different from Nazi Germany, their son suffers the same fate. To his brother, Yankel Rosenbaum was killed "for no other reason than that he was a Jew!" (94). To Reuven Ostrov, the Crown Heights rioting follows the legacy of the pogroms, the persecution that followed the Jews, against all logic, from Russia to Germany to America: "It's like you're trapped, everywhere you go there's Jew haters" (131). An ominous hatred, inescapable and inexplicable, pursues Jews everywhere. Anti-Semitism spurs a paranoia oddly parallel to the xenophobia that created it.

Just as a Jewish interpretation fits the Crown Heights disturbances into a recurring historical pattern, an African American version considers Blacks, as they have been throughout American history, innocent victims, while Jews are the aggressors, the perpetrators who would, according to Reverend Al Sharpton, kill a child and "walk away like [they] just stepped on a roach!" (115). Gavin Cato's death is placed within the larger historical pattern of Middle Passage, slavery, and lynching, of utter disregard for Black life. From this perspective Jews are a small, privileged group avoiding its neighbors, demanding and getting special treatment from the

city and the police, and secretly controlling events while pleading innocence. Again the implication lingers of something larger than a simple
accident, or even than a privileged group abusing its power. Jews are dehumanized as cold-blooded murderers detached from the nature of their
crime: the opposite of the myth of savage, emotion-charged Blacks, but
with the same dehumanizing result. The facts emphasized here are utterly
different than in the Jewish version. According to the Blacks of Crown
Heights, the Rebbe regularly cruised city streets at seventy miles per hour
with no objection from police; crucial streets were often closed to make
way for Jews; the driver of the Rebbe's car immediately fled to Israel
without being questioned; a Jewish ambulance refused to treat the dying
Cato; and police systematically harassed Blacks but left Jews alone. Sonny
Carson asserts that "it is just getting intolerable for me to continue to
watch this small arrogant group of people continue to get this kind of
preferential treatment" (104). He sees no equal justice, no equal treatment, for Blacks. To the continued suppression of Black rights is added
the connivance of a small minority; an insidious, pervasive Jewish power
controls events, with the term "arrogance" implying insolent Jewish power.
The boundary between resentment of Jewish status and full-fledged anti-
Semitism is fluid and difficult to locate. As Cato's father exclaims, "[T]he
Jewish people, they are very high up . . . they runnin' the whole show
from judge right down" (138). The placement of this quotation at the end
of *Fires in the Mirror* is an ominous sign of continuing division.

     The apparently antithetical Black and Jewish views of the Crown
Heights affair, then, turn out to have remarkable similarities. Both groups
perceive history as a closed system continually repeating itself in which
their people are victimized and abused by ubiquitous outside forces. Each
draws on dominant cultural stereotypes to explain the other's pernicious
role. Categories invented in Europe prove extremely effective in providing mutual scapegoats for groups originally victims of these stereotypes.
Of course, given the history of both Blacks and Jews there is much reason
for paranoia. Monolithic reductions of history have an archetypal allure.

     Such reductionist ideologies are a recurring feature of human history.
They are not, however, inescapable; Smith's portrayal reveals contradictions and complexities that undermine essentialism. A Jewish occupant
of Crown Heights, Roz Malamud, is able to separate herself from her
Black neighbors in one sentence ("I don't love my neighbors"), then immediately acknowledge their commonality: "[T]he people in this community want exactly what I want out of life" (Smith 1993, 123). Rabbi
Shea Hecht similarly expresses beliefs that simultaneously separate Jews—

"we are different, and we think we should and can be different"—and acknowledges that "we're all children of God" (110). Local Jewish reaction does not blame anti-Semitism alone, but attempts to understand some of the frustration that led to the disturbances. While blaming outside agitators for the rioting, Roz Malamud searches for an alternative explanation: "[I]f you're sitting on a front stoop and it's very, very hot and you have no money and you have nothing to do with your time and someone says, 'Come on, you wanna riot?' You know how kids are" (125). By individualizing the problem, stepping briefly into the mind of a fictionalized "you," she begins to explore some of the greater social problems that led to the rioting. Through the vehicle of Smith's imaginative performance, the audience sees Malamud make a performative transposition of her own. A relatively privileged position provides room for understanding and sympathy; economically secure, knowing that the police, in the final instance, will protect her, Malamud feels safe enough to study and analyze, to explore different versions of events. Of course many privileged people remain oblivious to the marginalized; the Jewish history of oppression helps to provoke Malamud's speculation. From a safer distance, the writer Letty Cottin Pogrebin plays the perceiving liberal eye, discussing how Jews provide a venue for African American frustration: "[W]hen they [Blacks] have anything to say about the dominant culture nobody listens! Nobody reacts! To get a headline, to get on the evening news, you have to attack a Jew" (51). One marginalized group, disregarded to the point of invisibility, must attack another historically persecuted group to attain a reaction, employing an emotional reflex to gain some recognition. Such mutual acrimony further serves to deflect attention away from education and employment issues that might actually benefit the poor of Crown Heights.

To community organizer Richard Green a sociological analysis of the Black underclass, for whom rioting is the only means of visibility, overshadows Jewish fears of anti-Semitism:

> Those young people out there are angry and that anger has to be vented. . . . And they're not angry at the Lubavitcher community they're just as angry at you and me. . . . They have no role models, no guidance. . . . When you ask 'em who Hitler was they wouldn't even be able to tell you. (119–20)

In stark contrast to Jewish perceptions, the invocation of Hitler is ahistoricized, dismissed as an attention-grabbing device. The Black underclass is desperate for reaction, positive or negative. Neglected by the larger community, young African Americans develop their own anarchistic society, rather like the children in *Lord of the Flies*. These particular children, however, do not exist in a historical vacuum, but have a memory of oppression, passed down by the adult world, to further embitter them. The promise of taking part in an affluent society seems eternally deferred, a circumstance generating new depths of despair. So, according to one observer, Cato's death "was just the match that lit the powder keg. It's gonna happen again and again" (77). Anticipating the Los Angeles riots, this statement reveals economic and social disenfranchisement, rather than the presence of Jews, as the motivating factor.

Jews, then, act as a vehicle for expressing frustration, as scapegoats for an oppressed group. Against continuing economic disenfranchisement there is no breaking down of barriers, none of that movement into other communities which Angela Davis endorses. *Fires in the Mirror* is itself a possible exception through its presentation of multiple perspectives. The performance is akin to shock therapy, a naked gazing at hate. By exploring the wellsprings of both sides, their historical identity and their humanity, the conflict is exposed as a tragedy of errors. In Crown Heights the terms "identity" and "humanity," though overlapping, are in mutual tension, simultaneously defining and rupturing each other. Crown Heights, then, is an extreme microcosm of larger social tensions. Historical identity is a foundation of any human being, guiding language, perceptions, and daily actions; without it we could not exist as people. Yet besides a specific ethnic history, "humanity" implies a transcendence, a set of common traits—jealousy, love, passion—played out in daily life, a shared drama. As Roz Malamud says, "We want what they want." The tension between ethnic specificity and a common humanity drives the reactions of both Hasidim and Blacks. More than for the Hasidim, the Black reaction is impelled by external forces, in larger terms by racism and economic stratification, in smaller terms by Hasidic exclusivism. Yet the maelstrom of Crown Heights seems tilted toward ethnic separatism: toward misunderstanding, paranoia, and the threat of violence.

IV

In Crown Heights Jews have retained a historical identity in the most stringent form—in clothing, eating habits, religion, political stance—while Blacks are an irregular Caribbean and American assortment, cut off from a central homeplace through the history of slavery. It is no wonder that some Blacks consider Jews as both a model and a rival for their own people. The Jewish ability to maintain identity over thousands of years of oppression leads to Mohammed's resentful claim "that *we* are the chosen of God. *We* are those people that almighty God Allah has selected as his chosen, and they are masquerading in our garment—the Jews" (Smith 1993, 58). This odd historical parallel draws on Jewish notions of identity, only to claim these notions for Blacks and reject them for Jews. Jews become phantoms or doppelgängers who have stolen the whole of Black diaspora history even before it has occurred. Long reduced to a shadowy absence by the Jewish usurper, in this doctrine Blacks must now reclaim their true historical identity. African Americans may use religious and historical identification with Jews to project their own dreams of succeeding as Americans while remaining true to historical identity.

The extreme contradictions that mark Black Muslim images of Jews are not as anomalous as they might first appear, but rather intensify paradoxes inherent in the relationship between the two peoples. Hence the complex portrait Henry Louis Gates Jr. assembles of Farrakhan, a figure who simultaneously reviles and reveres Jews, magnifying and reducing them, enlarging them to superhuman status while shrinking their emotional range to archetypes of good and evil:

> Jewish people are the world leaders, in my opinion. They are some of the most brilliant people on this planet. The Jews are some of the greatest scientists, the greatest thinkers, the greatest writers, the greatest theologians, the greatest in music, the greatest in business.

And Jews "can do very good things or they can become very base, evil, and use the revelation for wicked purposes" (Gates 1996, 125). The creatures thus described are not human but an extrahistorical force controlling human destiny. Similarly a frustrated mind, or a social group, may latch onto astrology or other supernatural forces to decipher the vicissitudes of history and to explain its own problems. Farrakhan describes a small cabal of Jews who control the world through international conspiracy, the implicit assumption being that Blacks are manipulated out of power and affluence, and out of their historical destiny.

If, as Louis Althusser defines it, ideology is an *imaginary* relationship, albeit one operating with real power over material conditions, then Farrakhan's mythic Jewish cabal is an imaginary condensation of an already imaginary ideological system, a double displacement from whatever material conditions actually exist (though since material conditions are defined and distributed through ideology, their significance is largely embedded in social structure).[4] The Jewish cabal may seem more real, more tangible, than any other reality. This simultaneously fictitious and all too real construction becomes an eternal reality undermining Black efforts. As Farrakhan says, "But it's like I'm locked now in a struggle. It's like both of us got a hold on each other, and each of us is filled with electricity. I can't let them go, and they can't let me go" (128). Although this transhistorical struggle is quite imaginary, in the perceiving mind it is intensely real. This same struggle is given only slightly more physical presence in Jewish fiction discussed throughout this book: the rabbi and minister in Neugeboren's "Elijah," Spearmint and Lesser in *The Tenants*, Eisen and the Black thief in *Mr. Sammler's Planet*. These scenes of archetypal conflict exemplify a Jewish need to confront the Black presence. In creating themselves as Americans, Jews must struggle with their own history of marginalization, of which African Americans are a continuing reminder. The trajectory of these works, from Black aggression in "Elijah" to the muscle Jew of *Mr. Sammler's Planet*, illuminates the increasing comfort and power Jews hold in American society. If within the literary establishment Jews feel free to explore such depictions, within the African American community only "fringe" figures employ such imagery. Farrakhan's obsession with Jewish power results from African American powerlessness, while Jewish depictions of conflict with Blacks indicate an underlying anxiety regarding Jewish status. What Gates describes as "Farrakhan's peculiar mixture of insight and delusion" (128) is not so peculiar, not as individual a phenomenon as that statement implies. It is rather an extreme manifestation of the fight for identity and status within a society from which Blacks have long been excluded, an identification with Jews gone awry.

The current impasse in Black-Jewish relations is largely created by differing economic and social status. While still flirting with Jewish nationalism, with pride in historical and religious tradition, most American Jews live the life of the assimilated American. An uneasy compromise with contrary historical forces leads to the continuance of a mainstream Jewish American liberalism, one supporting the rights of other minorities to education and the ability to compete for a piece of the American dream, yet conflicted regarding the practicality of government intervention. The African American position is just as conflicted as the Jewish, while marked by greater anxiety. As Ellis Cose documents, Black professionals often feel isolated from and underappreciated by their White colleagues. Economically successful Black professionals may be unable to explain their

perceptions of racism, or even to differentiate actual racism from lingering paranoia.

A more coherent message emanates from Louis Farrakhan, who speaks
to and for a different audience, one simultaneously politically weak and
united in its needs, the Black urban poor. Like that of the Jewish leadership, Farrakhan's rhetoric corresponds to the social position of his primary audience, who may consider Jewish Americans as comfortable hypo-
crites passing judgment. The failure of 1960s attempts to solve ingrained
economic problems, the breakup of old coalitions, and the silencing of
old leaders have led to a power vacuum with only Farrakhan to fill it.
Farrakhan himself voices this: "[T]hey have forced other black leaders
into silence on the basic issues of race and color and economics, and
Farrakhan now has emerged as the voice that speaks to the hurt of our
people" (Farrakhan 1994, 25). Marginalized and ignored, this imperative
voice becomes, at its most extreme, the voice of paranoia. Objectified as
the cause of Black impoverishment, the figure of the Jew substitutes for a
network of social and historical factors an easily containable sign of difference.

Rather than dwelling on Farrakhan's message, exaggerating its extent, I can only repeat the oft-repeated yet never acted-upon maxim that
social problems will never disappear until attacked at their structural roots.
Gates concludes his article:

> One black man graduates from college for every hundred who go to jail.
> Almost half of black children live in poverty. People say that Farrakhan
> is now the leading voice of black rage in America. One day, America
> will realize it got off easy. (1996, 131)[5]

As Jews assimilate, Black attitudes toward Jews remain conflicted, balanced
between admiration, legitimate political grievance, and ancient stereotypes.

In defining group identity within America, economic status is always
a key factor, one that denotes social status. Economic status influences
the balance between group identity and social comfort: high status encourages a belief in assimilationist possibilities, while poverty provokes
alienation and ethnic nationalism. If tensions between Blacks and Jews
have been explored, and perhaps eased, through dialogic literary processes,
economic status is always present in literary representations, demarcating
group perceptions and psychological needs. So economic status maintains representations of Blacks as a "problem" minority, in contrast to
Jews, whose ethnic identity has been normalized as a colorful variant of

mainstream American identity. As America enters the new millennium, Jews and Blacks can no longer be posited as sympathetic doubles. However much literature may stimulate understanding, its effects are overshadowed by economic difference.

As long as gross economic inequities provide a breeding ground for hatred, it is difficult to believe that stresses between Blacks and Jews will disappear (although they may dissipate as the two groups become decreasingly relevant to each other). If Jewish proclamations of historical sympathy began the political alliance, by the 1980s the visible dynamic had reversed to one of Black action and Jewish reaction. If Jewish Americans, satisfied with their status, feel decreasingly concerned regarding African American affairs, current Black stances stem largely from a position of weakness. While earlier Jewish roles may still provide an ennobling conception of suffering fraught with meaning, current Jewish status may be perceived as a betrayal, as well as a prize seeming forever out of reach. Yet Jews, too, continue to feel resentment at African American hostility following the Civil Rights era.

Despite lingering resentments, Jewish-Black relations should be viewed in a larger context, one in which a variety of ethnic groups interact, cooperate, and clash, as part of the formation of a new American culture and, hopefully, a more inclusive world. Certainly, multiculturalism is a defense against the ethnocentrism of the past, which exoticized and dehumanized groups deemed outside the social mainstream. And certainly, hybridization allows for rich, exciting new cultural formations. The works discussed in this book are part of a lurching, uneven evolution toward this new world. Mythologizing and misunderstanding are inevitable, yet attempts to represent not only one's own culture but those that exist alongside it are critical to developing interlocking new voices. Immersed in the ideals of the Civil Rights movement, Jewish and African American writers intimated future developments as they struggled to represent each other as part of a community, to depict a rich, complex humanity replete with virtuous idealism as well as with ugly faults. Between a leveling assimilationism and a fragmenting ethnocentrism, our society faces a delicate balancing act. Blacks and Jews, mysteriously paralleling each other's histories while remaining apart, are paradigmatic of the strain between evolving theories of respect for difference and socioeconomic facts that can only divide.

Glossary
A Few Fictions Defined

Terms dealing with race and ethnicity are constructs, mythic signifiers that, if interrogated, prove unstable and finally fall apart. Such terms are, however, very real in their effects, pervasive in their usage, and hence a necessary starting point. To be constantly unsure of language, to be wary of misspeaking, to fear a misstep at any turn, is to be silent. The following definitions of terms critical to this book—terms historically contingent and ever evolving—provide a framework for discussion.

African American: Of African descent but living in the United States and habituated to American culture. "African American" is a cultural term more than a racial one, since a person may be Black but live outside of America and since African Americans are often racially mixed but share a historical and social context.

Anti-Judaism or Anti-Jewish: To hate the Jewish people merely for being Jewish; to consider Judaism as, by definition, evil. Conventionally, anti-Judaism constructs Jews as paradigmatic of greed, conspiracy, and duplicity. For this book's purposes, the terms are interchangeable with anti-Semitism.

Anti-Semitism: A Eurocentric, semantically inaccurate term derived from the only Semitic (or partly Semitic) people living within Europe's borders prior to the twentieth century. For the sake of convenience this book maintains the term's conventional meaning of anti-Jewishness.

Black: Belonging to a racial group with highly pigmented skin derived from Africa.

Blackness: In conventional European usage blackness is associated with witchcraft, Satan, and evil, a meaning often transferred to Africa's people. In twentieth-century America blackness refers to a host of attributes associated with Black people, including such qualities as primitivism, spirituality, and physical prowess. Though associated with people of African descent, blackness is an ideological construction.

227

Enlightenment: A complex historical process considered to constitute the awakening of the modern mind, the individual, rationalism, and the scientific method. The process is generally considered to have begun during the Italian Renaissance with its rediscovery of classic Greek and Roman texts and to have reached its peak in the eighteenth and nineteenth centuries. The Enlightenment was a multifaceted, evolving historical process (or group of processes) with its own idiosyncrasies and internal conflicts and disjunctions. For the purposes of this book the term "Enlightenment" generally refers to doctrines of racial hierarchy and hegemonic dominance. This is of course a limited perspective, but one very relevant to the concerns of colonized and marginalized peoples.

Ethnicity: Belonging to a group of people with a unified national and cultural background (an amorphous term, since there are many definitions of "unified"). "Ethnicity" tends to be more of a cultural term than a racial one.

Ideology: A system of thought or way of viewing the world. In traditional Marxist thought ideology acts to create, reinforce, and justify a state's power hierarchy, which in the last analysis is always generated by society's material base. Such a view may lead to an inflexible notion of ideology as a monolithic, oppressive force.[1] Later Marxist and post-Marxist theorists have posited the concept of ideology more flexibly, allowing multiple, contestatory ideologies that may reflect various class interests, may be fractured within one class, and may overlap classes.[2] Such a view risks overstating the power of individuals and social subgroups; status within a social hierarchy continues to be crucial in structuring ideology.

Jewish: A term that may refer to religion, heredity, genealogy, or culture. The term is so contested, so filled with meanings, as to be maximally overdetermined. Allen Guttman points out that Jews originally "defined themselves as a biological group, as the seed of Abraham" (1971, 4) but one to which conversion is possible, and that Orthodox Judaism is "a way of life rather than a series of definitions and beliefs" (5). Despite such cultural and biological definitions, religion is the key stable feature of Judaism, which otherwise takes on different features in different historical contexts. From the perspective of pseudo-scientific racial theory, generally adopted by anti-Semites, the term "Jewish" is racial. In this book, at least when discussing Jewish American literature, the term refers to an ethnic and cultural group.

Liberalism: A philosophy that upholds individual autonomy and freedom as the highest good. While virtually all forms of liberalism include such basic features as a democratic government (usually through a representative system) and free expression, liberalism nevertheless exists in multiple forms, particularly regarding implementation. Most prominent is a split between classical liberalism, which believes that government can best assure individual liberties by minimal interference, and a more modern liberalism that supports government intervention to empower the poor and disenfranchised. In the United States, at least since World War II, the former kind of liberalism has been recast as conservatism, while the latter has been associated with such programs as public education, welfare, and more recently affirmative action.

Minority: A group or member of a group defined by society as in a minor position, as not considered primary in constituting a larger society's power structure, particularly economic and social. Who constitutes a minority is largely defined not by actual numbers but by positioning within a hierarchical arrangement. Although the number of White, upper-class, heterosexual, Protestant males is relatively small, in America this group is never considered a minority.

Race: A group of people from common genetic stock with a common genealogy. Henry Louis Gates Jr. contends that the term is a social construction, "that 'races,' put simply, do not exist" (1988, 403). I would argue that races do exist, but only through superficial genetic characteristics, most obviously in skin pigmentation. The concept of "race," however, is compromised by the tremendous variety of characteristics within one racial group, as well as by the constant flux of racial groupings. African Americans, for instance, may have a great deal of "White," as well as Native American, inheritance. The biological significance of racial difference, furthermore, is puny compared to the meaning given by social and cultural assumptions. This is why race may be considered a cultural construct. Nineteenth-century pseudoscientific definitions by which Whites, Blacks, Jews, and Orientals were each considered to belong to a specific race, with specific physical, intellectual, and emotional characteristics, still shape contemporary concepts of race.

Racism: The belief that race is a preordained, metaphysical category, that such human traits as rationality, emotional stability, physical strength, and moral worth are primarily inherited through racial lineage. Anti-Semitism may be considered a form of racism, derived as it is from the same pseudoscientific racial theory that characterized Blacks and Orientals as inferior.

White: The European-derived racial group, lacking in pigmentation, generally considered to constitute the dominant culture in America. White is associated with rationality, stability, and morality; the countermyth, however, is of a cold, overly intellectual, cruel people.

Notes

Introduction

1. Irving Howe describes the political novel as one with an explicit awareness of ideology, in which

> the *idea* of society, as distinct from the mere unquestioned workings of society, has penetrated the consciousness of the characters in all of its profoundly problematic aspects, so that there is to be observed in their behavior, and they are themselves often aware of, some coherent political loyalty or ideological identification. (1957, 19)

In practice the concept of a political novel is not always easy to differentiate from that of a "nonpolitical" novel.

Chapter 1. Monologues and Dialogues

1. For Jews the Holocaust is the ur-trauma, an event interpreted, at least with hindsight, as an originary suffering occurring, paradoxically, at a chronological end rather than a beginning point, a unique catastrophe uniquely inflicted upon the Jewish people. Slavoj Žižek describes the Jews as "a people like any other, no more and no less corrupted, living their ordinary life—when suddenly, like a traumatic flash, they came to know (through Moses . . .) that the Other had chosen them" (1989, 115).

2. Someone fond of complex diagrams could add more categories distinguishing, for example, between Indians, Arabs, Irish, Poles, and so on as they fall between Black and Jewish extremes. Gender could be added, with the masculine associated with Europe in its rational strength, as opposed to the feminized Other (although aspects of the feminine are sometimes considered as humanizing through their selfless, nurturing traits). Homosexuality would fall, perhaps, close to the Jewish or Oriental headings as highly feminized, overly gestural, and emotionally and mentally unstable.

3. Ethnic and national conceptions of "true self" are, of course, social constructions increasingly mythologized as they fade into the past. James Joyce's *Ulysses* parodies such conceptions in its description of Ireland as idyllic paradise:

> A pleasant land it is in sooth of murmuring waters, fishful streams where sport the gurnard, the plaice, the roach, the halibut the gibbed haddock, the grilse . . .

[etc., etc.]. In the mild breezes of the west and of the east the lofty trees wave in different directions their firstclass foliage, the wafty sycamore, the lebanonian cedar, the exalted planetree, the eugenic eucalyptus and other ornaments of the arboreal world with which that region is thoroughly well supplied. Lovely maidens sit in close proximity to the roots of the lovely trees singing the most lovely songs while they play with all kinds of lovely objects. . . . (1986, 241)

This mythic land, described through the use of static, archaic lists, is one version of the homeplace for which colonized peoples may yearn.

4. Prior to the twentieth century the minute number of Jews in America tended to conform to dominant society in regard to racial matters. So for instance at the time of the Civil War Southern Jews generally supported slavery while Northern Jews opposed it (Sloan 1971, 100). Such reactions are explicable among a people anxious to fit into American society.

5. The presumption inherent in speaking for others and the dangers of usurping a position not one's own, of reducing complex social positions to a mirror of one's own perceptions and needs, were generally unremarked in a period that still believed in the possibility of an objective scholarship able to position itself outside ideology. Only recently has there been a fuller discussion of the problems inherent in liberal patronage. As Linda Martín Alcoff explains, "[T]he practice of speaking for others is often born of a desire for mastery, to privilege oneself as the one who more correctly understands the truth about another's situation" (1995, 116). Speaking for others may continue dominant practices of analysis and control; modern liberalism, after all, is in many ways an extension of classical rationalism.

6. To be sure, the literature described by Bakhtin includes vistas of possibilities, while Deleuze and Guattari's "minor" literature operates within a "cramped space" forcing an immediate political awareness (1986, 17). Operating on a borderline between multivocality and necessity, "minor" literature is at times compelled toward a narrow political purpose, yet it remains inscribed by multiple subject positions.

Bakhtin's dialectic has extended to modern forms beyond the novel; poetry, for instance, has become increasingly open-ended and experimental.

Chapter 2. Black (E)Masculinity and Anti-Semitism

1. Wright expanded this anecdote for his final short story collection, *Eight Men*.

2. Shelby Steele is skeptical about the long-term productivity of African American masculine ideals, describing them as a form of "compensatory grandiosity" used to hide racial and personal vulnerability (1990, 64).

However, African American society has long provided its own alternatives to White patriarchy, largely through storytelling and music. bell hooks describes her fascination, dating from childhood, with Black men who resisted or ignored dominant masculine ideology, "who were not obsessed with being patriarchs: by Felix, a hobo who jumped trains, never worked a regular job, and had a missing thumb; by Kid, who lived out in the country and hunted the rabbits and coons that came to our table; by Daddy Gus, who spoke in hushed tones, sharing his sense of spiritual mysticism" (1992, 88). Resistance and hope are further expressed in musical traditions, most prominently blues, jazz, and gospel. Dismayed by the brutal life of his nephew in the Newark ghetto, the writer Don Belton invokes this music through his record collection: "It was as though through the voices of these black male artists I was calling a phalanx of ancestors to rise and protect my nephew" (1997, 114).

3. In a 1970 interview Himes makes a similar point more diplomatically, explaining that "in a basically anti-Semitic country like America the most available market for a poor Jew on the lower rung of business was the black man" (Williams 1970b, 83). Himes acknowledges the Jewish position while implicitly criticizing Jews willing to profit from a social structure that has historically abused them. This same interview displays enormous inconsistencies: "Even today a Jew will make a fortune out of the race problem, and this builds up a subconscious resentment—although most of the white people I do business with, who help me, whom I love and respect, are Jews" (84). This astonishing contradiction is only slightly immoderate given the wildly fluctuating perceptions of Black and Jewish Americans regarding each other.

Chapter 3. Jewish Assimilationism

1. Bellow's use of autobiographical incidents in his fiction has been often remarked: "As we know, Bellow is highly autobiographical in the selection of his themes and characters. More often his stories are based on certain real events, and his characters are modeled either after himself or after people close to him" (Singh 1997, 26). For instance, in *The Dean's December* the protagonist's wife, a Romanian astronomer, parallels Bellow's wife at the time, a Romanian mathematician. Furthermore that novel's central event, as Brent Staples explains, is taken from an actual murder (234). Staples further discusses how Bellow's physical descriptions were lifted from actual people: "He sometimes snatched bodies whole, but mainly he cannibalized them, taking only the choicest parts. He stole from himself as well, giving characters his own enormous eyes and unflattering teeth" (218).

2. These psychic terrors are allegorized in Charles Johnson's satirical *Middle Passage,* which makes of unexplored zones a terrifying enigma:

> Three quarters of the world's surface . . . is covered by that formless Naught, and I dislike it, Calhoun, being hemmed in by Nothing, this bottomless chaos breeding all manner of monstrosities and creatures that defy civilized law. These waters are littered with wrecked vessels. And I've seen monsters, oh, yes, such things are real down there. (1990, 42)

3. In 1990 Bellow further explained that "simply because you read Malinowski and Company didn't mean that you now knew the Trobriand Islanders. What you knew was the vision of an educated civilized European" (1994b, 303).

4. Bellow's early characters, in such novels as *Dangling Man* and *The Victim*, are Jewish versions of T. S. Eliot's paradigmatic modern figure, J. Alfred Prufrock, occupying a bleak modernist landscape "like a patient etherized upon a table." Later works portray a more multifaceted Jewish American identity.

5. Individualism is, in general, a male entitlement in this novel. Only the man takes on a quest for identity; women remain at home, the symbolic placeholders of civilization,

by their mere presence subverting the male quest. *Henderson the Rain King* again parallels *Heart of Darkness* in favoring a European gender hierarchy, wherein women "live in a world of their own, and there has never been anything like it, and never can be" (Conrad 1989, 27). Of the Arnewi queen Mtalba, Henderson exclaims "Maybe she didn't even know where America was, as even civilized women are not keen on geography, preferring a world of their own" (Bellow 1976a, 76). The blank spaces of the map are available only to men in what Johanna Smith, commenting ironically on *Heart of Darkness*, calls "a manly encounter with truth" (1989, 189), while women serve to construct a fanciful facade, a "beautiful world" (194) that excuses and hides the ugly deeds of imperialism. Women represent the facade of civilization, petty, perhaps, in its pretense and triviality, yet necessary. Even knowledge of the blank spaces is denied women; logical and spatial categories belong to men, while women, like primitives, exemplify irrational thought. Simultaneously, however, it is women who enact the social artifice. Lilly embodies and enacts all the hypocrisies of civilization, being "not naturally truthful" and "something of a blackmailer" (Bellow 1976a, 245). All the strains and contradictions of society are placed upon woman, a weight that, not surprisingly, she cannot sustain, or rather Henderson cannot excuse in her.

Bellow has often been attacked for his portrayals of women. Ada Aharoni, while admitting that, as perceived through the consciousness of the always male protagonists, Bellow's women "do not have the same depth of emotional, moral, and intellectual complexity as the heroes," argues that as they have evolved the novels have "given us a vast and rich gallery of convincing and vivid women of all kinds" (1989, 95). In a similar defense of Bellow, Gloria Cronin upholds his portrayals of women as ironically deconstructive: "[I]n spite of Bellow the author, the text has its own agenda as it deliberately examines the Western intellectual traditions of misogyny that have so clearly marked Sammler and Bellow both" (1992, 100).

6. Emily Miller Budick convincingly argues that Malamud's "The Jewbird" is an allegory for race relations in America: "[T]he fact that the Jewbird is a blackbird named Schwartz [Yiddish for "black"] seems to me to make this link inevitable" (1998, 14).

7. See John Edward Philips's "The African Heritage of White America" for a further discussion of the banjo's history in America.

8. Ruth Wisse defines the schlemiel as "a fool, seriously—maybe even fatally—out of step with the actual march of events." From a position of vulnerability, this characteristic allows the schlemiel to subvert authority, "to challenge the political and philosophic status quo" (1971, 3). As an agent of the status quo the schlemiel is merely a fool, though Malamud uses his naïveté to point to systemic social problems.

Chapter 4. Ambivalent Estrangements

1. The protagonist of Abraham Cahan's *The Rise of David Levinsky* (1917) echoes the protagonist of James Weldon Johnson's *The Autobiography of an Ex-Colored Man* in wishing for an identity commensurate with what he considers the soul of his people. At the close of Cahan's novel, David Levinsky reflects, "[M]y past and my present do not comport well. David, the poor lad swinging over a Talmud volume at the Preacher's Synagogue, seems to have more in common with my inner identity than David Levinsky, the

well-known cloak manufacturer" (1960, 530). In *Hungry Hearts*, Anzia Yezierska similarly portrays a struggle to find American identity that ends in a reversion to the cultural
worth of the Jewish people, exemplified in the protagonist's invocation of "the age-old
music of the Hebrew race," of "my own people—crying in me" (1985, 249).

2. For the writers discussed in this chapter, Lorraine Hansberry and Paule Marshall,
their status as women is a complication in their attitudes toward largely male Jewish benefactors. Writing prior to the emergence of such figures as Alice Walker and Toni Morrison
and to the rediscovery of Zora Neale Hurston, the two had little to draw on in the way of
acknowledged foremothers. For the viability and recognition of a minority literature, the
ascendancy of a Jewish literary community stood as an additional source of inspiration—
though again a male-dominated one. As Michael Rogin comments, "Jews were middlemen not only in their economic and cultural positions but also in their racial and sexual
identification: they were positioned between white and black and between men and women"
(Rogin 1996, 68). In the conundrum of borrowing from marginalized male writers to give
voice to doubly marginalized females, the less conventionally masculine Jewish persona
may have provided an additional element of identification for Black women writers.

3. To Baldwin it is the "power of revelation which is the business of the novelist,
this journey toward a more vast reality which must take precedence over all other claims"
(1955, 15).

Chapter 5. Burning Bridges

1. The wedding of artistic form to culture and politics, a recurrent Black nationalist
concept, has only recently become a truism in academia. Linda Martín Alcoff points out
that "The discursive style in which some European poststructuralists have claimed that all
writing is political marks the claim as important and likely to be true for a certain (powerful) milieu, whereas the style in which African American writers made the same claim
marked their speech as dismissable" (1995, 103).

2. Among the rich variety of African American musics Black Arts thinkers reserved
the highest place of honor for modern jazz; it was considered an astonishingly complex
artform that upheld the Africanist standard of immediate, spontaneous creation. A. B.
Spellman claims that "all of the writings of Ellison, Jones, Baldwin, et al., all of the paint-
ings of Lawrence, do not weigh as much as one John Coltrane solo in terms of the force of
its thrust, the honesty of its statement, and in the originality of its form" (1968, 164).
Ironically, Afrocentric theory cannot explain the complex, hybrid nature of this music,
missing the *American* nature of African American culture.

3. Cruse ignores DuBois's promotion of the "Sorrow Songs" as the only uniquely
American music, as well as Zora Neale Hurston's celebration of Black folk tales. Prefiguring Cruse by over a decade, James Baldwin writes, "[T]he fact is not that the Negro has
no tradition but that there has as yet arrived no sensibility sufficiently profound and tough
to make this tradition articulate" (1955, 36).

4. Lisa Jones explains of herself: "My mother is white. And I, as you may or may
not have figured out, am black. This is how I choose to define myself and this is how
America chooses to define me. I have no regrets about my racial classification other than
to lament, off and on, that classifications exist" (1994, 28).

Chapter 6. Jewish Backlash

1. Malamud asked the young James McPherson for help rendering Spearmint: "Malamud was worried over whether he had done justice to Willie Spear's [sic] idiom; but beneath the surface, during our exchange of letters, he was deeply concerned about the tensions that were then developing between Black intellectuals and Jewish intellectuals" (1989, 15). Possibly Malamud included his asymmetrical differentiation of "Willie" and "Lesser" as a conscious attempt at designating social status.

2. Howe writes of *Native Son*, "[B]oth truth and terror rested on a gross fact which Wright alone dared to confront: that violence is central in the life of the American Negro, defining and crippling him with a harshness few other Americans need suffer" (1990, 125). Ralph Ellison, in "The World and the Jug," takes Howe to task for his narrow view of Black literature, his slighting of Black America's rich culture.

3. Such an incursion into the aesthetic facade of European civilization is a frequent theme of modernism: "Malamud's world is an intensified realistic version of Eliot's wasteland" (Kernan 1968, 198). Contemporary New York, far in time and place from the European Enlightenment, accelerates the desecration inherent in Eliot's modernscape.

4. Perhaps to rectify the imbalance between saintly Jew and angry Black, Malamud has included another mythic Jewish figure, the landlord. If "Black Is My Favorite Color" embodies in one character the sympathetic Jew striving for solidarity with Blacks and the exploitative property-owner, *The Tenants* divides these roles. Opposed to Lesser is Levenspiel, the landlord, with his repeated cajoling—tinged with threat—to depart the building. Yet Levenspiel, too, is problematic, depicting himself as a suffering Job figure. Malamud seems unwilling or unable to fashion an indisputably reprehensible Jewish landlord and so qualifies the stereotype with his recurring trope of virtuous suffering. The reader can't know which Levenspiel to believe and is given few guidelines to the truth of his complaints. Certainly Levenspiel is self-serving and untrustworthy. He claims to be losing money from his Harlem tenement: "Rent control, if you aren't afraid to listen to the truth, is an immoral situation. The innocent landlord gets shafted" (Malamud 1971, 19). While Levenspiel acts as the voice of property, of the exploitative Jew, Lesser's obstinate refusal to leave an empty building is also grating. Joining the innumerable Malamud characters suffering inexplicable woes, elsewhere Levenspiel is pitiable, especially during his daughter's abortion. Levenspiel's ambiguity—is he exploitative Jew, minor Job, or insightful social critic?—stems not from a richly crafted modernist irony, but from the unresolved state of Jewish American society.

5. This critique prefigures that of Allan Bloom, Bellow's University of Chicago colleague, who describes the end product of centuries of rationalist thought as an atomistic, atavistic individual saturated by sexuality and rock music,

> a pubescent child whose body throbs with orgasmic rhythms, whose feelings are made articulate in hymns to the joys of onanism or the killing of parents; whose ambition is to win fame and wealth in imitating the drag-queen who makes the music. In short, life is made into a nonstop, commercially prepackaged masturbational fantasy. (1987, 75)

6. Responding to Norman Mailer's "The White Negro," James Baldwin critiques the mystique of Black sexuality:

But *why* should it be necessary to borrow the Depression language of deprived Negroes, which eventually evolved into jive and bop talk, in order to justify such a grim system of delusions? Why malign the sorely mentioned sexuality of Negroes in order to justify the white man's own sexual panic? (1961, 230)

7. The criminal/prince brings to mind Harlem Renaissance poet Helene Johnson's description of a Black dancer, a minstrel figure initially ridiculous whom the poet finally imagines dancing in Africa "black and naked and gleaming. . . . Gee I bet he'd be beautiful then all right." Johnson compares this figure to a bottle of sand from the Sahara desert displayed in the Harlem library: "That's what they done to this shine, ain't it? Bottled him. / Trick shoes, trick coat, trick cane, trick everything— / all glass—" (1981, 79).

8. The antithesis of the warrior Jew is the figure of the Fool, a representative of the diaspora, the ghetto Jew. The Fool's meekness and patience are celebrated, though often with a measure of parody, in such figures as Isaac Bashevis Singer's "Gimpel the Fool." The satire becomes bitter in I. L. Peretz's "Bontsha the Silent," which portrays such humility as pathetic and futile.

9. Bellow's nonfiction work *To Jerusalem and Back* (1976) pleads for "the survival of the decent society created in Israel within a few decades" (1976a, 25), but is riven by guilt at the treatment of Arabs. The Egyptian dead described in *Mr. Sammler's Planet* reappear, in virtually the same language, in Bellow's experience as a battlefield correspondent, where he sees corpses that "swelled, ballooned, then burst their uniform seams. They trickled away; eyes liquefied, ran from the sockets; and the skull quickly came through the face" (1976a, 59). Bellow agonizes over Israel's militarism but stringently maintains his final justification for Israel; the need to assure that the Holocaust not repeat itself, for Jews "amongst the peoples of the earth, had not established a natural right to exist unquestioned in the lands of their birth" (26).

Chapter 7. Aftermaths

1. Recently more attention has been paid to the Middle Passage, as the simultaneous appearance of a movie and opera on the Amistad rebellion indicates.

2. Of course, Jews are quite capable of adapting dominant cultural racism. Discussing Saul's sensitivity toward Bournehills, Merle unfolds contradictions in the Jewish situation, and in her own understanding:

[P]erhaps it's because you're a Jew and that's given you a deeper understanding. After all, your people have caught hell far longer than mine. But I doubt it. Because I got to meet quite a few Jews in London: the East End was overrun with them in my time; people were saying they were taking over England. . . . most of them were as bad as the English and had no use for black people. (Marshall 1992, 262)

Whatever their history, Jews, like other people, are individual and various, good and bad, and open to assimilationist pressures, even while facing discrimination.

3. In a discussion with Henry Louis Gates Jr., Louis Farrakhan claims that his relatives likely "were members of the Jewish community" (Gates 1996, 125) through the

same geopolitical migration by which Saul Amron claims a Caribbean link. Farrakhan's statement exposes the contradictory nature of Black anti-Semitism, based as it is on a partial identification.

4. Zutkin may be a fictionalized version of Irving Howe, a similarly esteemed Jewish intellectual who supported Richard Wright's rise to prominence.

Chapter 8. A New Dispensation

1. Three of Paley's stories—"Samuel," "The Little Girl," and "Lavinia"—written from the Black perspective, are atypical of her in focus and narratorial voice. Though interesting explorations, these stories lack the sparkle of Paley's best. The psychic distance of these characters from Paley seems to limit her, to make her self-conscious.

Judith Arcana identifies Paley's friend Bill Dixon as a key source for these stories: "Grace says it was through Bill that she learned much of what she uses in her Black characters, much of what she puts into her Black voices; she speaks through him" (1993, 107).

2. This account is somewhat utopian. The problems faced by children of mixed marriage are articulated in Ishmael Reed's anthology *MultiAmerica: Essays on Cultural Wars and Cultural Peace*. Karla Brundage explains the difficulties of her intermediary role: "I was born with a cross to carry, so to speak" (Brundage 1997, 117), and "In a weird way I have been passing for something all my life" (118). Allison Francis similarly claims, "I am sometimes forced to occupy a nether space, a third race, that mediates between the color politics of black and white communities. I become an abstraction, rather than an actual person, through which other people confront their color" (Francis 1997, 124). In a contrary vein, Robin Washington validates Paley's story: "The lesson of Black Jews in America is that we are a part of both worlds and full members of each. We are not the internally torn souls of so many tragic mulatto movie characters" (Washington 1997, 142).

Chapter 9. Fragmentation and Multiculturalism

1. Ishmael Reed characterizes African American and Latino conflict as the critical overlooked story of contemporary ethnic relations: "The fact that the media sensationalizes a quarrel between blacks and Jews while ignoring a much more serious fight between blacks and browns indicates the value that the media place upon black and brown life" (1997, xxiii).

2. This disclaimer carries the benefit of historical hindsight; as Donna Rifkind points out, the discussions around this point "sound much more like those of a novelist in the 1990s than a cafe owner in the 1940s" (1993, 29). Bailey's Cafe is, however, tinged with magical realism; it is presented as a place outside the ordinary limitations of time, so perhaps such decontextualization is appropriate.

3. Its satiric form did not protect the novel from attack. Michiko Kakutani describes the novel as exhibiting "a paranoid position with disturbing implications" that do "a disservice to Mr. Reed's own notable career" (Kakutani 1986).

4. See *This Bridge Called My Back* (edited by Gloria Anzaldúa and Cherríe Moraga) for further critiques of White feminism from Black and Latino perspectives.

Chapter 10. Parallels and Paralysis

1. Philip Roth satirizes Kahane in *The Counterlife* (1986) in the figure of Mordecai Lippman, whose rhetoric extends fear of the Black Other onto an Israeli West Bank settlement: "[B]etween the hammer of the pious white American Christian and the anvil of the dirty foreigner, the Jew in America will be crushed—if he is not slaughtered first by the blacks, the blacks in the ghettos who are already sharpening their knives" (1986, 124). Lippman, with his monolithic view of Jewish history, denies that a gentile society can ever accept Jews. Simultaneously, in his fear of Blacks he assigns the imagined outbreak of anti-Semitism to those most marginalized, those devoid of historical responsibility for persecuting Jews.

2. Although neoconservatism has considered itself a movement only loosely, and although it has included many non-Jews, its original formation was dependent on a Jewish group bred on radical grounds: the New York intellectuals. Neoconservatism is largely a reaction against the New Left, itself less Jewish in character than earlier radical movements.

3. All quotations are taken from A. D. Smith 1993, the book version of Smith's video; the book includes numerous line breaks that convey the poetry of the language, but for convenience' sake these line breaks have been eliminated here.

4. Farrakhan's search for a monolithic explanation of history resembles a Marxist definition of ideology, suggested and then declined by Louis Althusser as simplistic, as created by "a small number of cynical men who base their domination and exploitation of the 'people' on a falsified representation of the world which they have imagined in order to enslave other minds by dominating their imaginations" (1971, 163). This tidy, containable explanation is transposed to the Jews to explain the continued misery of the African American underclass.

5. The picture painted here runs counter to recent statistics that show increased Black graduation rates from both high school and college, a contradiction demanding further study.

Glossary

1. Louis Althusser defines the Ideological State Apparatus as "the system of the ideas and representations which dominate the mind of a man or a social group" (1971, 158), the bundle of ideas that reinforce and justify a society's economic relations: "Ideology is a 'Representation' of the Imaginary Relationship of Individuals to their Real Conditions of Existence" (162). An actual, material universe is assumed, with ideology as a kind of fantasy to be unveiled by scientific Marxism.

2. Stuart Hall discusses Antonio Gramsci's revisions of conventional Marxist notions of ideology, part of a movement toward a more complex, decentered definition:

He [Gramsci] altogether refuses any idea of a pre-given unified ideological subject—for example, the proletarian with its 'correct' revolutionary thoughts or
blacks with their already guaranteed current anti-racist consciousness. He recognizes the 'plurality' of selves or identities of which the so-called 'subject' of
thought and ideas is composed. . . . This complex, fragmentary and contradictory conception of consciousness is a considerable advance over the explanation by way of 'false consciousness' more traditional to Marxist theorizing.
(1996, 433)

Bibliography

Adorno, Theodor, and Max Horkheimer. 1993. *Dialectic of Enlightenment*. New York: Continuum.

Aharoni, Ada. 1989. "Women in Saul Bellow's Novels." In *Saul Bellow in the 1980s,* 95–112. East Lansing: Michigan State University Press.

Alcoff, Linda Martín. 1995. "The Problem of Speaking for Others." In *Who Can Speak?* edited by Judith Roof and Robyn Wiegman, 97–119. Urbana: University of Illinois Press.

Althusser, Louis. 1971. "Ideology and Ideological State Apparatuses (Notes towards an Investigation)." In *Lenin and Philosophy and Other Essays*. New York: Monthly Review Press.

Anzaldúa, Gloria, and Cherríe Moraga, eds. 1982. *This Bridge Called My Back: Writings by Radical Women of Color*. New York: Kitchen Table, Women of Color Press.

Arcana, Judith. 1993. *Grace Paley's Life Stories*. Urbana: University of Illinois Press.

Arnold, Matthew. 1960, *Culture and Anarchy*. 1869. Reprint, edited by J. Dover Wilson, Cambridge: Cambridge University Press.

Avery, Evelyn Gross. 1979. *Rebels and Victims: The Fiction of Richard Wright and Bernard Malamud*. Port Washington, N.Y.: Kennikat.

Bakhtin, Mikhail. 1981. *The Dialogic Imagination*. Austin: University of Texas Press.

Baldwin, James. 1955. *Notes of a Native Son*. Boston: Beacon.

———. 1961. *Nobody Knows My Name*. New York: Vintage.

———. 1993. *The Fire Next Time*. New York: Vintage.

Balogun, F. Odun. 1985. "Mythopoetic Quest for the Racial Bridge: The Radiance of the King and *Henderson the Rain King*." *The Journal of Ethnic Studies* 12, no. 4 (winter): 19–32.

Baraka, Amiri. 1963. *The System of Dante's Hell*. New York: Grove.

———. 1979. *Selected Poetry of Amiri Baraka/LeRoi Jones*. New York: William Morrow.

————. 1984. *The Autobiography of LeRoi Jones/Amiri Baraka.* New York: Freundlich.

————. 1991. *The LeRoi Jones/Amiri Baraka Reader.* Edited by William J. Harris. New York: Thunders Mouth.

Bauman, Zygmunt. 1991. *Modernity and Ambivalence.* Ithaca: Cornell University Press.

Baumgarten, Murray. 1993. "Urban Rites and Civic Premises in the Fiction of Saul Bellow, Grace Paley, and Sandra Schor." *Contemporary Literature* 34, no. 3 (fall): 395–424.

Bellow, Saul. 1970. *Mr. Sammler's Planet.* New York: Viking.

————. 1976a. *Henderson the Rain King.* 1959. Penguin.

————. 1976b. *To Jerusalem and Back.* New York: Viking.

————. 1977. "Looking for Mr. Green." In *Mosby's Memoirs and Other Stories.* Reprint, New York: Penguin.

————. 1981. *The Dean's December.* New York: Harper and Row.

————. 1994a. *It All Adds Up.* New York: Viking.

————. 1994b. "A Talk with Saul Bellow: On His Work and Himself." Interview by Michiko Kakutani. In *Conversations with Saul Bellow,* ed. Gloria Cronin and Ben Siegel, 181–89. Jackson: University Press of Mississippi.

Belton, Don. 1997. "Voodoo for Charles." In *Black Men Speaking*, edited by Charles Johnson and John McCluskey Jr. Bloomington: Indiana University Press.

Berman, Paul. 1994. "The Other and the Almost the Same." In *Blacks and Jews: Alliances and Arguments,* 1–28. New York: Delacorte.

Bhabha, Homi K. 1994. *The Location of Culture.* New York: Routledge.

Bloom, Allan. 1987. *The Closing of the American Mind.* New York: Simon & Schuster.

Bloom, Harold. 1988. Introduction to *Richard Wright's Native Son.* Edited by Harold Bloom. New York: Chelsea House.

Boyarin, Daniel. 1997. *Unheroic Conduct: The Rise of Heterosexuality and the Invention of the Jewish Man.* Berkeley: University of California Press.

Brantlinger, Patrick. 1986. "Victorians and Africans: The Genealogy of the Myth of the Dark Continent." In *"Race," Writing and Difference,* edited by Henry Louis Gates Jr., 185–222. Chicago: University of Chicago Press.

Brown, Lloyd W. 1973. "LeRoi Jones (Imamu Amiri Baraka) as Novelist: Theme and Structure in *The System of Dante's Hell.*" *Negro American Literature Forum* 7:132–42.

Brundage, Karla. 1997. "Passing." In *MultiAmerica: Essays on Cultural Wars and Cultural Peace,* edited by Ishmael Reed, 116–22. New York: Viking.

Budick, Emily Miller. 1998. *Blacks and Jews in Literary Conversation.* Cambridge: Cambridge University Press.

Cahan, Abraham. 1960. *The Rise of David Levinsky.* 1917. Reprint, New York: Harper and Row.

Carmichael, Stokely. 1968. "Toward a Black Liberation." In *Black Fire: An Anthology of Afro-American Writing*, edited by LeRoi Jones and Larry Neal, 119–32. New York: William Morrow.

Carson, Clayborne. 1992. "Blacks and Jews in the Civil Rights Movement: The Case of SNCC." In *Bridges and Boundaries: African Americans and American Jews*, edited by Jack Salzman, 36–49. New York: George Braziller.

Cleaver, Eldridge. 1992. *Soul on Ice.* 1968. Reprint, New York: Delta.

Cobbs, Price, and William Grier. 1968. *Black Rage.* New York: Basic Books.

Conrad, Joseph. 1989. *Heart of Darkness.* 1899. Reprint, edited by Ross Murfin, New York: St. Martin's.

Cose, Ellis. 1993. *The Rage of a Privileged Class.* New York: HarperCollins.

Cronin, Gloria. 1992. "Searching the Narrative Gap: Authorial Self-Irony and the Problematic Discussion of Western Misogyny in *Mr. Sammler's Planet.*" In *Saul Bellow: a Mosaic,* edited by L. H. Goldman et al., 97–122. New York: Peter Lang.

Crouch, Stanley. 1996. "Introduction: Barbarous on Either Side: The New York Blues of *Mr. Sammler's Planet.*" In *Mr. Sammler's Planet,* by Saul Bellow, vii–xxvii. New York: Penguin.

Cruse, Harold. 1969. "My Jewish Problem, and Ours." In *Black Anti-Semitism and Jewish Racism,* edited by Nat Hentoff. New York: Baron.

————. 1984. *The Crisis of the Negro Intellectual.* 1967. Reprint, New York: Quill.

Deleuze, Gilles, and Felix Guattari. 1986. *Kafka: Toward a Minor Literature.* 1975. Reprint, Minneapolis: University Minnesota Press.

Diner, Hasia. 1977. *In the Almost Promised Land.* Westport, Conn.: Greenwood.

Dittmar, Kurt. 1991. "The End of Enlightenment: Bellow's Universal View of the Holocaust in *Mr. Sammler's Planet.*" In *Saul Bellow at Seventy-Five: A Collection of Critical Essays,* edited by Gerhard Bach, 63–80. Tübingen: Gunter Narr Verlag.

Dolgin, Janet. 1977. *Jewish Identity and the JDL.* Princeton: Princeton University Press.

Dubois, W. E. B. 1989. *The Souls of Black Folk.* 1903. Reprint, New York: Bantam.

Dunbar, Paul Laurence. 1968. "We Wear the Mask." In *Dark Symphony: Negro Literature in America,* edited by James Emanuel and Theodore Gross, 41. New York: Free Press.

Dworkin, Andrea. 1974. *Woman Hating.* New York: Plume.

Ellis, Trey. 1989. "The New Black Aesthetic." *Callaloo* 12, no. 1 (winter): 233–43.

Ellison, Ralph. 1966. "The World and the Jug." In *Shadow and Act,* 115–47. New York: Signet.

―――. 1972. *Invisible Man.* 1947. Reprint, New York: Vintage.

―――. 1986. "What America Would Be Like Without Blacks." In *Going to the Territory,* 104–12. New York: Random House.

Fanon, Frantz. 1967. *Black Skin, White Masks.* 1952. Reprint, New York: Grove.

Farrakhan, Louis. 1994. Interview. *Time,* 28 February, 24–25.

Faulkner, William. 1989. *Light in August.* 1932. Reprint, New York: Vintage.

Fiedler, Leslie. 1960. "Negro and Jew: Encounter in America." In *No! in Thunder,* 231–50. Boston: Beacon.

Fires in the Mirror. 1993. Video. Performed by Anna Deavere Smith. American Playhouse.

Foucault, Michel. 1977. *Discipline and Punishment: The Birth of the Prison.* Harmondsworth, U.K.

Francis, Allison. 1997. "Why Am I Still Onstage at the Cotton Club?" In *MultiAmerica: Essays on Cultural Wars and Cultural Peace,* edited by Ishmael Reed, 123–26. New York: Viking.

Friedman, Murray. 1995. *What Went Wrong? The Creation and Collapse of the Black-Jewish Alliance.* New York: Free Press.

Furman, Andrew. 1996. "Saul Bellow's Middle East Problem." *Saul Bellow Journal* 14, no. 1 (winter): 40–67.

Garvey, Marcus. 1991. "African Fundamentalism." In *African Fundamentalism,* edited by Tony Martin, 4–6. Dover, Mass.: Majority Press.

Gates, Henry Louis, Jr. 1988. *The Signifying Monkey.* New York: Oxford University Press.

―――. 1992. "Trading on the Margin: Notes on the Culture of Criticism." In *Loose Canons: Notes on the Culture Wars,* 173–93. New York: Oxford University Press.

―――. 1996. "The Charmer." *The New Yorker,* 29 April and 6 May, 116–31.

Gibson, Donald. 1972. "Wright's Invisible Native Son." In *Twentieth-Century Interpretations of Native Son,* edited by Houston Baker, 96–108. Englewood Cliffs, N.J.: Prentice-Hall.

Gilman, Sander. 1986. *Jewish Self-Hatred, Anti-Semitism, and the Hidden Language of the Jews.* Baltimore: Johns Hopkins University Press.

―――. 1991. *The Jew's Body.* New York: Routledge.

―――. 1993. *Freud, Race, and Gender.* Princeton: Princeton University Press.

Gilroy, Paul. 1993. *The Black Atlantic.* Cambridge: Harvard University Press.

Giovanni, Nikki. 1970. *Black Feeling, Black Talk, Black Judgement.* New York: William Morrow.

Glazer, Nathan. 1969. "Blacks, Jews, and the Intellectuals." *Commentary* 47 (April): 33–39.

———. 1996. "The Campus Crucible: Student Politics and the University." 1969. Reprinted in *The Essential Neoconservative Reader,* edited by Mark Gerson, 41–63. Reading, Mass.: Addison-Wesley.

Goldberg, David Theo. 1990. *The Anatomy of Racism.* Minneapolis: University Minnesota Press.

Goldman, L. H. 1983. *Saul Bellow's Moral Vision: A Critical Study of the Jewish Experience.* New York: Irvington.

Guttmann, Allen. 1971. *The Jewish Writer in America: Assimilation and the Crisis of Identity.* New York: Oxford University Press.

Hall, Stuart. 1996. *Stuart Hall: Critical Dialogues in Cultural Studies.* Edited by David Morley and Kuan-Hsing Chen. London: Routledge.

Hansberry, Lorraine. 1987. *A Raisin in the Sun and The Sign in Sidney Brustein's Window.* 1958. Reprint, New York: New American Library.

Harap, Louis. 1987. *Dramatic Encounters: The Jewish Presence in Twentieth-Century American Drama, Poetry, and Humor and the Black-Jewish Literary Relationship.* Westport, Conn.: Greenwood.

Hartman, Geoffrey. 1997. *The Fateful Question of Culture.* New York: Columbia University Press.

Hayden, Robert. 1985. *Collected Poems.* 1962. Reprint, edited by Frederick Glaysher, New York: Liveright.

Himes, Chester. 1986. *Lonely Crusade.* 1947. Reprint, New York: Thunder's Mouth.

Himmelfarb, Milton. 1969. "Is American Jewry in Crisis?" *Commentary* 47 (March): 33–42.

Hodges, Graham. 1986. Foreword to *Lonely Crusade,* by Chester Himes. New York: Thunder's Mouth.

hooks, bell. 1992. "Reconstructing Black Masculinity." In *Black Looks: Race and Representation,* 87–114. Boston: South End.

Howe, Irving. 1957. *Politics and the Novel.* Cleveland, Ohio: Meridian.

———. 1976. *World of Our Fathers.* New York: Schocken.

———. 1990. "Black Boys and Native Sons." In *Selected Writings, 1950–1990,* 119–39. New York: Harvest/HBJ.

Huggins, Nathan Irvin. 1971. *Harlem Renaissance.* New York: Oxford University Press.

Hurston, Zora Neale. 1984. *Moses, Man of the Mountain.* 1939. Reprint, Urbana: University Illinois Press.

Isaacs, Neil. 1990. *Grace Paley: A Study of the Short Fiction.* Boston: Twayne.

James, Caryn. 1990. "Spike Lee's Jews and the Passage from Benign Cliché into Bigotry." *The New York Times*, 16 August.

Johnson, Charles. 1990. *Middle Passage*. New York: Plume.

Johnson, Helene. 1981. "Bottled." 1927. Reprinted in *Black Sister*, edited by Erlene Stetson, 78–79. Bloomington: Indiana University Press.

Johnson, James Weldon. 1989. *The Autobiography of an Ex-Coloured Man*. 1927. Reprint, New York: Vintage.

Jones, LeRoi. *See* Baraka, Amiri

Jones, Lisa. 1994. "Mama's White." In *Bulletproof Diva*, 28–35. New York: Doubleday.

Joyce, James. 1986. *Ulysses*. 1922. Reprint, New York: Random House.

Kahane, Meir. 1987. *Uncomfortable Questions for Comfortable Jews*. Secaucus, N.J.: Lyle Stuart.

Kakutani, Michiko. 1986. "Gallery of the Repellent." *New York Times* 5 April.

Katz, Shlomo. 1967. *Negro and Jew: An Encounter in America*. New York: Macmillan.

Kellman, Steven. 1987. "*The Tenants* in the House of Fiction." In *Critical Essays on Bernard Malamud*, edited by Joel Salzberg. Boston: G. K. Hall.

Kernan, Alvin. 1986. "*The Tenants:* 'Battering the Object'." In *Bernard Malamud*, edited by Harold Bloom, 193–206. New York: Chelsea House.

Kimball, Roger. 1990. *Tenured Radicals: How Politics Has Corrupted Our Higher Education*. New York: Harper and Row.

Klonsky, Milton. 1948. "The Writing on the Wall." *Commentary*, February, 189–90.

Kristol, Irving. 1995. "Welfare: The Best of Intentions, the Worst of Results." 1971. Reprinted in *Neoconservatism: The Autobiography of an Idea*, 43–49. New York: Free Press.

Kundera, Milan. 1988. *The Art of the Novel*. 1986. New York: Harper and Row.

Ladner, Joyce. 1971. "What 'Black Power' Means to Negroes in Mississippi." In *The Black Revolt*, edited by James Geschwender, 202–16. Englewood Cliffs, N.J.: Prentice-Hall.

Lasher, Lawrence. 1991. *Conversations with Bernard Malamud*. Jackson: University Press of Mississippi.

Lee, Don L. 1970. Introduction to *We Walk the Way of the New World*. Detroit: Broadside Press.

Lester, Julius. 1988. *Lovesong: Becoming a Jew*. New York: Henry Holt.

Levi, Primo. 1961. *Survival in Auschwitz*. 1958. Reprint, New York: Collier.

Lewis, Daniel Levering. 1984. "Shortcuts to the Mainstream: Afro-American and Jewish Notables in the 1920s and 1930s." In *Jews in Black Perspectives*, edited by Joseph Washington Jr. Madison, N.J.: Fairleigh Dickinson University Press.

Lipsett, Seymour, and Earl Raab. 1995. *Jews and the New American Scene*. Cambridge: Harvard University Press.

Mailer, Norman. 1957. "The White Negro." *Dissent* 4, no. 3 (summer): 276–93.

Malamud, Bernard. 1971. *The Tenants*. New York: Farrar, Straus & Giroux.

———. 1984. *The Stories of Bernard Malamud*. Reprint, New York: Plume.

Marre, Diana Katherine. 1988. "Traditions and Departures: Lorraine Hansberry and Black Americans in Theatre." Diss., University California at Berkeley, 1987. Ann Arbor, Mich.: UMI.

Marshall, Paule. 1981. *Brown Girl, Brownstone*. 1959. Reprint, Old Westbury, N.Y.: Feminist Press.

———. 1988. *Soul Clap Hands and Sing*. 1961. Reprint, Washington, D.C.: Howard University Press.

———. 1992. *The Chosen Place, the Timeless People*. 1969. Reprint, New York: Vintage.

Marx, Karl. 1978. "On the Jewish Question." In *The Marx-Engels Reader,* edited by Robert Tucker, 26–52. New York: Norton.

McCluskey, John, Jr. 1984. "And Called Every Generation Blessed: Theme, Setting, and Ritual in the Works of Paule Marshall." In *Black Women Writers (1950–1980),* edited by Mari Evans, 316–34. Garden City, N.Y.: Anchor.

McFarlane, James. 1978. "The Mind of Modernism." In *Modernism: 1890–1930,* edited by Malcolm Bradbury and James McFarlane. Hassocks, Sussex, U.K.: Harvester.

McPherson, James. 1989. "To Blacks and Jews: Hab Rachmones." *Tikkun* 4, no. 5 (September–October): 15–18.

Memmi, Albert. 1967. *The Colonizer and the Colonized*. 1957. Reprint, Boston: Beacon.

Meyer, Adam. 1994. "Faith and the 'Black Thing': Political Action and Self-Questioning in Grace Paley's Short Fiction." *Studies in Short Fiction* 31, no. 1 (winter): 79–89.

———. 1995. "Memory and Identity for Black, White, and Jew in Paule Marshall's *The Chosen Place, The Timeless People*." *Melus* 20, no. 3 (fall): 99–119.

Milliken, Stephen. 1976. *Chester Himes: A Critical Appraisal*. Columbia: University of Missouri Press.

Morrison, Toni. 1970. *The Bluest Eye*. New York: Pocket.

———. 1989. "Unspeakable Thoughts Unspoken." *Michigan Quarterly Review* 28 (winter): 1–49.

———. 1990. *Playing in the Dark: Whiteness and the Literary Imagination*. New York: Vintage.

Motley, Willard. 1951. *We Fished All Night*. New York: Appleton-Century-Crofts.

Muller, Gilbert. 1984. *John A. Williams*. Boston: Twayne.

————. 1989. *Chester Himes*. Boston: Twayne.

Naylor, Gloria. 1993. *Bailey's Cafe*. 1992. Reprint, New York: Vintage.

Neal, Larry. 1971. "The Black Arts Movement." In *The Black Aesthetic,* edited by Addison Gayle Jr., 272–90. Garden City, N.Y.: Doubleday.

————. 1989. *Visions of a Liberated Future*. New York: Thunder's Mouth.

Neugeboren, Jay. 1966. *Big Man*. Boston: Houghton Mifflin.

————. 1969. "Elijah." In *Corky's Brother,* 159–95. New York: Farrar, Straus & Giroux.

————. 1970. *Parentheses: An Autobiographical Journey*. New York: E. P. Dutton.

————. 1974. *Sam's Legacy*. New York: Holt, Rinehart & Winston.

Ozick, Cynthia. 1983. *Art and Ardor*. New York: Knopf.

Paley, Grace. 1974. *Enormous Changes at the Last Minute*. New York: Farrar, Straus, & Giroux.

————. 1985. *Later the Same Day*. New York: Penguin.

Peretz, Isaac Loeb. 1963. "Bontsha the Silent." In *Great Jewish Short Stories,* edited by Saul Bellow, 128–37. New York: Dell.

Philips, John Edward. 1990. "The African Heritage of White America." In *Africanisms in American Culture,* edited by Joseph E. Holloway. Bloomington: Indiana University Press.

Podhoretz, Norman. 1966. "My Negro Problem—and Ours." In *The Commentary Reader,* edited by Norman Podhoretz. New York: Atheneum.

Pratt, Mary Louise. 1992. *Imperial Eyes: Travel Writing and Transculturation*. New York: Routledge.

Raab, Earl. 1969. "The Black Revolution and the Jewish Question." In *Black Anti-Semitism and Jewish Racism,* edited by Nat Hentoff, 15–41. New York: Baron.

Rampersad, Arnold. 1986. "Langston Hughes's Fine Clothes to the Jew." *Callaloo.* 9, no. 1 (winter): 144–57.

Randall, James A., Jr. 1971. "Jew." In *The Black Poets,* edited by Dudley Randall, 278–79. Toronto: Bantam.

Reed, Ishmael. 1986. *Reckless Eyeballing*. New York: Atheneum.

————. 1988. *Writin' is Fightin'*. New York: Atheneum.

————.1997. Introduction to *MultiAmerica: Essays on Cultural Wars and Cultural Peace,* edited by Ishmael Reed, xv–xviii. New York: Viking.

Reed, Tennessee. 1997. "Being Mixed in America." In *MultiAmerica: Essays on Cultural Wars and Cultural Peace,* edited by Ishmael Reed, 113–15. New York: Viking.

Rich, Adrienne. 1986. "Split at the Root: An Essay on Jewish Identity." In *Blood, Bread and Poetry,* 100–123. New York: Norton.

Richman, Sidney. "The Stories." In *Modern Critical Views: Bernard Malamud,* edited by Harold Bloom, 71–100. New York: Chelsea House.

Rifkind, Donna. 1993. Review of *Bailey's Cafe. Gloria Naylor: Critical Perspectives Past and Present,* edited by Henry Louis Gates Jr. and K. A. Appiah, 28–30. New York: Amistad.

Rodrigues, Eusebio L. Koheleth. 1974. "The Quest for the Real in 'Looking for Mr. Green'." *Studies in Short Fiction* 11:387–93.

Rogin, Michael. 1996. *Blackface, White Noise: Jewish Immigrants in the Hollywood Melting Pot.* Berkeley: University California Press.

Rorty, Richard. 1989. *Contingency, Irony, and Solidarity.* Cambridge: Cambridge University Press.

Rosen, Steven J. 1995. "African American Anti-Semitism and Himes's *Lonely Crusade.*" *MELUS* 20, no. 2 (summer): 47–68.

Rosenbaum, Alan, ed. 1996. *Is the Holocaust Unique?* Boulder, Colo.: Westview.

Roth, Philip. 1967. *Portnoy's Complaint.* New York: Random House.

———. 1986. *The Counterlife.* New York: Farrar, Straus, & Giroux.

———. 1989. "Goodbye, Columbus." 1959. Reprinted in *Goodbye, Columbus and Five Short Stories,* 1–136. Boston: Houghton Mifflin.

Russell, Mariann. 1973. "White Man's Black Man: Three Views." *CLA Journal* 7:93–100.

Said, Edward. 1979. *Orientalism.* New York: Vintage.

———. 1993. *Culture and Imperialism.* New York: Knopf.

Sanford, John. 1995. *The People from Heaven.* 1943. Reprint, Urbana: University of Illinois Press.

Sartre, Jean-Paul. 1976. *Anti-Semite and Jew.* 1948. Reprint, New York: Schocken.

Schwenk, Kathryn. 1994. "Lynching and Rape: Border Cases in African American History and Fiction." In *The Black Columbiad,* 312–24. Cambridge: Harvard University Press,.

Segal, Lore. 1985. *Her First American.* New York: Knopf.

Singer, Isaac Bashevis. 1981. "Gimpel the Fool." In *The Collected Stories,* 3–14. New York: Noonday.

Singh, Sukhbir. 1997. "Meeting with Saul Bellow." *American Studies International* 35, no. 1 (February): 19–31.

Sloan, Irving. 1971. *The Jews in America: 1621–1970.* Dobbs Ferry, N.Y.: Oceana Publications.

Smith, Anna Deavere. 1993. *Fires in the Mirror.* New York: Anchor.

Smith, Johanna. 1989. "'Too Beautiful Altogether': Patriarchal Ideology in *Heart of Darkness.*" In *Heart of Darkness: A Case Study in Contemporary Criticism,* edited by Ross Murfin. New York: St. Martin's.

Sollors, Werner. 1978. *Amiri Baraka/LeRoi Jones: The Quest for a "Populist Modernism."* New York: Columbia University Press.

Solomon, Eric. 1987. "Counter-Ethnicity and the Jewish-Black Baseball Novel: The Cases of Jerome Charyn and Jay Neugeboren." *Modern Fiction Studies.* 33, no. 1 (spring): 49–63.

Spellman, A. B. 1968. "Not Just Whistling Dixie." In *Black Fire: An Anthology of Afro-American Writing,* edited by Leroi Jones and Larry Neal, 159–68. New York: William Morrow.

Spillers, Hortense. 1987. "Mama's Baby, Papa's Maybe: An American Grammar Book. *diacritics* 17, no. 2:65–81.

Staples, Brent. 1994. *Parallel Time: Growing Up in Black and White.* New York: Pantheon.

Steele, Shelby. 1990. *The Content of Our Character: A New Vision of Race in America.* New York: St. Martin's.

Stewart, James. 1968. "The Development of the Black Revolutionary Artist." In *Black Fire: An Anthology of Afro-American Writing,* edited by LeRoi Jones and Larry Neal, 3–10. New York: William Morrow.

Thomas, Laurence. 1993. *Vessels of Evil: American Slavery and the Holocaust.* Philadelphia: Temple University Press.

Van Deburg, William. 1997. Introduction to *Modern Black Nationalism: From Marcus Garvey to Louis Farrakhan,* edited by William Van Deburg. New York: New York University Press.

Wald, Alan M. 1994. *Writing from the Left: New Essays on Radical Culture and Politics.* London: Verso.

Walker, Alice. 1976. *Meridian.* New York: Harcourt Brace Jovanovich.

———. 1994. "In Search of Our Mothers' Gardens." 1974. Reprinted in *"Everyday Use,"* edited by Barbara Christian, 39–50. New Brunswick, N.J.: Rutgers University Press.

Wallace, Michelle. 1979. *Black Macho and the Myth of the Superwoman.* New York: Dial.

Washington, Robin. 1997. "Black and Jewish Like Jesus and Me." In *Multi-America: Essays on Cultural Wars and Cultural Peace,* edited by Ishmael Reed, 138–42. New York: Viking.

West, Cornel. 1993a. Introduction to *Fires in the Mirror,* by Anna Deavere Smith. New York: Anchor.

———. 1993b. *Race Matters.* Boston: Beacon.

Wideman, John Edgar. 1989. "Valaida." In *Fever,* 27–40. New York: Penguin.

Wilkins, Roger. 1980. "Speaking Out." *Perspectives: The Civil Rights Quarterly* 12 (spring): 2–3.

Williams, John A. 1964. *This is My Country Too*. New York: NAL-World.

———. 1967. *The Man Who Cried I Am*. Boston: Little, Brown.

———. 1970a. *The King God Didn't Save: Reflections on the Life and Death of Martin Luther King Jr*. New York: Coward-McCann.

———. 1970b. "My Man Himes." In *Amistad 1*, edited by John Williams and Charles Harris, 25–94. New York: Random House.

———. 1982. *!Click Song*. Boston: Houghton Mifflin.

Williams, Robin M., Jr. 1971. "Social Change and Social Conflict: Race Relations in the United States, 1944–1964." In *The Black Revolt*, edited by James Geschwender, 24–32. Englewood Cliffs, N.J.: Prentice-Hall.

Wisse, Ruth. 1971. *The Schlemiel as Modern Hero*. Chicago: University of Chicago Press.

Wright, Richard. 1960. *Eight Men*. New York: Pyramid.

———. 1966. *Native Son*. 1940. Reprint, New York: Perennial.

———. 1977. *American Hunger*. New York: Harper and Row.

———. 1989. *Black Boy*. 1937. Reprint, New York: Perennial.

Yezeirska, Anzia. 1985. *Hungry Hearts and Other Stories*. 1920. Reprint, New York: Persea.

Žižek, Slavoj. 1989. *The Sublime Object of Ideology*. London: Verso.

Index

253